WITHDRAWN

Out of the Psychic Closet

The Quest to Trust My True Nature

By Toby Fesler Heathcote

Twilight Times Books
Kingsport Tennessee

Out of the Psychic Closet: *The Quest to Trust My True Nature*

Twilight Times Books
P O Box 3340
Kingsport, TN 37664
www.twilighttimesbooks.com/

First Edition: September 2009

Library of Congress Cataloging-in-Publication Data

Heathcotte, Toby Fesler
Pending

Cover art by Ardy M. Scott

Printed in the United States of America

To Marcia Stoner for inspiring my search

Contents

Preface

You picked up this book probably because you've struggled to understand some unsettling occurrence in your life, maybe one named in the table of contents.

Most of the experiences described here happened to me or to people I know and trust. We don't have any special credentials. We're ordinary people who've had uncommon experiences.

For many years mine scared me. I wish a book like this had been available for me to read then because my fear diminished my psychic abilities. However, having acknowledged my fear—with it "up front and labeled," as William Faulkner advised—I shall now set it aside, for I want to write objectively for my readers, without my fear weighing on me, skewing my words.

I don't pretend to have had all the experiences I've written about in these pages, but I've had many, enough to understand the process involved in coming to terms with them. I like to think of myself as normal, just as I'm sure you think of yourself as normal, too. That's hard to remember when people look at me like I'm crazy. Or when I think, *I must be nuts!*

After much research and introspection, I came to this conclusion: Normal people sometimes know things that they can't possibly know. That's when gooseflesh races along our arms and legs, alerting us that we're in touch with a mighty power.

You and I might both have the same experiences. The only difference between us is that I'm reckless enough to write about mine. In fact, it's the writing craft that gave me the idea for this book. Not long ago, I published a novel called *Alison's Legacy* about an innkeeper in the eighteenth century. She has a psychic friend who can see the past in a blazing fireplace and also has an uncanny flair for showing up when the heroine is in jeopardy.

To promote the novel, I arranged a book signing in the library of a neighboring town, Scottsdale. Eight people showed up. My Glendale librarian said she'd host me, but she'd have to fit me into a series on New Age topics. Could I speak about psychic events in our lives? I agreed. Eighty people showed up.

That large turnout convinced me that most people prefer to explore their own psychic potential rather than read about the abilities of some fictional character. They want a narrative that they can relate to, that they can interpret as being of relevance to themselves; they want to read about experiences that touch their own lives, experiences in which they have a personal interest, perhaps because they have been in similar situations themselves, or perhaps because something similar has happened to their friends or relatives. They want to *identify*. And so I have written this book about myself... about *us*.

The text appears in two parts. The first tells how psychic experiences happened to me. You can compare where your story and mine intersect. The second part includes research, history, other people's stories, and comments on what's worked and what hasn't in my own search to make sense of the paranormal. Resources follow each section in the second part along with books and websites for further research in case you want to follow up in depth. You'll also find an index at the end of the book to help you shuttle around.

Out of the Psychic Closet isn't necessarily a validation of your paranormal events. We all have to look to the integrity of our own hearts and minds for that. But, when you finish reading, I hope you too will step proudly out of the psychic closet, your consternation transformed into awe and your fear into gratitude for living in the flow and sharing the interconnectedness of the universe.

Toby Fesler Heathcotte
Glendale, Arizona

PART ONE

HOW IT HAPPENED TO ME

Psychic awareness seems to happen to us, makes an indelible imprint on our memories, and throws our worldviews into chaos. The experiences provoke reassessment of who we are, what our capabilities are, and what impact others will have on us.

With nurturing, psychic awareness can grow and help us live our lives in rewarding and insightful ways. Without nurturing, we struggle against ourselves.

Chapter One

Witness to Another World

Ghosts

Now, I know I'm not crazy, but I spent years trying to believe what people told me was the truth and trying even harder not to believe what I knew within myself was real.

Maybe I'd started on that path by the age of three. Sleet bit my face. My bare arms felt numb in the cold air. "Wait, Daddy!" I screamed and staggered across our backyard away from our house toward my grandparents' house in Ovid, Indiana.

Daddy's jacket billowed when he turned toward me and opened the screen door. "Go back home."

Hurrying to him, I slipped and fell on frozen grass.

He let go of the door. It clattered as he dashed down the steps and engulfed me in his arms. "You can't go in there."

"Why not?"

He bit down on his quivering lip. "Grandpa's dead."

"What dead, Daddy?" I sobbed. "What dead?"

It turned out to be something awful. "Dead" took Grandpa away; then a few weeks later it took Grandma too. Where did they go? Why did they leave us alone? I was scared.

Daddy and Mother acted sad. The next summer they sold both houses, and we moved to Pendleton, a town five miles away. I missed Grandma and Grandpa, but I felt glad that I got to see my other grandparents, Mom and Pop Crosley, a lot more.

One day Mother and Daddy took me to stay with Mom at the Crosley house. Mother looked very pretty in her blue dress with the fluffy peplum around the middle, but her face looked like she had a bellyache from eating too many green apples. Daddy held her waist. Their footsteps made hollow sounds as they walked off the porch.

Mother called back, "Don't worry. I'll be all right."

I loved to stay with Mom Crosley because she told me stories about her family and sang songs in her deep, trembling voice. Not today. She folded her arms over her starched gingham dress and paced around the dining room table. The shiny wooden floor creaked beneath her soft slippers.

I sat at the table where we ate fried chicken every Sunday and tried to fold dress tabs on paper dolls. The grandfather clock ticked loudly. "Is Mother sick?"

"We don't know. We'll just have to wait and see." Mom nibbled a mint from the cut-glass bowl. "She's got a baby inside her, and it might be sick."

After a long time Daddy brought Mother back. I thought she would bring the baby with her, but she didn't. I felt happy anyway. I didn't want her to go away anymore.

Many times, I went with Daddy to the little graveyard across the road from a country church. We never went inside. He mowed the grass while I sat on a tombstone and played with my dolls. In the fall, I picked dead blooms off the magenta peonies Daddy had planted beside the graves of Grandma and Grandpa. Nearby lay Daddy's brother who died as a baby and a sister dead at the age of ten. I tried to picture the children, lying beneath the earth in their little boxes. I felt afraid for them.

Daddy didn't cry as he told me about his family. He said we had to keep their resting places nice. That way we could show our love. Some other people's graves had high grass on them. A few had overgrown weeds, the tombstones cracked and broken. I wondered why no one loved those people.

The summer I turned six, my parents took me to a rodeo where my dad bought an all-black Shetland pony named Rocket. We took the backseat out of our 1941 Chevrolet, squeezed the pony in, and drove home with him whinnying or nibbling our hair all the way.

Ostensibly Daddy bought Rocket for me and my little sister, Trena, who was born the same summer, but he treated the pony like his own pet. He taught the pony to stand up on his hind legs and to drink grape soda from a bottle. He let us feed Rocket sugar cubes, apples, and potato peelings with salt on them. Rocket tried to bite the buttons off everyone's shirts and gulped down Daddy's Lucky Strike cigarettes. That pony had some poor nutrition habits.

My dad raised hunting dogs and fed any cat that wandered by, but Rocket was my special pet. Daddy taught me to drive a sulky in summer and a sleigh in winter. I gave the other children rides two at a time.

One of my best friends in the neighborhood was Marcia Stoner. By second grade, she and I had acquired two passions—roller skating and Brownie Scouts. Our mothers took turns giving us rides.

Just my size and very pretty, Marcia had long blond curls with a ribbon. I wore a bow in my black hair. New Year's Eve, instead of going skating as we had planned, Marcia visited relatives with her aunt and uncle. In those days before seat belts, she lay asleep in the backseat on the way home late on a snowy Indiana night.

A car driven by a drunk driver hit them. On impact Marcia flew out the back window. All her major bones broke, and her skull fractured.

Two days later, Marcia lay in a casket lined with pink rosebuds for the viewing in her family's living room. She wore the brown uniform of a beginner scout. I gazed at her, horrified, imagining all the broken bones I couldn't see. Her mother sobbed beside my mother and me. Others sat about, whispering and crying, including Marcia's two little sisters and several neighbors.

Because Marcia couldn't, I vowed that day never to go through the ceremony that conferred the right to wear the green uniform of a full-fledged Girl Scout.

At the funeral in the stone-walled Methodist church, I refused to go down to the altar to look at her again. The organist played the strains of Brahms' *Lullaby*, which sounded ugly to me at the time. The stench of hothouse gladiolas and roses blended with the musty smell of carpet soggy from snow boots. Nauseated, I sat on a wooden pew and cried.

In the weeks that followed, Mother encouraged me to play with other children, but I missed Marcia and kept to myself.

One sunny day, warm enough that the ground had thawed and started to green, I lay in my backyard, watching soft, white clouds move across a gray sky. The scent of first cherry blossoms carried on the air.

Suddenly Marcia appeared on a large cloud. Her curls bobbed over the side as she leaned down and grinned at me. Funny, she didn't wear a hair ribbon, but the impish voice sounded just like hers. "Hi."

I scrambled up and shouted, "Marcia, is that you?"

"Yes, this is a good place. I'm having fun here." Marcia turned away from me and disappeared into the cloud.

I went tearing into the house. "Mother, Mother?" I found her shelling peas in the kitchen. I shouted, "I saw Marcia. She's alive up in heaven, and she said she's all right!"

'Now, Toby," Mother said as she set down the colander. Her pretty face looked sad. "You know Marcia can't talk to you. You're just imagining that."

Her words didn't make sense. How could I see Marcia if she wasn't there? How could I hear her?

Mother hugged me. Her body felt skinny now and her hug warm, but I remembered before my sister's birth how Mother's hugs had felt awkward over the huge mound of her stomach.

A memory clicked in my mind, and I asked, "What happened to that other baby?"

Mother's pale green eyes clouded with some emotion I didn't understand. "There wasn't any other baby. You must be thinking of something else." Mother sighed as she straightened my hair bow. "Why don't you go find out if some of the other kids can play?"

I trudged outside and started up the gravel alley. Mom Crosley and I were wrong about the other baby. If there had been one, Mother would have told me. Now she said I had not seen Marcia, and so, obviously, I was wrong about that, too—even though Marcia on the cloud looked as clear and real to me as when she sat next to me in school. I'd believed she was there—but it seemed I had been mistaken.

If I ever saw Marcia again, I would know it was my mind playing a trick on me. I'd make her go away, and I would definitely never tell anyone. When people are dead, they are gone forever.

Later that summer, Daddy and I took peonies for Marcia to the big cemetery in Pendleton with all the graves mowed and tidy. I felt glad to know that Marcia was still loved even though she was dead. I stood silently there and didn't talk to her. What would have been the point? Marcia wouldn't hear me, anyway.

Near-death Experiences

About the time I turned ten, my thirteen-year-old cousin Judy contracted Hodgkin's Disease. Everyone said we looked just alike, both with freckles, except she had red hair while I had black.

Big lumps raised on Judy's body. I felt the one on her neck. It was like she had a hot golf ball under her skin. I don't know what the doctors tried by way of medication, but eventually they gave up hope. In desperation, her parents took Judy to a man who laid his hands on people and tried to heal them. Judy screamed under his touch. She said it felt like heat going through her and cried that she didn't want to go back. So her parents didn't take her. They all feared the healer's power. He might be of the devil.

The day before Judy died, she said Jesus stood at the end of the bed. He told Judy He was waiting for her.

At her wake, relatives and friends filled Judy's living room with its hardwood floors and knickknack shelves on the walls. The mourners sat on folding chairs borrowed from the church and fanned themselves with paper palm fronds.

Daddy held my little sister on his lap while I hovered near him, scared and uncomfortable. Tears fell down his cheeks as he squeezed her arms repetitively. I was stunned. I'd never seen him cry before.

The story whispered about Jesus seemed to comfort Judy's mother but not Daddy. Or me. Actually, I knew better. Nobody came to talk to the living, not Marcia or Jesus. Judy thought she saw Jesus, but she couldn't really have done so. He probably took her, like He took Marcia. I could be next. *I knew that when people died, they were dead, and that was that.*

The summer of my eighth-grade year, my remaining grandfather, Pop Crosley, fell ill, and went to the hospital. Things were bad because Mother and my two uncles took turns staying with him. One afternoon I watched from the front door of our gabled house on Adams Street as they all got out of the car at the same time. I knew Pop had died or they wouldn't have left him alone.

They seemed mystified that, at the last minute, Pop had sat up in bed and yelled out, "I'm not going with you!"

My mother's brother, Uncle Sonny, called Pop, "A fighter to the end."

But Pop had fallen back on the bed, lapsed into unconsciousness, then died.

"Who was he yelling at?" I asked.

"We don't know," Uncle Noonie whispered mournfully.

Mother turned away with a fearful look. "The drugs made him crazy. He didn't know us at the end."

Retrocognition

I wished I could have some hope of seeing Pop again, but I couldn't.

Mom Crosley stayed with us for a few nights after his death and slept with me. She didn't really sleep. She walked the floor while I lay in bed and alternately dozed and watched her. Finally, about the time of my fourteenth birthday, she announced that she needed to go home. Mother insisted that Mom should not stay in the house alone, so they talked it over and decided that someone should go with her. My parents couldn't do it, with Daddy working and Mother taking care of my little sister. So it was decided that I should go.

The plan called for me to stay in the front bedroom while Mom returned to the bed where she had slept with Pop for over forty years. Later she must have considered that a mistake because in the night she climbed in bed with me. Still she couldn't sleep and ended up telling me stories.

One fascinated me, about her father, Joseph, who saw a banshee, a dark-cloaked woman who paced back and forth in front of the house as a warning when someone was about to die. Mom said people came to him for advice about things not understood. If Mom ever tried to communicate with the dead, she never mentioned it. I didn't mention Marcia either.

Mom told me about the cedar chest at the end of the bed. The chest contained all the memorabilia of her older son and daughter and their days of singing gospel music all over Indiana, even on the radio. I had never met this aunt and uncle, Mom and Pop's two older children. The girl died pregnant with her first child at twenty-one. I hadn't even been born yet, but I felt like I knew her because Mom talked about her daughter so much. Her clothes still hung in Mom's closet. The dead daughter had worn size three shoes and size three dresses. My feet and body were already too big for them. The oldest son had had a squabble with Pop and moved to Anderson eight miles away, but he might just as well have moved to the other side of the world.

Mom hadn't finished grieving the loss of her daughter and son. Now Pop was gone, too. She told me over and over how much she loved them, how she missed them, how she had tried to get her son to come home. She had begged him to come to see his sick father or even just come home for a visit, but he wouldn't. To grieve for the living seemed worse even than to grieve for the dead.

Those gospel singers inherited their voices from their mother. While we sat up in the bed at night, the room glowed from the pinks and greens refracted through the hand-painted lamp globe. Mom sang, in a big contralto that belied her tiny body, *The Letter Edged in Black* and some song about a train bearing a corpse in a coffin. She sang *The Battle Hymn of the Republic* and *The Old Rugged Cross*. I felt sorry for Mom, but her songs made me afraid to go to sleep.

Eventually, I moved to the back bedroom with her. Mom's grown son, Uncle Sonny, and his wife lived next door and were expecting a new baby. One night, I awoke and saw Mom wedging a crib between the bed and the wall. She put their eighteen-month-old, Stana, into it and shook me. "Wake up, Toby. The new baby's been born, and it's dead. Sonny and I are going to the hospital. You have to take care of Stana." Mom ran out, leaving the bellowing child in the crib.

I scrambled to the end of the bed, confused, thinking at first that I heard the dead baby crying and wondering how a dead baby could cry. Then I realized it was Stana whom Mom had wanted me to watch, so I crawled out and grabbed her. I felt scared for Uncle Sonny, for his wife, and for the little baby, dead before it ever got to live. I feared for myself. Cuddling Stana, I walked for hours. Every time I put her down, she started screaming again. Finally, Mom came home again. Stana and I fell immediately into exhausted sleep.

When Uncle Sonny's wife returned from the hospital, I went next door to visit her. With my still-immature psychic eyes, I saw the dead baby lying on the bedroom floor. I never walked into that room again and never told anyone why. Like a sniper, death took people in pairs—five pairs in quick succession—first my grandparents, then Judy and another cousin, now Pop Crosley and Uncle Sonny's baby.

A man down the street died; his widow survived him by only three months. Our neighbors across the street, a couple, were killed in a car wreck together. They left an only daughter, my teenage babysitter. I could end up alone like her.

Eighteen deaths touched me personally by the time I was thirteen. Except when they were my relatives, Mother sent me out to collect flower money. I hated the sorrowful looks on the neighbors' faces when I explained my mission almost as much as I hated the clink of coins in the coffee can. Even more did I loathe the familiar, mauve viewing room in the funeral home, the sickening sweetness of fresh-cut flowers banked around a coffin, and the pasty, made-up face inside.

Why, I wondered, did Jesus keep taking people away? How could He take our loved ones and leave us so sad here below? To say they were in a better place or to see death as the natural end of life meant nothing to me. Death was a horror that beset me. I feared its power to rob me of my loved ones or to take me helter-skelter.

If only Marcia had really talked to me, everything would have been all right. Then I'd have proof of the afterlife. That connection between us would have become my salvation. Without it, I felt doomed to live in fear of life as much as in fear of death.

The Spiritualist Camp in Chesterfield lay a ten-mile drive from our home, but everybody rolled their eyes and laughed at any mention of the mediums there, believing them all to be fake and crooked, not to be trusted.

Until I graduated from high school, I continued to attend church. I listened to the Sunday School lessons and even taught a class of four-year-olds, but none of the lessons sank in. I grew to resent the fact that my parents made me go to church but didn't attend themselves. When I asked why, they said they didn't need to. And neither, in my opinion, did I. Running away seemed the only way to make my own choices. The only place I could think to run to was college.

But when I suggested going to college, Daddy refused to allow it. He assumed I'd get married and thus waste the money spent to educate me. He also objected because he thought I'd lose any belief I had in God and become a Communist. But Mother overrode him by promising to sew clothes for people to help pay my room and board.

So, I enrolled at Indiana University, ninety miles from home and a universe away. Daddy had been right to worry. I lost my belief in God. Happily for all of us, though, I didn't become a Communist. I became a Democrat instead.

In an effort to find some new basis for understanding, I enrolled in a philosophy class and sat beside a handsome chemistry major. To say Bryan was bright and sexy with excellent spouse potential didn't touch the reality of my attraction to him.

We studied the Tao, existentialism, nihilism, other philosophies, and literary ideas. We explored the frameworks we'd been taught. As I had spurned a Protestant religion that failed to address my core needs, Bryan rejected the rigid, unquestioning faith that Catholicism required. We found intellectual answers in rationalism and empiricism.

Even though Bryan wasn't a Communist, he embodied my dad's worst fears about the dangers of college and its intellectual life. Besides, Bryan grew up in the inner city and looked more than a bit Italian. He had been overseas in the Army. He was smart and worldly. I considered him a perfect mate. My parents seemed less convinced.

Chapter Two

Fleeting Connections

<u>Dreams</u>

When my parents got to know Bryan better, they really liked him. We married soon after graduation and moved into an apartment in Bloomington. He changed his major to finance and went to graduate school. Soon our first child came, a beautiful boy we called Brandy. My earlier questions about my lack of trust in myself and about the futility of life under the control of a capricious deity receded. I saw some answers to my old, disturbing questions in my son's hazel eyes, and I began to trust my ability to understand what life was about. The responsibility to care for my child and to make a good home with his father gave my life meaning.

I got a call from Mother that my childhood babysitter, Helen, the one whose parents had died in a car wreck, intended to visit. I hadn't seen her since those tragic times. On Helen's arrival, we sat down to dinner in my parents' kitchen. I put Brandy in a high chair and excitedly shared the news of my second pregnancy.

Mother hoped for a girl, but Bryan and I along with my dad hoped for another boy as a playmate for Brandy.

Helen turned to Mother. "What was that baby you lost? A boy or a girl?"

Those questions floored me. I never heard Mother's answer. I was a little girl again back in Mom Crosley's dining room, listening to the clock chime, worry and fear in my heart. So there *had* been another baby all those years ago.

I got through dinner somehow, and after Helen left I asked Mother why she had told me she had not lost a baby.

Tears stood in her eyes as she whispered, "I didn't want to upset you. You were so little."

Where could my anger go in the face of Mother's sadness? I hugged her and set the matter aside in my mind.

A few months later, Brock, our second son, arrived.

High achievers in an environment where we thrived, Bryan and I fit in well together at Indiana University. Student loans came through when we needed them. I earned my master's degree. I always found a teaching job to augment our income. Bryan worked on his doctorate with a residency. Our sons were healthy and smart.

Our life flowed just as it should, but I couldn't rest. I often awoke in the night. Despite the abundance of my daylight life, night thoughts and nightmares filled me with fear of death. At times I wondered if I would ever get a decent night's sleep.

During his bid for the presidential nomination, Bobby Kennedy came to Bloomington where I saw him speak. A staunch fan, I worked on his campaign.

One night I dreamed I was passing out papers for his funeral. An easy explanation came to mind: Not long before, Jack Kennedy had been assassinated, and people feared a copycat crime. It happened, of course, the next week when Bobby went to California to campaign after he won the Indiana Primary.

Brandy, five at the time, hugged me and said, "We're all sad about Bobby, Mommy, but it's okay. We all have to die sometime."

Where had that wisdom come from? Because of my own childhood experiences, I had intentionally shielded my children. I didn't mention death to them. They'd never been to a funeral or seen a corpse.

Doubles

One night soon after, a rustling sound awoke me. I saw Brock, the four-year-old, scurry into the bathroom. I sat up and called to him then felt ridiculous. He looked transparent and wore an Indian-style feather on his head as little boys often do. Neither boy had such a feather in his toy box. I got up to go check on him. I went into the bathroom to find it empty. Sure enough, he lay in his bed, sleeping restlessly.

Clearly, I had seen an apparition of my son's physical body, often called a double, but I refused to admit the fact. I rationalized that I could have been dreaming. After all, I had been asleep before seeing the image. I dismissed the incident. In fact, I found it a relief to do so. I hated the intrusion of any possible psychic information.

A few days later, I saw a similar apparition of my friend Connie. She and I both taught at the local high school. Her husband also attended graduate school. She had a baby girl. While our kids played in the meadow between our married-housing apartment buildings one Saturday morning, Connie and I planned to attend a bridal shower for another teacher that afternoon.

I volunteered to drive and told her I would pick her up at one-fifteen. Connie wore a red sundress with matching scarf around her head. Because I wore shorts, I asked her if she intended to change clothes. She said yes, and we agreed to dress up more for the bridal shower.

At one-ten, wearing a dress, I drove into the turnaround of her apartment building and saw Connie walk through the door. I assumed she'd changed her mind because she still wore the red sundress. I glanced at the curb as the car came to a stop then looked back to find her gone. Perplexed, I wondered what had happened to her. In a moment she came through the door, actually wearing the same clothes.

As she approached the car, I called, "Did you forget something?" She shook her head. "Did you look out and then go back to get a drink of water or something?"

"No." Connie looked at me suspiciously. "I just came down the elevator. I've not been outside since I saw you this morning."

"I meant just now. You said you were going to change your clothes."

"What's the matter with you, Toby?"

The matter was that I didn't want to admit that I had seen her double. My conscious mind had anticipated that she would wear different clothes.

I couldn't use the excuse of being asleep this time. I'd seen her while wide awake, with the engine running on my car. I mumbled something inadequate, and we headed off to the bridal shower. I didn't forget, nor did I understand, what had happened. I rationalized that my imagination had worked overtime. I couldn't have seen Connie before she came through the door, therefore I didn't see her. In essence, I lied to myself.

When I returned home and described the two occurrences to Bryan, he agreed with my analysis. In fact, he thought my overactive imagination intruded as a result of my career choice, speech and drama teacher. However, he failed to convince me.

Soon after, I began to have unsettling dreams. In one, I walked along a clapboard sidewalk with Bryan. We went in and out of stores and looked at opals because he wanted to buy one for me. We tried to decide which we liked best of all the opal pieces, a ring, a bracelet, a necklace, or earrings.

When I came downstairs to the main floor of our apartment in the morning, Bryan sat at the Formica-topped table with a cup of coffee and the Sunday paper. He showed me an ad for opals and suggested he should buy me one. The ad featured a variety of stones set in different pieces of jewelry. With a laugh, I described my dream and its similarities. He laughed, too. After all, it was October, the month of my birthday. Just a coincidence. Not even remarkable.

Then another night, I dreamed that I stood in a public place with shower stalls set in a row. I tried to turn one shower on but it didn't work. I proceeded to the next, which wouldn't work. I finally got the eighth one to work.

The next day I went with some other mothers and children to a public swimming pool where I had never been before. After I changed into my swim suit, I stepped up to a shower stall and couldn't get the faucet to turn on. None worked until the eighth. The dream faucets lined up in a row. At the pool, eight shower heads came off one main pipe, two heads to serve each of four stalls.

When I became aware of having precognitive dreams, fear took over. One dream in particular haunted me because I believed it would happen.

I dreamed a young man I had grown up with and loved died in a car wreck. The image of twisted steel, broken glass, and his mangled, bleeding body sickened me.

Even though we lived in different states and hadn't talked since marrying other people, the dream so filled my mind with dread that I called to warn him. Fortunately, he seemed all right and promised he'd drive carefully. How could I ever know if my call had averted a disaster, anyway? If he did die, I might not know for a long time.

Afterward, I dreaded the dreams that filled my mind with awful images. I worried about what people would think of me should I wave a danger flag at them because of my dreams. I feared witnessing something terrible with no ability to change the outcome. The responsibility burdened me. Would I be to blame?

I decided I didn't want to know the future and began to suppress the dreams. On awakening, I busied my mind with the coming day's activities, deliberately crowding out any memory of unwanted dreams of what might happen in the future. Something inside me wanted to come out, a part of myself that didn't follow society's expectations or even my own, a part of myself I couldn't understand and feared.

I had an irrational desire to run away from the life I had known for twenty-nine years, as if a change of place would make it easier to push down the images and feelings from my unconscious mind. Now I realize how immature a response that was. How I imagined that simply moving away would solve my problems remains a mystery.

In any event, when Bryan began to interview for a permanent teaching position, I encouraged him to take one that got us as far from Indiana as possible. He wanted to leave the area too, so he interviewed only in states outside the Midwest. He was an excellent doctoral candidate and received several offers.

Arizona appealed to us most because of its dynamic environment, growing status in the country, and good climate for raising children. I hardly looked back, intent on establishing a life where I thought I could control the dynamics. Bryan and I obtained great teaching jobs, he at Arizona State University in Tempe and I at Carl Hayden High School in neighboring Phoenix. We focused on building a new house, amassing furniture, cars, clothes, and all the accouterments of prosperity.

Déjà Vu

Although I had rejected religion, I began to read, primarily academic works on reincarnation, yoga, and experiments in extrasensory perception (ESP), a safe path, I thought. I hoped science might fill the empty place. Instead children did, my own and my students.

One day I sat at my office desk during a publicity meeting with members of my drama club. A drama student named Patrick sat on a stool next to me and across from two senior girls on plastic kitchen chairs left over from a previous show. Because I needed a clipboard, I rose and started toward the classroom.

Patrick yelled, "Don't move." He sounded gruff.

The other students glanced up, and I turned to my usually mild-mannered student in surprise.

Shoving the stool aside, Patrick gestured around the room. "I remember this. We've done this before. You were sitting over here," he said to the girls, "beside each other, and Mrs. H. got up to leave."

We'd not had this particular meeting before with the same people present. "Did you dream it?" I asked.

"I must have." Patrick looked confused.

I recognized Patrick's experience—déjà vu, meaning "already seen" in French, a sense that one has previously witnessed or experienced a new situation. Naming the experience did not reassure me that either Patrick or I understood. Whether he dreamed the event before it happened or simply knew in a waking state seemed moot.

"Maybe you just made a mistake," one of the girl students offered.

Although we let the subject slide and continued with our committee meeting, I felt unsettled.

One afternoon not long after, I cooked dinner while my sons played outside.

"Mommy, Mommy, come out here," Brandy screamed.

Hastily, I set the lid on a skillet of fried potatoes and hurried out the back door to the patio where the washer and dryer hummed.

"Look at this!" Now six, Brandy stood beside the sandbox, both arms pointed toward its center with a flourish, like the announcer on *Miss America*. A grinning Brock sat inside surrounded by toys.

With a practiced eye, I scanned the children for injuries but saw none. "What is it?"

"The toys. The red truck and the green one." Brandy's tone sounded like he thought he was delivering the revealed word of God.

With a merry nod, Brock picked at brownie leavings around his lips. His manner indicated that he knew something was up.

What did my sons have on me? I looked over the sandbox and the toys with care. "What is it? I don't see."

"It's just like in my dream." Brandy said. "The red truck sat over there," he pointed at one toy, "and the green truck lay on its side." He pointed toward the other toy. "And Brock was sitting beside it. It's the same. Just like I dreamed it."

"You mean you put them in the same places just now?" I asked.

"No, the dream did it." Brandy's expression revealed that he believed the miraculous had happened.

My son gave me a wake-up call. He had demonstrated déjà vu or precognitive dreaming, abilities I'd been attempting to deny. It looked as if I needed to take these events more seriously. I could no longer rationalize them as mistakes or imaginings.

That summer I visited in Indiana and sought out Uncle Noonie. He had once dreamed his friend had a heart attack and died on the street in front of the bank in Pendleton. The friend did die of that cause in that place within a week. Uncle Noonie didn't understand precognitive dreams any better than I did. Neither did we understand where the line fell between déjà vu and precognitive dreams, whether they were the same or merely similar.

Since we knew so little about psychic abilities, we had no notion of whether or not they could be inherited. If they could be, we assumed we'd inherited the talent or curse from our common ancestor: His grandfather and my great-grandfather, Joseph Hayden, the one who had seen the banshee walk back and forth in front of a house when someone inside was about to die. People came to Joseph with problems, and he gave them psychically obtained advice. Joseph did not earn his living as a psychic. He was a farmer and raised ten children, including my grandmother, Mary Elizabeth Hayden Crosley.

With no friends or family in Arizona with whom to explore these issues, naturally as a teacher I turned to books as mentors. I began to read, primarily about precognition, doubles, astral projection, and dreams. My fascination paced my growing knowledge.

I wanted to experiment with some of the things I'd been reading. I wanted to go to a hypnotist and have a past life regression. I wanted to have my fortune told. I wanted to consult mediums and perhaps even get to know them personally.

Bryan had little patience for such exploration. He found my interest in these matters annoying and distracting. I had, after all, renounced spiritual searching before we married. This dispute was one of the reasons why our marriage ended.

Although I knew that Bryan and I needed to live separate lives, I felt heartbroken. I cried a lot, drank a lot, sat alone in my apartment a lot. I spent a good portion of my time feeling sorry for myself. I failed to comprehend my true emotions. It took a psychic event to reveal them to me.

Visions

One evening, overwrought, I looked in the bathroom mirror and saw two images of myself. One image looked like me with tears on my face. The other appeared to be an idealized version of me. I thought she was an angel. She asked if I wanted to stay alive. I realized then that thoughts of suicide had crept into my mind and I had not acknowledged them. I knew that I had to regain control of my life. My sons were teenagers, and they needed me alive, not dead.

I cried with relief, for just knowing that I had the choice between living and dying empowered me and gave me the strength to choose to live. I felt more peaceful and willing to work through my emotional pain. I had faced the thought of death, and paradoxically my fear of it was lessened. If I could even consider taking my own life, then I couldn't be as frightened of death as I thought I had been. I wasn't afraid of life, either. This experience had strengthened me, and I knew I could go on after the divorce and build a meaningful future for myself.

There was some force within me, and even though I couldn't comprehend it, I knew I had just for a moment seen a manifestation of it in the mirror.

Chapter Three

Speaking and Listening

Glossolalia

After my marriage ended, I needed support. Most came from other women teachers who had been through a divorce, but I also looked for spiritual underpinnings. The teachings of the Methodist Church hadn't stuck. I don't know why I felt I could find solace in a funda-mentalist Christian group, except for the fact that my roots lay there. I had been baptized in an Evangelical United Brethren Church that my parents once attended. I doubted they found much comfort in it or they'd have returned when they faced so much heartache during my childhood, but I tried anyway.

For a while, I helped a gospel singer with his ministry, scheduling concert dates and attending some of his concerts. I had the chance to listen to two different congregations speaking in tongues, one a charismatic Catholic group, the other Pentecostal. One person began to chant, others joined in, and soon almost the whole congregation chanted. Although they used unintelligible words, a powerful rhythm emerged, a contagious swell of sound. I felt swept along on a wave of group energy.

Voices

The gospel singer charmed me in part because he believed in the efficacy of altar calls to accept Jesus and a set of beliefs that assured one's salvation. I attended his church, similar to Baptist, but began to feel alienated because their message seemed like pastoral nostalgia to me. Their simple explanations of the beyond didn't satisfy me.

One evening before a Bible study, which I didn't want to attend, I heard a voice in my head say, "Toby, go to the Bible study." The voice, neither male nor female, sounded crystal clear.

Of course, I went. That could have been Jesus commanding. I waffle on His general instructions from time to time, like a failure to love my neighbor as myself, but a direct order I would never disobey. Amazingly, the Bible study concerned the Old Testament story of the boy Samuel, who heard the voice of God.

When I asked the pastor if he thought it possible to hear voices in our times, he said, "Oh, no, only the prophets of the Bible. People who think they hear voices now are deceived by the devil. That's witchcraft."

I left the church because I didn't want to associate myself with restrictive ideas, particularly ones that denied my own experience and described me by implication as evil. Besides, the inner voice had been on my side.

<u>Retrocognition</u>

Not so my next psychic experience. During the first year of separation from my husband, I lived in a condo on a major thoroughfare where anyone with an interest could find out my daily routine. I returned from school around four o'clock on regular days and six on rehearsal days.

Once during final exam week I came home early, about two-thirty, to find the front door standing ajar. Someone else had entered the house. It didn't take a premonition to know that.

Drawers stood open on my desk in the living room. The condo had a shotgun floor plan with all the rooms opening off a central hallway. I got nervous as I crept along, looking first in the bathroom, then in Brock's bedroom, then in Brandy's. I sensed another person in the house.

When I walked into my bedroom, the patio door stood open, the drapes swinging. The yard was empty, but the back gate remained locked. Whoever had been inside must have gone over the wall.

As I turned away from the patio, I saw a vision, or maybe a psychic remnant, of a man lying on the carpet among articles of my underwear strewn all over the floor. He held a pair of my panties up to his face. He wore jeans and a plaid shirt. I could pick him out of a crowd, he appeared so clear to me—about thirty years old, five-ten, one-hundred sixty pounds, brown hair tied back in a pony tail, a white guy with a bit of acne, a wide forehead, and a long, narrow nose.

Of course, I immediately called the police. While I awaited them, I searched for anything missing. The thief had ignored an envelope lying on my desk with a hundred dollars inside. He'd left with a camera and my peach-colored panties. Why he stole those items is still unknown. When the police arrived, I described the events and what I'd found. I also told them what the thief looked like.

The policeman asked, "You actually saw him?"

"Well, in a way...." I explained how I'd seen him psychically, and I used the technical term for the phenomenon: retrocognition

The policeman gazed at me with what I interpreted as wrenching disregard.

Nothing came of the police investigation. I never got my camera back, or my peach panties. But I began to see the irony of searching for truth outside myself while seeing and hearing it inside.

Precognition

I stopped denying my own experiences. Still, I didn't know where the voice came from, or the image of the burglar, or whether I might be going crazy. Accepting one's experiences for what they are and accepting them as genuine phenomena weren't quite the same. I could at least admit I'd had a dream or vision or other experience. I felt less and less willing to deem them as symptomatic of psychosis or even neurosis although doubt continued to plague me. At this point in my life I became more open to exploration. I believed I had to or never get to a place where I could understand myself.

I began to experiment with psychic phenomena and generally delved into the occult. I paid for a session with a trance medium who told me of a past lifetime as an Arab dancing girl. Something about owning such an identity both attracted and repelled me, but I didn't have any reference points for evaluation. Dick Sutphen, a local author and teacher, held a seminar on reincarnation in Sedona, and I attended. Sutphen regarded past life memory as something anyone could attain with some effort and led us in guided meditations. I only saw hazy pictures of myself in other times and place, but I still recall the exultation of a hundred people holding hands and chanting the word om.

Next came a class designed to help me experience astral projection. Arranged in pairs, eight students sat in the teacher's living room.

I followed the instructions to hold the hands and touch the knees of a person I did not know, a young man who sat on an ottoman in front of my chair. I imagined myself floating into my partner's home and described what I saw, images that included peacock feathers. Later my stunned partner confirmed that he had a stuffed peacock in his living room, not a normal decoration. Despite the successful demonstration, I had no sense of having traveled through the astral plane. I merely saw pictures with my eyes closed.

Not long after, I injured my neck while exercising and went to the health center for electro-massage. Before the treatment, I lay on a heating pad. The nurse suggested I close my eyes, relax, and let the machine do its work. Then she went away.

After relaxing, I noticed a woman looking down at me. More precisely, her face seemed to hover above my own. I had the uncanny feeling that the nurse had not returned because the image looked like my own face. I thought, *My goodness, I'm out of my body.*

Then I popped back inside my body, amazed at the momentary glimpse of myself from above. I could see myself from both inside and outside my body. That little incident seemed a real instance of astral projection. I didn't feel afraid. I felt thrilled.

By far the most important change I made during this period of exploration was to begin recording my dreams. I'd always remembered dreams from time to time, recording an occasional interesting or unusual one. When I read Patricia Garfield's book called *Conscious Dreaming,* I decided I might be missing something important, so I began to keep a notebook by my bed and make notes when I recalled a dream or scrap of one in the morning.

Dreams mentored me more than any book or person. I had to learn to see connections to my waking experience and apply what I learned.

One evening I fell off a chair from which I precariously balanced to replace a light bulb in a ceiling fixture. The glass of the crushed bulb cut deeply into my hand and severed an artery. Blood dripped from my hand into a mixing bowl. Brock, now a teenager, drove the car as we sped through the deserted Phoenix streets that gloomy night. Once I was admitted to the emergency room, I counted twenty stitches before losing track in the glaring white brilliance of the hospital lights.

Later, when I read my dream journal for another purpose, one entry from two months earlier jumped out at me:

I had dreamed I was bleeding from my hand.

A brusque warning not to be careless of my hand nestled obscurely between two other dreams. It can be enlightening to keep track of one's dreams, for had I not been recording them, I would never have recalled the warning at all. As I became more aware of the information available to me in dreams, I tried to pay better attention.

One time I dreamed about driving my car through roadblocks. On awakening I considered roadblocks a metaphor for some difficulties I'd experienced at the high school where I taught. Maybe, but on the way to work I had a fender bender, the first I'd had in years.

The dream of the roadblocks was probably prophetic in a general way. One dream that left no doubt occurred a few weeks later.

When I awoke one morning, I went to the door to let in Clete, our white cat, but he was not in sight. I lay down on the couch and fell back to sleep. In a dream with very bright colors I saw Clete in a plastic bag. The next day I learned he had been killed by a car and put in a plastic bag by the caretaker at the condo complex. The actual event happened within an hour after my dream.

That dream I had had of Clete tested Brandy's ability to believe me. He kept insisting I'd written the dream down after the event happened, but I hadn't. No amount of his saying the precognitive event didn't happen altered the fact that it had happened. His reaction hurt me. I'd always prided myself on my honesty, and it frustrated me to have someone I loved disbelieve me.

Even though I reminded Brandy of his childhood precognitive dreams, he denied my experiences so he could keep on denying his own. I tried to understand. After all, I had done the same for years. For the most part, I still didn't know how to distinguish prophetic dreams from any other kind, but this one I could not dismiss because of the intense colors. There was an otherworldly brilliance to the dream as if I had stepped into another reality. Days later the experience haunted me.

Channeling

Every time I faltered in the process of writing this book, I reminded myself of what I had said in the Preface, namely that I wanted to write objectively. I wanted to write as true an account as I could. What follows was the most difficult segment for me to include because it provoked the greatest fears about my sanity and about my acceptance by family and friends.

> *Dreams are poems... symbols of the good life... hope for the future. Drink milk. You can do automatic writing. Try it.*

Jarred awake, I watched my hand hold a pen and travel across the page of a spiral notebook. I lay on my left side in the bed where I had slept several hours of the night already. I stretched to reach the notebook lying on the bedside table. Blue light from the swimming pool shimmered through slatted window blinds.

I marveled at the meaning of the words filling the page.

> *Many times I have encouraged you, but you lose for lack of confidence. Don't analyze so much. Just let it flow. Automatic writing is the beginning of mediumship. Pay attention to it. Hold the pen loosely in the hand and doze. You have to hold the thought in your mind, not think it. Just hold it and let it come out the pen.*

What on earth was happening? Why couldn't I control my hand? I wanted to cry out but felt fascinated by my hand holding the pen in a rigid, upright position and sliding across the page. This bizarre episode couldn't continue. Grabbing my right hand with my left, I stopped the trail of progressively more indecipherable squiggles.

Sitting up, I turned on the bedside lamp, looked around at the familiar lavender walls, blue draperies, and pillows piled in the corner. My fear diminished as I realized no real harm had come to me. I felt less disoriented than after a dream but far more astonished. In such an agitated state, I knew I couldn't go back to sleep and walked downstairs to drink a glass of milk as advised. I paced the floor and smoked a cigarette.

Despite my struggles with precognition, telepathy, and other ESP, I perceived this experience as remarkable because of its physicality.

I'd always pooh-poohed physical mediums with their séances and ectoplasm. But I had watched my own hand write across the page, knowing I had no previous thought or knowledge of the words written. I had to read the page to discover their meaning.

The next day I called a friend who seemed much more comfortable with the unknown than I and explained the event in the night. She suggested I talk to an acquaintance of hers named Janet, a psychic who knew about such things. When I phoned, Janet declined to listen to my concerns. She preferred to speak to me face to face so that her intuition would function better.

A few days later, I sat nervously in a window booth at Denny's, rolled my napkin into a cylinder, and sipped iced tea with lemon.

"You must be Toby." A short woman in a crisp white blouse and dark skirt stood by the booth. When I nodded, she sat down. A gentle smile lit a round face framed by reddish brown hair. "You could do automatic writing if you wanted to."

Surprise is too weak a word for my reaction. "That's what I wanted to talk to you about." Feeling foolish, I gave her the details of my dream's teaching about automatic writing and confessed my nervousness at the whole prospect. "I hope I'm not going crazy."

When the waitress arrived, Janet ordered coffee then turned to me. "You are honored to have the gift." Her demeanor commanded belief. "Why don't you just make a private time to relax with a pen and paper handy, quiet your thoughts, and see what happens. What have you got to lose?"

"Nothing, I suppose," I mumbled. *Besides my mind.*

Janet patted my hand. "Automatic writing is Spirit's manifestation through you, and that's good."

"That sounds great, but I'm not sure I believe it."

The waitress set the coffee on the table and raised a questioning eyebrow at me. I waved her away.

While Janet drank coffee, she described her fear and doubt when dead people first spoke with her. After testing the messages and discovering how often they were true, she accepted the gift as a positive one. She suggested that I might come to the same conclusion about automatic writing, should I decide to give it a try.

I appreciated her willingness to share and thanked her. Then we said good-bye.

It's one thing for a medium to profess belief in Spirit's manifestation, but it was quite another thing for it to happen to me. Janet seemed to believe that spirits from the other side communicated with us. I needed proof. Was another mind involved dictating to me from the beyond, or had my wits abandoned me?

A part of me wanted to convince myself that the dream instructions had been *just a dream* and not worthy of such extensive follow up as I was giving it. My own illogical reaction annoyed me. After all, I had recorded my dreams for quite a while and knew them to be by turns fanciful, insightful, and even creative in solving problems. Now, I was the recipient of dream instructions, and I felt alarmed, for it seemed to me that there was another intelligence involved.

I followed Janet's suggestion the next evening, feeling silly, certain nothing would happen. Comfortable at my homey roll-top desk, I idly gazed at the wooden pigeonholes filled with stapler, scissors, note cards, ads for theatrical performances, and other paraphernalia. With a spiral notebook open and a pen poised above it, I tried to empty my mind. My eyelids felt heavy.

The pen moved across the paper just as it had in the night. To my astonishment, words appeared on the page.

> *It comes to me. Just wait. I am Agnes. Okay. Hollywood late 1930s, gold and white Cadillacs abound. Furs are in. Laughter is in. Excitement of parties and pools. Cold nights and hot days. Stage lights are merciless on the makeup and complexion. But I wouldn't trade it for any other life. Parts come to me with abandon, and I accept the ones I like. The play is important, but the player is more so.*

Fascinated, I began to read the words, grasping meaning only upon the reading, not during the act of writing.

> *When I was a young girl I saw horses killed and wept. I wanted to groom them and be part of their nature, but my calling was elsewhere. My calling was the stage with all its gaiety and pain, fraught with frustration.*

Who spoke in first person point of view? *Not I, Toby.* Another personality had authored these words. By some miracle, I remained calm
and continued to read the efforts of my right hand, which exhibited a
volition disconnected from my brain.

> *The pool of life is full of ripples too rare to understand.*
> *But we are intertwined, you and I, in a fine web of the*
> *future.*
> *To be free and ride in the wind with Charles in his*
> *roadster or on the back of the mare I love. This is wisdom;*
> *this is happiness; this is life in its magnitude.*

Agnes Moorehead came to my mind as the only actress with that
first name. I knew nothing about her except that she played the mother of the main character on the television show *Bewitched.* I had also
seen her perform once at Indiana University during my undergraduate
days. I knew of Hollywood, of course, and like everyone else imagined
what it would be like to work there.

When I read other people's efforts to prove psychic experiences
through research, I wondered if they might have slid off into wishful
thinking and fiddled a bit with the facts. As a result, I approached
the research with a high level of self-assurance that, if I uncovered
anything evidential that revealed Agnes Moorhead to actually be the
source, I would recognize it because I believed the contents of my own
mind. And what I knew about Agnes Moorehead was pretty much
nothing. In the Phoenix Public Library I searched for a biography to
see if I could substantiate any of the automatic writing. I found just
one, *Agnes Moorehead: A Very Private Person,* written by Dr. Warren
Sherk. The dust jacket said the author lived in Arizona. On a chance,
I looked him up in the Phoenix phone directory and learned that he
lived within a mile of my home, though I'd never heard of him.

Both excited and afraid of what I might find, I brought the book
home. If nothing fit, then I'd be able to dismiss the entire episode of
the automatic writing as a fantasy—a relief of sorts, though I'd then
have to deal with the possibility that I might have mental problems.

On the other hand, the facts might fit. What then? Might I be tapping into knowledge from another reality? What would that mean?

The automatic writing expressed a love for horses. The biography
said Agnes loved all animals. In the 1930s she rode a horse often. In

later years she had a favorite appaloosa mare, Endora, named for her part on *Bewitched*.

The automatic writing placed Agnes in Hollywood in the 1930s. The biography listed her first film there in 1939, *Citizen Kane* with Orson Welles, but she had already established her reputation as an actress during her radio days early in the decade.

The automatic writing said she liked to ride in a roadster with Charles. The biography named Charles Laughton as one of the most influential men in her life. Following that clue, I looked for information about his life. I knew little about him, though I had enjoyed his films.

In *Charles Laughton: An Intimate Biography* by Charles Higham, I found a story of the tour of *Don Juan in Hell*, the show I had seen while in college. Laughton and Moorehead performed with Charles Boyer and Sir Cedric Hardwicke. It seemed both Agnes Moorehead and Charles Laughton, who also loved cars, wanted to drive the tour bus very fast and laughed at Boyer for being afraid of the speed. A bus wasn't a roadster, but the actors had many opportunities to ride together in the eighty weeks of the tour or at many other times back in Hollywood.

The facts in the automatic writing certainly fit Agnes's life. Her biographer gave details. The most unsettling information came from the number of personality traits and habits she and I had in common, little things that struck the heart and not the mind:

- She taught speech, drama, and English before becoming an actress. I had followed the same teaching career for eighteen years.
- We both hosted annual Christmas parties.
- As adult women, Agnes and I stood five feet, three inches, weighed about one-hundred thirty pounds, and had freckles.
- We both had startling blue eyes that unsettled people when we stared too long at them. My Hispanic students found the color of my eyes unnerving, especially, I noticed, when I stared into theirs after they broke a classroom rule.
- Both Agnes and I spoke French as a second language.

- Lavender was our favorite color.
- We each took an intellectual approach to our dramatic work, she as an actress and I as a teacher of drama and a director of plays at the high school.
- Agnes and I both liked to philosophize about religion.
- We were compulsive workers, conscientious, loyal, prompt, and honest.
- Agnes and I loved horses. She had her Endora, and I had my Rocket.

After doing the research, I felt a kinship with Agnes born of similar character traits and interests. I also became more comfortable about the process of automatic writing. I lost my fear of the source although I still worried about my sanity. I didn't tell most of my family members and friends because I feared their ridicule or rejection. To be honest, if they'd told *me* such a yarn, I might not have believed *them* either.

I couldn't prove Agnes spoke into my mind and caused me to write about her, but something happened. It couldn't be a case of reincarnation because she and I had been alive at the same time. However, she might have communicated with me as a discarnate, a disembodied spirit. Was I an unwitting medium communicating with the dead? And this was only the beginning.

Chapter Four

The Presence of Power

Telepathy

Two years after the divorce, my sons and I lived in a condo in Phoenix. They had just begun college and traveled back and forth between there and Tucson. I began seeing Mike, a man I met. We had much in common in temperament and interest. He had written his master's thesis on dreams. Because I was opening more to my psychic potential, his interest in and openness to the unknown made him irresistible to me.

I read an article about an experiment done in dream telepathy. I'd long had an interest in telepathy, dream or otherwise. Over the years my sister and I had had a running joke about who got the long-distance charges between Indiana and Arizona since we generally talked for close to an hour. As a result I learned that, when I felt a strong urge to call her, I could delay to see if she would call me. Then she would have to pay, and I could have the laugh. It often worked the other way too, and she had the laugh.

Mike and I embarked on an experiment. While he slept in his bedroom several miles away, I focused on a particular picture. We decided a hit would be any dream he remembered with content that seemed similar to my pictures. I didn't tell him I intended to use album covers. We figured one hit would prove dream telepathy existed. That's not too scientific, but we didn't care.

Out of the fourteen attempts, five nights he had no dream recall. We termed all of the nine remembered dreams hits because they had some common elements with the album covers I had pictured. We more than proved dream telepathy to my way of thinking based on just one amazing hit. He dreamed of a family picnic at a patriotic holiday. His sister carried a turkey on something inappropriate like a paper plate, causing the juice to drip all over the place. My focus album? Charlie McCoy's album entitled *The Real McCoy* with the cover image of a harmonica in a hot dog bun on a paper plate embossed with the American flag.

We had other good hits, such as one night when Mike dreamed a very complicated story with no relationship to the album cover. Then, he laughed and said just at the end of his dream the actor George C. Scott popped in. My focus album had been *Patton*, the movie score with Scott's picture on the cover.

Spirit Guides

One evening while the dream experiments were in progress, I sat at my desk, pen and paper ready. I had only a short while before leaving for a graduation ceremony, something high school teachers attend year after year. I always enjoyed the event because I could kiss the senior speech and drama students good-bye and wish them a happy life.

In addition, I had told the medium Janet that I would practice automatic writing. I also wanted to find out what would happen. Would Agnes continue to write through me, or was that experiment over? I carefully avoided looking at the paper so I wouldn't influence what appeared on the page.

> *I am not Agnes but another. She is elsewhere engaged but profitably so. I am here to show you new directions for your impetus to fulfillment. I am Emmons. I come to you in dreams and see you as the one who can give life to my utterances. Trust the flow and we will end some good place. Farewell and happy graduation.*

I went to graduation and put the transmission out of my mind, but in the following days I took time for reflection on the arrival of a different personality. The change in writing style and focus fascinated me. The new personality seemed to have intentions greater than my curiosity.

Although I had never known anyone called Emmons, I remembered having dreamed about someone with that name. I skimmed through my dream journals for the past year and found a recorded scrap that said, "a man whose name is Emmons. Do exactly as he says." It appeared that I had known of his coming, however obliquely.

At the same time, I noticed another dream dated the year before that said, "This forgotten little redhead named Janet has something important to tell me." That note obviously referred to the medium I had just met for the first time at the restaurant. The year before, I definitely had not known her name, her occupation, or the color of her hair.

The next time I tried to do automatic writing, I felt intrigued and nervous at the same time and continued to keep my eyes shut so I couldn't consciously influence the composition.

> *There is a modicum of difficulty in transmission. I wish you would look at the paper while we do this, and that way we can see the progress.*

I opened my eyes.

> *Now, isn't that better? Relax. Don't force the flavor or the content into a mold that cannot carry the message. Don't worry about grammar and syntax. They will follow the thought as geese follow the wind.*

Emmons continued to teach me the process of automatic writing, taking up where my dreams left off. For my subconscious mind to teach my conscious mind seemed awkward, but I wondered if perhaps that turnaround happened more often than acknowledged, by me and by others. In any case, I wanted to find out where the path would take me.

A subsequent transmission identified Joshua Emmons, an Englishman who lived in the 1700s. He explained the relationship among Agnes, himself, and me.

> *We are faces of the mind. We are developmental rings of consciousness. The psyche fans out and overlaps with other psyches in concentric circles of psychic activity. As one grows and expands, more and more gain becomes available. Agnes and Toby share psychic space. I dip in and out.*

The use of the phrase "psychic space" helped me think of Agnes, Emmons, and me as connected to each other through thought rather than through anything physical. Defining our relationship in that way led me to believe that Agnes's appearance was a good introduction to automatic writing. Because she and I had so much in common, I felt less threatened than if Emmons had presented himself first. I'd needed proof. Agnes's life had been easily verifiable, and I had the confidence of my own previous ignorance of it.

After three or four sessions, I still doubted anything would come through every time I sat at my desk. I remained agitated about the format. Should I write or type? I tried them both. After I had tried to use a tape recorder, Emmons said,

> Be of good cheer. The words will come as they will. I
> impress on you ideas. It is yours to put them into the English
> language.

I stopped to light a cigarette then continued. Sometimes I felt tense and drank a gin and tonic, which relaxed me enough to do the light trances but not enough to feel tipsy.

Emmons began to impress his ideas although I felt awkward with the process. I finally decided to write in long hand on Tuesday and Thursday evenings then type the manuscripts on the weekend since I was teaching summer school.

The experience of automatic writing felt qualitatively different from the voice I'd heard the day of the Bible study. That voice sounded clear and loud at the back of my head, almost as if another person was speaking behind me.

Emmons's thoughts and words, on the other hand, had no sound to them. Neither did there seem to be any forethought on my part. The words simply flowed through my fingers onto the notepad. I found keeping my eyes open difficult since I often had rapid eye movements, a signal of my altered state of consciousness.

Sometimes I had difficulty maintaining focus because I feared interruption by one of my sons. Not that I didn't want them to know about my experiment with automatic writing. Rather, I feared upsetting them or having them worry about something they didn't understand. I didn't understand it all that well either and wouldn't be able to explain it with any kind of confidence.

I felt a lot of concern about not being in control of the process. However, I talked my fears out with another teacher, my friend Nancy, who shared an interest in the paranormal. She pointedly asked me who put the pen to paper anyway, if not I? Nancy encouraged me to keep a record of the sessions by dating them and making comments and references to my personal life at the end. Later there might be new perspectives on the material that I didn't see at present.

Her support gave me courage. I too believed in keeping a complete record of the transmissions and my reactions to them. If my experience with Emmons proved to give solid indicators of immortality, then my work would have great value. If my story became a treatise for psychiatrists tracking the descent into madness, then it would still have value.

One evening I sat at my desk, waiting to sense Emmons's presence. Our calico kitten scratched at the screen door, and I got up to let her in. I tried to do so without altering my relaxed state of mind. Brandy had named the cat Lucius in honor of one of his favorite football players. The cat was female—an example of my son's sense of humor.

> *In Lucius resides the essence of my message. I am the moment point for you—the onset of thought when you release all else that involves your life. I arise from your need to know the reach of human potential. You and she share in this moment of time. The impulse to movement and gratification is strong and propels you into action, thus she scratches at the screen door and you sit down to reach for me.*

Not long after, Emmons stated his desire to write a book on interpreting past life memories to help people grow spiritually. That prospect filled me with both apprehension and excitement. I had always wanted to write—plays, short stories, and essays, but not books. In fact, as an undergraduate, I majored in creative writing. Once I had intended to become an author, but teaching had taken first place in my time and effort. I regretted that shift but considered it an economic necessity. With my sons in college, writing could now become a higher priority for me. I worried about what my family and friends would think of me and to what strange places I might have to go psychologically. But, not to go was out of the question. The search meant everything to me.

Emmons gave a rationale for his book:

> *The belief in reincarnation provides a long view. There is much that can be gained from attention to this area of*

growth. It has validity and is manageable for the human mind to contend with.

To see oneself as an outgrowth of previous incarnations is to see oneself as a culmination of certain acts and thus an end product. That idea on its own has great value for the self-image and aids in the ability to develop self-confidence and self-assertion in the world. Reincarnation is not the ultimate explanation of your reality, but it is certainly a valuable tool by which to learn of yourself and to reach into your own history.

Again, I doubted myself. Who was I to think I could advance the spiritual search of others? That seemed so presumptuous of me, but to Emmons it appeared to be a life's work, or rather many lifetimes' work. I didn't know where I began or ended.

Considering how much energy I expended in teaching, I wondered where the stamina would come from to write a book. If Emmons were merely a part of my subconscious mind, wouldn't he also feel exhausted? Of course, I considered the outside chance I was masochistic, so I decided to talk the matter over with my friend Jacque, a counselor at the school where I taught.

When I presented my case to her, we'd stretched out on lounge chairs on the patio of my condo, she with a beer and I with a martini. June evenings were lovely in Phoenix. Even if the temperature had hit a hundred and ten during the day, nights seemed to have no weather at all. The air felt like my own skin, a perfect fit.

Jacque rumpled her tight brown ringlets. "So, what's so tough about writing a book? You've already committed to the time for transmissions two nights a week."

"I know, but that doesn't take any energy at all. I just sit down and relax. Then the words come. Writing a book's a whole different animal."

"It might be a bit of work, but what's the advantage in doing it?" Jacque always asked counselor-type questions, because she was trained that way.

I answered the question because I knew that Jacque would insist that I did. "If I managed to complete the book, I'd feel really good about myself. But it's a huge task and I'm not sure I've got the ability. Emmons seems to think I have."

"He can't do it without you. He needs you to do the writing."

"I know." But the whole idea seemed to me to be ludicrous. Who was I talking about, my inner self or some being from another reality?

"What do *you* want from all this, Toby? What will you get out of writing the book?"

In the garden space around the patio grew fragrant roses—pink, yellow, and red. Feathery bamboo plants trembled in the faint breeze; I trembled slightly myself. "Having something I can publish, I suppose. Writing's what I've always wanted to do, but I've believed I didn't have anything valuable to say."

"Emmons does." Jacque settled back and spoke softly. She had already accepted Emmons as a separate personality from me. "He wants to talk about reincarnation. What's more important than that?"

"Nothing. If it's true, then I can get rid of my fears about death."

"You feel that you fear death any more than anybody else?"

I sighed and picked up my empty glass. "I don't know if I'm ready to deal with all of this or not." Glad for an excuse to end the conversation, I headed toward the kitchen to fix dinner.

After dinner, Jacque went home, but she'd left me with a difficult question. Did I fear death more than other people? An honest look back at my childhood, with the death of Marcia and so many family members, persuaded me that I most probably did have greater fear than normal. I had worked through some of it when I dealt with my suicidal thoughts but not nearly all.

Over a period of a few months Emmons dictated the book during our Tuesday and Thursday sessions. He retained something of a human ego but not to the point of conceit, and he seemed kind and knowledgeable. He also gave messages about matters pertaining to my life and the lives of those around me. He interacted with me personally, a spirit essence who could just as easily have been a part of my psyche or a part of the ether.

Once I felt comfortable with him, I had the impulse to let Emmons speak through me. I never went into an unconscious state. I always seemed to stand aside and remain alert while Emmons communicated through me. It felt much the same to do automatic writing or to allow Emmons to speak through me. Both required a contemplative alteration of consciousness, not as deep as hypnosis.

While Emmons spoke through me in direct voice trance, I maintained awareness though without control over the thought processes and the words produced by it. My consciousness seemed to remain perched over my right shoulder. I never once felt afraid or threatened. I just waited passively.

Subjectively, the trance made Emmons more real to me than the automatic writing had. His personality came across much more prominently, distinctly different from mine. I liked him and found him charming, clever, wise, and more mature than I. More importantly, I trusted him.

One doubt daunted me. Emmons made a reference to Seth, a spirit personality who spoke through a medium named Jane Roberts. I had read her books, *The Seth Material* and *The Nature of Personal Reality.* At first, I'd thought the whole business bizarre, but Seth's ideas tantalized me, far more than did the preachers I had listened to in church: Reincarnation is a fact. We incarnate into physical form to learn to manipulate energy. We create our own reality through our beliefs. Our beliefs inform our emotions; they can make us sick or well. We communicate telepathically asleep and awake. Our conscious minds are powerful. The inner self has all the answers.

Was the experience with Emmons simply a copycat at so deep a level I didn't recognize my own mental processes? Or, did Emmons say the truth, that he and Seth came from the same reality?

Earth Mysteries

Two hours' drive away from my home lay Sedona, with its incredible red rock formations. I could feel the energy in those mountains. I was lucky enough to have a friend with a condo there, and for years I often went for weekend getaways. I always found the power of the place worked on my health. If I felt bad, perhaps with a backache, when I arrived, the pain worsened. If I felt good when I went, I felt wonderful there. More dreams came to me while in Sedona, several per night. The place intensified events and emotions for me—as well as my physical state. I can't account for the area's influence on my sense of well being with any scientific proof. However, many psychics believe Sedona amplifies their energy. That's why so many make it their home.

One time while Jacque and I sat on a blanket among the red rocks in Boynton Canyon in Sedona, a new spirit guide named Richard spoke into my mind. I felt as if his voice traveled through an ephemeral pipeline from a great distance. The top of my head seemed to reach the sky. I felt tall, expanded, a conduit for a mighty force. I feared that the force would swallow me up, that I would lose my individuality in the process. I felt very removed while channeling him.

Jacque posed questions to Richard, and I spoke his answers. She met Richard on an intellectual level. When she asked him about her path to God, he said through me:

There are no paths to God. We are all in God playing.

Richard presented a higher perspective on life. I believe he meant that because we are all a part of God, different manifestations of God, we can learn our spiritual lessons in a joyful way.

The experience of channeling Richard made me think more seriously about the repercussions of direct voice trance, unadulterated mediumship. I didn't want my family or Mike to know I'd gone that far. I relied on Nancy and Jacque to keep me grounded, and they accepted the new bent to my experience as genuine and not too bizarre. Once I became accustomed to the practice, I realized I hadn't faced anything new. This was the same experience as automatic writing. Perhaps it should be called automatic speaking.

In fact, Emmons came to my psychological rescue by giving me a personal message:

> *Long life induces laughter more than anything else.*
> *It's fun to be Emmons. It's fun to be, and that is a most*
> *important idea. Rejoice in being. I do. I love life. Live*
> *it zestfully wherever you are—in whatever stage of*
> *development. Only by totally exploring and enjoying where*
> *you are now will you advance. See how that works? Only if*
> *you are in the now can you pass on.*

However comforting those words, I knew not everyone channeled disembodied spirits. I was an oddity in my own mind as well as in other people's. At this time Mike decided our relationship wasn't working for either of us and ended it. He said his reasons had nothing to do with my psychic experimentation, and I believed him. But it would take a pretty dumb woman not to know I came to any relationship as a pretty big gulp.

Whatever the reasons, I missed Mike and wanted him back. Emmons told me:

> *Wisdom grows through pain, unfortunately. But pain can often be diverted through attention to viewing the underbelly of the situations of one's life. Look for the secret gift always to be obtained from the harsher realities, and know that growth comes, wisdom comes, through self-knowledge, your acceptance of self.*
>
> *In your private place, admit your inadequacies because never will they be eliminated if one does not admit to them, if one does not confront and diffuse them.*
>
> *No one is perfect who remains on the earth. If you are there, you know there are imperfections still. So freely admit them; freely seek them out. Only thereby can you improve yourself and become worthy of advancement to a higher plane.*

No one knew better than I my imperfections. Despite the disappointment of losing Mike, I continued to do automatic writing and received messages for many people. Jacque found hers helpful. She said they brought her peace of mind through understanding problems with a broader perspective. Nancy reacted the same way.

Once, Emmons gave a message for a teacher named Dave whose mother lived out of state. I didn't think he believed in psychic events, but I called him anyway. "How're you doing, Dave? It's Toby."

"Fine." His voice registered surprise. We rarely talked outside work. "What's up?"

"I was just thinking about your mother and..."

"My mother?"

"...uh, have you talked with her lately?"

"What's this about?" No doubt Dave thought I'd overstepped myself. I thought so, too, but Emmons had said Dave needed to receive the message.

I plunged on the best way I knew. "I've got a feeling, a really strong hunch, that your mother wants to talk to you, and I'm just encouraging you to call her." I could hear him clear his throat. "I think she wants you to call. Something about legal matters."

"I don't want to be rude, but how is this your business?"

"It's not really. I just had the message, the... uh... intuition, and I wanted you to know."

Dave's voice rose. "This is really bullshit. What's gotten into you? I don't believe in this kind of thing." In a barely softened tone, he added, "See you." The phone clicked in my ear.

He had figured out I was giving him a psychic message, something he despised. I felt so angry I could have crawled through the phone and wrung his neck, as my mother used to say. He had a colossal nerve to shut me off like that. Then, I remembered my own reservations about receiving psychic messages from Emmons. If it unnerved such a perceptive person as I, what would it do to a bigot like Dave?

From then on, I resolved always to inquire first in a general way as to people's beliefs about psychic things before I plunged into conveying any messages. I found it particularly difficult to predict teachers' views on the subject, and they made up the bulk of my adult acquaintances. I decided I'd better find some friends among the local psychics and in the New Age churches.

When I began the automatic writing, I feared I'd get lost in the transmissions, but after a time realized I was in control. No one, in this world or the one beyond, could make me do automatic writing or direct voice trance if I didn't want to. Spending my time as a medium had some huge drawbacks: I would not be able to write and teach. There was no escaping the religious overtones of the material, and I didn't see myself as a religious leader. Emmons from time to time made predictions that didn't come true. People would constantly roll their eyes at me if I let people know that I was receiving messages and speaking for him. I'd have to confess to my family what I'd been up to and suffer their disappointment, derision, or worse their embarrassment. I didn't see how I could accept all of those changes.

The more I dwelt on the problem, the less I received. Emmons finished dictating his book material. I sat down at the desk to reach for him, but nothing came. He was gone.

I felt glad and sad at the same time.

Chapter Five

Exploring the Knowledge

<u>Past Life Memories</u>

Back in Indiana Uncle Noonie fell ill with cancer. The doctors gave little hope of his recovery, and he remained in the hospital for several weeks. One night I dreamed that I waded across a river with him. When Mother called the next morning to tell of his passing, I didn't feel surprised because he and I had made a contact of sorts. I had lost my first mentor from the days when we'd compared notes on dreaming true.

Six months later, I got another call, that Uncle Sonny lay dying. I felt that old dread of death's double-down trick. It seemed to always take my loved ones in pairs. In all the years of my sons' growing up, only Mom Crosley has passed away, regrettable yet predictable, because of her advancing years.

I went home to Indiana, more prepared to deal with the emotions than in earlier years. My experience with mediumship came closer to proving the existence of the other side than any teaching.

In his final hours, Uncle Sonny spoke to departed family members, as if they were in the room with us. I had read of research on near-death experiences and considered us all lucky to witness Sonny's transition with his loved ones gathered on both sides of the veil. I held his hand when he died and felt a great sense of peace. I could almost see his spirit leave his body.

When I later described the moment to Mother, she got that old look of alarm in her eyes and asked in a trembling voice, "Are you a medium, Toby?"

"I don't know," I answered. Her fear for me unraveled my resolve. The pieces that had begun to fit crumbled into a pile again.

On returning to Phoenix, I failed to receive any psychic impressions that comforted me in my grief about Sonny. I also wanted to write something for the family about him but couldn't make myself sit and write it. Disappointed, I visited a Spiritualist Church, hoping for a message from him.

One of the psychics who worked at the church said to me, "Someone from the other side says he wants to give you a long-stemmed, red rose. Is that significant to you?"

"Yes." I remembered the one I'd given him.

"He sends you love and says you have a problem that he is going to help you with. There's a blond-haired woman with him. Would you know who that is? I have a feeling the woman is still alive."

"His wife."

"He says she needs some help and encouragement."

I felt relieved and the next day called my aunt to tell her of the message. My call meant a great deal to her and, I hoped, made her sorrow a bit easier to bear. The aid the psychic mentioned did come to me. That weekend I wrote my tribute to Sonny. He may have helped me because the words came easily. When I passed it out to the family, they all loved it.

Although I felt only an indirect connection with Sonny, a very satisfying dream came to me that helped dissipate my grief regarding Noonie:

> I dreamed I walked through a beautiful wood on a summer evening. I heard a campfire crackling and came upon Mom Crosley and Uncle Noonie sitting on a log before the fire. They turned toward me and gave me wonderful, loving smiles. Their skin glowed luminously in the firelight. Incredibly, they both looked about thirty years old and in excellent health.

Of course, I remembered from my own childhood what Uncle Noonie looked like in his thirties, but I'd never seen Mom Crosley at that age. Still, I recognized her. I wanted to believe that I had seen them and not constructed an image of them. So long as I could maintain that fragile belief, the dream consoled me.

In part to avoid my grief over the loss of my beloved family members, I set about preparing Emmons's book for publication. I welcomed the task I'd so dreaded before and began to compile the transcripts, separating the personal messages from book material. I discovered that my experiences during the time of the transmissions supported the ideas Emmons presented about reincarnation. They intertwined so that I couldn't decipher which caused the other. In Emmons's view, past life memories served to illuminate facets of our character, our needs, and our pursuits in the present lifetime. That made sense to me. What point would there be in remembering past lives if I could not gain some understanding of my present lifetime?

In the transcripts Emmons offered a way to gain perspective and self-confidence through understanding past lives. It suggested validating the incarnation through the life story told and gave some guidelines for analysis:

- Does the past life memory feel right?
- Is it close enough to the person's personality to allow assimilation?
- Can the material be integrated with the present self?

Three past life memories came to me—one in a regression with a hypnotist named Frank Baronowski, who wrote about some of his clients, one in a dream, and one in an automatic writing.

In the regression, I remembered a lifetime in the first part of the nineteenth century. As Susan Richards, I lived in a small town named Windsor, but the state remained unclear. However, I named Zachary Taylor as president, making the time period 1840s. I lived with and kept house for my father, who ran a business, perhaps accounting. Susan led a boring life with few social outlets.

That didn't matter to me because the experience amazed me so. After the hypnotist counted me down, I felt a great emptiness, a void filled with silence. I'd have sworn my name was Toby, but when Baronowski asked, I answered "Susan." The hypnotist continued to quiz me, and my words came from a deep place inside me that had answers I didn't know I knew.

My conscious mind, or ego self, remained quiet but aware and often surprised by the answers Susan gave. I felt her low self-esteem. I even watched her gaze into a cheval mirror. She called herself plain and indeed she was, with mousy brown hair, a round shape, and a gray dress. I sensed Susan's fear when she opened the front door and peered out while a horse-drawn fire engine clattered by.

Even though I couldn't actually look up the death certificate of my Susan Richards incarnation, I used the three criteria that Emmons recommended:

- That Susan had a mid-western American upbringing as a female felt right.

- Her personality was close enough to mine to assimilate ideas: Susan was a lonely soul. I feared loneliness but also found it enticing. Although I wanted to stop teaching to write full time, I delayed because I lived alone and thought I'd be too lonely. On the other hand, my job teaching speech and drama was high pressure and time-consuming. While worried about hitting deadlines, I longed for the pace of life Susan experienced and the time to explore each small grain of knowledge and each passing thought.

- I integrated Susan's life with me in this way. Whether Susan actually lived in the 1800s or not, her personality came out of my mind. I found great benefit from carrying her persona within me. I felt more confident that I could live a quiet life alone and find value in it. My fear diminished and more options opened for me.

Much of my learning in this lifetime has resulted from crises and painful experiences that forced me to grow. To learn from past life memories involved a certain grace, an easiness and kindliness, if you will.

The second past life memory came in a dream with a quality different from most of my dreams. A burst of facts and feelings appeared instantaneously in my mind, although what I perceived in a flash took several minutes to write out in detail:

> I saw a dancer, very muscular, lying on her side, doing exercises. She wore an old-fashioned leotard with a shirt. A ballet dancer, she felt a need to be a matron, felt sadness and shame at wanting to dance. Miss Leslie, the dancing teacher, was strict and demanding. The dancer had a short life. There were mountains around and a mountain man. He goes with the dancer, is her husband. She killed herself at the seashore because she couldn't

bring herself to have a baby, ruining the body that she
had spent years developing. So she drowned herself. The
mountain man felt guilty that he was the one who had
brought on this circumstance. The dream has a turn-of-
the-century feel, about 1900.

Assessing the memory of the woman in repose, or Nora, as Emmons
named her:

- I could relate to a woman in earlier America, this one even
  fewer years preceding my birth as Toby.
- Close in personality, Nora was me at some level that I can't
  quite define. I knew her feelings, felt her anger at the man
  and at the depressing prospect of bearing a child. She wanted
  to dance more than anything. In my life as Toby, I wanted to
  take dancing lessons as a girl, but my family couldn't afford
  them. As an adult I took lessons and then started a program
  at Carl Hayden High, where I taught a class in dance and
  choreographed some musicals.
- In integrating with my personality, I found sharp counterpoints
  with Nora. Unlike hers, my legs have always been weak. I had
  surgery on them when I was in my twenties. In later years,
  tendonitis had me on crutches more than once. On the other
  hand, being a mother has been very important to me. I found
  the idea of giving up motherhood for the dance inconceivable,
  and I felt proud to have matured since the days of the Nora
  lifetime.

In an automatic writing session, Emmons told of the third past
life. During the eighteenth century, I had been a woman innkeeper,
Matilda MacPhearson, who lived in the area around Broad Hinton
in Wiltshire County, England, near Lambsden Downs. She had long
black hair and a short temper with men because her husband had run
off with a tavern wench. Emmons said that he had often frequented
the inn called the Dog and Blossom. He remarked on Matilda's soul
development.

*We will speak briefly of the role played by anger in
the soul's development. It is a spur to action and often
hinders development of consciousness but speeds access*

to the riches of the world. Anger breeds its own kind of karma and involves the soul in nagging commitments to the people harmed through the expression of the anger. Yours was vented on men, many of whom have appeared in your present lifetime to accept atonement.

Taking Emmons's criteria for analysis:

- The past life memory felt right. Despite the distance of two hundred years and separate continents, this memory of Matilda felt pertinent to my present life.

- Matilda's personality seemed very close to mine. She held tenaciously to the very emotion that caused her pain, but she expressed her anger through ambition; anger fueled her career. She gained social status above other women of her time because of her position as an innkeeper. She strove to compete in a man's world to provide for her own security, just as I competed with male teachers in the high school where I taught. I could certainly relate to Matilda's anger, so like my own when my marriage didn't work out as I had hoped and when the relationship with Mike fizzled.

- In the matter of integrating Matilda's experience into mine, I try to be accepting of situations I can't control, not that I'm always successful. Matilda had an enormous impact on me emotionally. If I were she in a former life, I wanted to know more.

Fascinated by the story of Matilda, I had another regression and remembered that she had come to England from Scotland with her father, Jonathan MacThune, a cloth merchant. As Matilda, I hesitantly named James as the king of England. In the trance I saw the inn where she worked, with gables, a door in the middle, and windows on each side. I had an intuition that the inn had been converted into a shoe repair shop during the 1920s.

Such details I could research, so I hit the trusty Phoenix Public Library. In the *Historical Atlas of Britain* I learned that George I, George II, and George III ruled England during the 1700s. But in 1715 and again in 1745, the Scots fought against English rule in two Jacobite Rebellions. Support for the wars came primarily from three areas—Scotland itself, northern England, and southwestern England where Emmons and Matilda lived.

Bonnie Prince Charles, son of James Stuart, led the 1745 rebellion to put his father on the thrones of England and Scotland. The Scots in Wiltshire fought for James. Matilda's error in saying that she thought James was king had significance for me, a telling error. It seemed likely that Matilda would respond to such a question as "Who is the king?" by saying the name of the monarch who provoked so much conflict in her lifetime. Her life dates of the 1700s coincided with the Jacobite Rebellions.

Also, woolens and linens, both cloths for clothes, were big industries in Scotland. It seems natural for her father to immigrate to an area of England with a similar business situation. Salisbury, the largest city in the Wiltshire County of those days, was the center of the woolen industry.

Since I knew very little about the culture of the period, I wondered whether the English welcomed Scots who immigrated in the 1700s. Scots were not only welcomed but courted early in the century. In fact, Scots held positions of power, including in the English Parliament. The government of Scotland barely functioned because of the English takeover. All of that changed after the Rebellion of 1749 when the English persecuted, deported, and executed many Scots.

In *A Shell Guide to Wiltshire*, I found a startling bit of evidence—a photograph of the inn I'd seen in my regression. What's more the sign on it said Boot and Shoe Repair. The building, built in the 1600s, existed long before Matilda's birth and so could have been the inn where she worked. The foreword of the book said that the pictures were taken in 1935, so the inn could have been a boot and shoe repair store as early as 1920, as I had believed.

I read also that a family named Methuen, a very similar name to MacThune, purchased Corsham Court, other buildings in the town, in 1745. The time period coincided as well. Members of the family still lived in Corsham as late as the twentieth century.

Added to that information were these facts: The inn stood in a town named Corsham, fifteen miles west of Broad Hinton where Emmons said he lived. A town named Lambourn Downs lay fifteen miles east of Broad Hinton. The place names all coincided with the automatic writing and the regression, if Lambourn Downs could translate to Lambsden Downs.

A critical question remained: Did I know these details of the history of the Scots in England or the geography of the English countryside before the onset of the automatic writing?

The answer: if I knew, I didn't realize it. I don't remember ever in my life poring over a map of southwestern England although I might have done so in my youth when I studied geography in school. However, I didn't know Wiltshire existed. I know for certain that I never looked at *A Shell Guide to Wiltshire* before. I drew a blank on all these details consciously. How then did I know them?

Feelings aren't proof, but it all felt right to me. I had a sense of Emmons in the town with a fleeting image of his bushy whiskers and gray-blue cloak. I could see Matilda with her squared shoulders, determined look, and long black hair done up in a bun. I felt the positive effect of the teachings Emmons gave me. His words encouraged me, guided me, and helped me grow.

I couldn't make a positive statement that the information came to me from a disembodied spirit or through clairvoyance or from deep recesses of my unconscious mind. All I knew was that the material came. It came into my head and would not be denied. Then it was gone. Regardless of the explanation for the method of receiving the information, the material had to stand on its own.

Once I'd finished Emmons's book, I tried to sell it to a publisher and failed. On Nancy's advice, I rewrote it and tried again. No luck. Discouraged, I set it on a shelf and plunged into teaching. I wrote a play about reincarnation and produced it at school. Probably because I had feared mediumship and repressed it, I had few psychic experiences. Intuition did creep through occasionally.

Intuition

One instance happened in my car on the way to school. My most common route was west on Glendale Avenue then south on Thirty-fifth Avenue. As I absently listened to a disc jockey, I felt an impulse to turn on Twenty-seventh Avenue instead, a parallel route. I soon regretted the decision.

An inordinate number of construction signs diverted traffic because of work to widen the roadway. While I inched along through the detours, I debated whether to stop at a Circle K and call the school secretary to say I would be late, all the while berating myself for having turned on the wrong street.

Then the traffic report on the radio warned drivers to avoid Thirty-fifth Avenue. Not one but two wrecks had stopped traffic there, one at Camelback Road and one at Indian School Road, the two major intersections.

Had I followed my normal route, I would have been detained even longer at one or both of those intersections. Worst-case scenario, I could have been involved in one of those collisions. Rather, I arrived at school two minutes before the bell, all the way reaffirming my intention to follow my intuition.

Another time I had just bought some magic elixir for my skin. As I stood at the sink about to make the first application of lotion, I heard a little voice—not a real voice, just a thought—say from the region of my belly, *This could hurt you.*

Moments before I'd thought in my head, *This is going to improve my looks.* So I went with that. Two weeks later I had a full-blown reaction with swelling and blisters on my face. Again, I resolved to pay attention to my intuition. It seemed I always told myself that, then failed to take my own advice.

Psychic Development Tools

My teaching buddy Betty talked me into taking a spiritual development class at a Religious Science Church. I really didn't want to because I had taken a previous class that had turned out to be a waste of time. Betty could be very persuasive. Her logic went sort of like this: what else did I have to do on Tuesday nights? I was single, no man in the offing, and my sons had already left home.

About the second night of class, I sat with Betty and three other students, waiting for the other students and the teacher to arrive. In a conversation with the nervous lady next to me, I mentioned psychometry.

"What exactly is that?" the lady asked as a blond student named John strode through the door. I knew little about his personal life.

I said, "It's where you hold an object in your hands and get psychic impressions about the owner."

"What do you get from these?" Grinning, John threw his keys at me. The real miracle in this story was that I caught them. I'm not very athletic.

His smile flattered me. John was a fox. Caught in the impromptu situation, I didn't question the pictures that came into my mind. "I see a corral, a horse breaking down fences."

"That's right." John dropped into the seat next to me. "I show horses with my son and daughter."

The good news—I received meaningful information. The bad news—he had children and might be married. He wasn't, and so began a chapter in my life.

I was ready for change, and John's enthusiasm for New Thought principles helped convince me that they constituted a good framework for my own swamp of beliefs. I found strength in the words of the founder, Ernest Holmes, who said, "All of your work begins and ends in your consciousness because mind is all there is."

My mind had been my greatest teacher and my greatest anxiety. Spiritual mind treatment and affirmations recommended by the Religious Science texts helped me come to a place of peace about my psychic experiences. I must confess, though, that I felt relieved that they seemed to have stopped.

John had wanted for a long time to live in San Diego. While we were seeing each other, he managed to set up a business and move there. Now I had the perfect out to satisfy my desire to leave teaching and try my hand at writing. And I could do so without fear of loneliness. After a year of visiting back and forth, I rented out the condo and moved to San Diego, too.

Somehow the physical move matched the movement of my psyche, freeing it. During that year I said good-bye psychologically to teaching by writing a handbook for speech and drama teachers. Even though I opted out, I passed along my best techniques to those who would follow me, for the good of the profession.

I wanted to pursue a writing career but didn't have the courage to rewrite the Emmons book and try again. Maybe it was the ocean air, but I felt very playful and decided to look in the white pages under W for writing. Only one entry seemed relevant, the Writing Center. So in good New Age fashion, I called. I'd have enrolled in play writing or screen writing if there'd been a class. They had an opening in a novel writing class.

That decision carried me through the next four years of my writing life. I've heard it said that when the student is ready, the teacher appears. My novel writing teacher, Mike MacCarthy, convinced me that I had a unique writing voice for fiction. He taught me writing techniques that allowed me to complete three novels and map a fourth.

Through fiction I found a vehicle for interpreting my psychic experiences. The characters in my novels all struggled with aspects of their psyches. One character could remember a past life and tried to atone for wrongdoing. Another character saw visions and struggled against derision from thoughtless friends and family. One had a near-death experience. I killed one character off for practicing witchcraft.

I loved hiding in my characters' psychic abilities and carrying them to all kinds of outcomes, good and bad. In imagination, I could track the rise and fall of psychic manifestations without suffering personal consequences. This book you're reading is part self-help, part memoir. I could make a case for saying all nonfiction is part memoir and all fiction is memoir in disguise.

While my writing life rode high, the relationship with John dissolved. A three-time loser, I went home to Arizona. Maybe a psychic experience would buoy me up. Something needed to.

Chapter Six

Possibilities

Mind over Matter

In the emotional quagmire of the end of the relationship, I gave up my image of myself as part of a couple. That wasn't easy because all my programming said I should have a mate, and I wanted one, but I no longer had the will to risk. I rewrote the book on automatic writing and failed to sell it. I regretted that I couldn't come through for Emmons but I ran out of ideas and energy for the project. I psychologically set aside those portions of my life, resumed writing novels, and joined a critique group. After buying a little house in Glendale near the Phoenix city line, I went back to work, this time teaching writing at a junior college.

Devoting myself to my family seemed an easy task because in slightly over a year I became a grandmother thrice. Brandy married Stephanie and brought her sweet eight-year-old Josh to the family. Then she gave birth to twins, Emily and Aaron. There's no greater assurance that you are alive than to have two squalling babies demanding a bottle at the same time. I forgot about loss and grief.

Then death dealt another double down, a big one this time.

Within six weeks, both my father and my cousin Larry, a childhood companion, died. Just as in the past, I decided to grieve later and fooled myself into believing I'd be all right. My predominant emotion was anger—that they had died, that I had been helpless, that I had not done things differently, that my sister and I couldn't console each other. I hardly wept, and something in my heart went as cold as the winter ground in which we laid my father in the little cemetery beside his family, the one I'd help him tend as a child. My cousin died in Canada with the ground so frozen that they put him in a drawer until the spring thaw allowed them to dig a grave; my own heart felt hardly less icy.

All those New Thought ideas I'd accepted, even touted, crumbled in the reality that death haunted me. The night fears returned more

ruthlessly than ever. My remembered dreams dropped off enormous-
ly. The ones I recalled often centered around torture, criminality,
and other horrible things. I went to three psychics, and they all told
me dismal things about my father's inability to resolve his lifetime.
I decided they were all quacks. Maybe they really read the denial I
nurtured in my heart.

Double down.

My mother died. A month later Martha, my mentor from the high
school district, died. At their funerals, I cried, but it was far too late.
Within three weeks, I began to experience enormous swelling and
pain in my joints.

At the time, Stephanie had a part-time job and I kept the twins
two days a week. I felt so much pain that I couldn't hold the children,
so she had to hire a babysitter. I continued to teach on crutches. By
mid May, I retreated to my bed and spent my time crying. My writing
buddies called to encourage me. My family and friends did the house
and yard work. They even went to the grocery for me

During that excruciating period, I had examinations by four different doctors: a general practitioner, two orthopedists, and a rheumatologist. Since it took two weeks to get an appointment, I spent
eight weeks as an invalid, getting progressively worse, unable to move
about the house by myself. I could not raise my arms to brush my
teeth. I had to have my hair cut off because I couldn't brush or curl
it. I could no longer wear my rings or any shoes except men's thongs.
Turning over in bed became an endurance test. Fortunately, one of my
former students who had become a friend worked during the day and
slept at my house at night in case I couldn't get to the bathroom by
myself, something that began to happen.

The constant pain traveled throughout my body—neck, shoulders,
elbows, hips, knees, ankles, and every space in between. Besides the
drugs, I tried warm showers, cold packs, relief creams. At times I lay
in bed, trying to figure out what body part hurt most. My busy, pro-
ductive life had disappeared.

I knew that I could not endure much more and gave myself until
the end of the summer. If the pain did not diminish by then, I would
"off" myself. I told my sons, so they wouldn't be surprised. I saw no
point in living another day if it presented only agony.

Making the decision calmed me. Pain had a clarifying quality. I feared it more than death.

The rheumatologist saved my life, literally, with the prescriptions he gave me. The diagnosis, sero-negative rheumatoid arthritis, set me thinking. Of course, I read everything available. As I am a writer, words have a great impact on me.

In rheumatoid arthritis, the immune system attacked the joints. The medication attacked the immune system, symbolic of my internal war. I could identify with having attacked myself—for not doing things well enough, for becoming overwhelmed with obligations, for failing to grieve. The war within me about my psychic abilities had continued as well.

Sero-negative also contained a hidden message. I didn't know for certain what that meant except that all the tests came back negative, as if I didn't have the illness. The rheumatologist explained to me that that sometimes happened, but no one knew why. Disregarding the medical context, I took the metaphorical value for use in creating an affirmation: "The disease has dissolved, gone, a part of my past. I am healthy and whole."

The literature on rheumatoid arthritis explained how stress reactions contributed to the illness. The flight-or-fight response shifted blood flow from internal organs to arms and legs. When they weren't used to run away or engage in a physical fight, the blood stayed in the arms and legs and caused swelling.

So, what did that say for me? Stay calm. Don't sweat the small stuff. It's all small stuff. I'd spent a good amount of time under stress at school with the problems of the inner city in addition to performance work in speech and drama. This was the time in my life to rid myself of that syndrome. Of course, any time would have been a good time, but now I wanted to do it. Now I could either let the activities of my life stress me or not.

Needing to delve more into the stinkin' thinkin' that helped cause the illness, I went to a practitioner at a Religious Science Church, a good decision. She made several suggestions, all of which I implemented: journal writing, becoming aware of thoughts, staying open to Divine guidance, praying for protection, loving myself, and living in the moment. I also worked to identify stressors, fix those I could, and affirm away those I couldn't. I admitted my resentments and forgave myself and others as best I could. I began to read Elisabeth Kubler-Ross. A psychiatrist, she wrote *On Death and Dying* and created a model, which outlined the steps in the grieving process.

I set my goal of a complete remission. Realizing much of the effort had to come from me, I willingly began a varied set of treatments, combining allopathic, that is, drugs to treat illness, as well as alternative healing approaches. After implementing one, I always saw improvement. Then I'd hit a plateau until I tried another. I went through many in succession:

- Spiritual counseling, which set me on the path of positive self-responsibility.
- Journal keeping where I confessed that I had stuffed my grief. I did forgiveness work for myself and others. Crying helped, too.
- Therapeutic Touch. When my progress on medication slowed, the rheumatologist suggested a more invasive medication. Fearing side effects, I opted for Therapeutic Touch. Those sessions gave me relaxation and increased energy. They also reduced the inflammation. At times, I could see the swelling diminish beneath the nurse's deft hands as she made passes over my legs then massaged them.
- Qigong, an easy exercise that got me moving better even though I missed my regular Jazzercise.
- Meditation with infinitesimally slow progress.
- A leave from teaching.
- Arthritis Foundation exercises, a six-week course at a local health spa that helped me believe I could some day return to normal physical functioning.
- Acupuncture. Generally, the acupuncturist inserted twenty to thirty needles in different areas, primarily in arms and legs while I lay on my back. With classical music playing, she left me to relax for fifteen minutes. Then she repeated the treatment while I lay on my stomach. From time to time, I felt some pain when a needle went in, similar to a pinprick, which is what it is, but that subsided in a moment. After three months of treatment, the swelling disappeared except in one ankle. My joints had returned

to such a comfort level that I fulfilled a dream of many years, to go sightseeing in Washington, DC. I walked all over the capital, like a person who had never had arthritis.

- A low-fat diet that decreased my cholesterol, eliminated twenty pounds, and relieved my leg joints.
- Weightlifting and, finally, my beloved Jazzercise again.

A part of the challenge involved my attempt to cope with the word "chronic" and the hopelessness it engendered. Many in American society consider arthritis a chronic condition; some, primarily the Chinese, believe it to be a curable one. Knowing the way belief turns into reality, I cast my lot with the Asian belief.

Fortunately, the rheumatologist worked with me to reduce medications. I still experienced bouts of sudden weariness but took that in my stride. Rather than complain or lament my weakness, I kept a stack of books beside a recliner and sat down to read for a half an hour. That practice had two positive outcomes: my energy returned and I stayed caught up on my reading.

I became well enough to have the twins with me again. Although I didn't return to teaching, I started some new writing projects, including this book. My approach to daily life definitely took a calmer turn, but from time to time I still found myself tensing up about some person or situation. I truly began to forgive myself for not being perfect and for not having it all figured out. Finally, after three years, the doctor told me I no longer needed any medication.

The experience with arthritis took away much of my fear of death. Certain ways of living were worse. I did have the ability to place mind over matter. I turned diseased into healthy flesh. Someone else might yank a picture off the wall without touching it, like a poltergeist, one kind of psychokinesis. I created the illness first in my mind. Then it manifested in my body. I created my cure first in my mind. Then it manifested in my body. That was the ultimate psychokinesis.

Mystical Awareness

Just when I'd given up on my psychic abilities and thought they'd gone away forever, I experienced the greatest of them all, mind over matter. After that I wanted to develop whatever abilities remained.

I joined a psychic development group with three other women: Jan, a hypnotherapist and the group leader; Vijaya, my friend and fellow writer; and Susan, the acupuncturist who had helped to restore my physical functioning. Together we explored our potential in an experimental style. I began to take delight in my psychic self.

On one occasion the four of us had planned a remote viewing activity. Susan's task was to sit at a pre-arranged time, seven in the morning, and focus on an object for an hour. Vijaya, Jan, and I meditated in the hope of visualizing the appearance of the object she had chosen.

At two-thirty the morning before we were to meet, I awoke and remembered the scheduled experiment. I gave myself a suggestion that my dreaming self would show me which object Susan would focus on later. I fell back to sleep but awoke with a start about forty minutes later with the image of a clock face, a cuckoo clock, in my mind.

At seven I did the requisite meditation: well, at least forty-five minutes of it. Never again would I volunteer for an hour-long meditation. I'm far too antsy for that.

I visualized myself floating over the houses and trees of Glendale. I imagined the freeway and Encanto Park, the area around Susan's house. I imagined myself going into her living room, where I have never actually visited. I saw her sitting in a chair with wooden arms, light brown colored wood, like natural walnut or pecan. She wore a silky robe or skirt. I saw the fireplace with an oval-shaped clock on the mantle. The face was dark as if discolored or in the shadows. Even though the clock looked different from the one in my dream, I still believed a clock was the focus.

I went through this scenario three times and didn't waver on the clock as the focus.

That afternoon when we got together, much to my embarrassment, Susan showed her focus object, a statue of a cherub holding a candle, something she had purchased in Disneyland.

The other women had visualized better than I. Jan had seen something ornate and old-fashioned, like an angel. Vijaya drew a sketch of something shaped like the candle beside a naked man, not a naked cherub. Of course, Vijaya is a grown-up lady. I missed the focus object, but we did discover that Susan sat in a wooden-armed chair and wore a silk gown during her meditation. At least my clairvoyance had worked to some extent.

My dream however made a major hit. Susan's cuckoo clock went off by accident in her bedroom at three-ten in the morning, the precise time I awoke with the image of the cuckoo clock in my mind. Some part of my awareness must have been there. Because of my good luck in having the remote viewing session scheduled, Susan could validate the facts for me.

I realized that psychic events accompanied the turning points of my life. They indicated the way to go or notified me that things were wrong. I have always needed a model of reality that at least included my psychic experiences whether it could explain them or not. Reading scientific research helped me accept the truth of my experiences. Spiritual biographies and treatises helped me understand the great scope of spiritual work available to all of us.

The conscious effort to initiate psychic activity spread into my dream life where I began to experience awakening. One night when the twins stayed over, I got my first chance at what scientists call lucidity.

In my dream a girl, supposedly my friend, had keys to my house. She opened the door and came in. When I confronted her, she said her mother intended to give the keys to Good Will and the girl didn't want to waste them. How nonsensical. I didn't know where Emily and Aaron had gone, and I feared the front door might be standing open.

Two men, one the girl's father, came down the hall toward my bedroom. I yelled, "What are you doing in my house?" They ignored me. I felt afraid for the twins and myself. Yet the whole situation seemed preposterous. I knew these were not my friends, like the dream pretended. I thought, *Hey, I'm dreaming.*

Suddenly my mind filled with an expansive whiteness and clarity. I thought, *If I'm lucid, I can change this dream anyway I want. What do I want to do?* I decided I would go check on Emily and Aaron. Then Emily began to cry

from another bedroom, and the whiteness went away,
but I didn't have to awaken. I was already awake.

While still dreaming, I dwelt on the dichotomy between the dream content and my opinions about its ludicrous quality. In the past the fact that I couldn't change my dreams had exasperated me so much that I awoke. This time I at least imagined myself capable of changing them.

Now I knew what other people meant when they spoke of clarity. It was wonderful. I wanted to have the experience again. I also considered it not a little miracle that my first *bona fide* lucid dream came while I was writing this chapter. I was on my way to owning the experience in a profound way.

One night when my writers' critique group had just ended, our hostess, Vijaya, departed to a meeting downtown. I lingered to chat with her husband, Dan, wanting his opinion about an extension to my patio.

"I just put this new sink in. Did you notice?" Dan filled a water glass from a gleaming, angular faucet in the kitchen work center.

Leaning on the ceramic counter, I peered at his handiwork. "Looks good."

From the doorway that leads to the living room, the swish of a skirt distracted me. Everyone had gone. I had waved good-bye to them at the front door. Dan and I were alone in the house, so I thought.

Staring at the entry, I became aware of an insubstantial presence. I could swear that presence stood about my height and wore cowboy boots and a long skirt.

A shiver ran through me, and I giggled. "Have you got a ghost?"

Dan, while crossing the kitchen, stopped mid-step. Water sloshed from his glass. The distressed look on his handsome face answered my question. "No one else has seen it," he whispered, "but, yes, I think we do."

Excited, I compared my perceptions with Dan's. His tumbled out along with concerns for his sanity. He felt greatly relieved to finally share his fears with someone. I had sympathy for Dan and his ghost and felt glad that my sighting, brief as it was, validated his experience.

Fifty-five years of self doubt had passed since Marcia's ghost peered down from a cloud at me. Now I had seen another. I no longer had to prove the world of ghosts existed, as nonsensical an idea as ghosts' having to prove our world existed. There was room in this universe for both worlds to exist side by side. In fact, they always had.

Now I could admit the fact that had always been present, if only I'd awakened to it. Some things were true whether I believed they were or not.

In *Illusions* author Richard Bach's exhortation, "Your only obligation in any lifetime is to be true to yourself," seems simple, but it's not. Before we can be true to ourselves, we have to know ourselves. For me that's taken a long time. I've had to face three major problems: low self-confidence, fear of death, and fear of my psychic nature, and they all influenced each other.

All three problems united for me. We don't just solve such issues once and then forget them. Like Shrek said in his first movie, "Ogres are like onions. Onions have layers. Ogres have layers." In revealing my layers, I hope to help you relax with yours.

During my childhood, my parents lived in an atmosphere that provoked them to deny my psychic abilities. They were in their twenties then. That seems so young to me now. In my family, an aura of mystery and fear surrounded any mention of my great-grandfather's psychic readings and of my uncle's prophetic dreams.

Seeing the same potential in their small daughter must have disconcerted my parents. In addition to so many deaths in our family, they had to deal with fears about the war. Four of my uncles fought in World War II. At home we had air raids and blackouts that kept everyone spooked. My parents didn't have the knowledge we have now that the United States and its allies would win the war. Against that background, they tried to protect me from emotional pain.

Instead of feeling comforted, like the little sponge I was, I absorbed their fears of death and of the psychic. I don't blame them. They did the best they could in a bad situation. Besides, I made mistakes with my sons and expect them to forgive me. Show me one set of parents that hasn't made a mistake. I'm grateful to my parents for theirs because it provoked a search that has given great meaning to my life.

After the angelic visit in my bathroom mirror, I began to dream of Emmons and then he presented himself in automatic writing. I struggled against myself for a long time, not wanting to accept the validity of inner messages or inner voices without understanding their source. I kept trying to blame the automatic writing on my emotional setbacks that were not that different from anyone else's and certainly not as bad as the series of deaths that undermined my beliefs as a child.

All the doubt, the questioning, the worry about my sanity came down to my inability to trust my perceptions. I imagined that I fooled myself. Somehow I didn't make the connection between the truth about the stillborn baby and the truth about seeing Marcia on the cloud.

At last I realized that, in every other way, my life went along well. I held down a job and helped my sons go to college. I maintained a social life and fulfilled my responsibilities to friends and family. I never doubted my sanity in any other area of my life. It seemed illogical to think of myself as crazy in this one aspect and sane in the rest.

I decided I had to trust myself. Even though I couldn't understand the source of the messages, they were valid, kind, and intelligent. Accepting the uncertainty finally helped me put the issues behind me.

Using hindsight, I wish I'd come to terms with the situation earlier. I wasted a lot of time and eventually lost the ability to do automatic writing. That's one of my reasons for writing this book. Maybe you won't make the same mistakes I made. I don't know whether I will take up automatic writing again, but any decision now can be made out of knowledge, not out of fear.

The experiences I've recorded are not definitive. Many people have far greater psychic abilities than I do. In fact, I think all people have them to a greater or lesser extent. These experiences are manifestations of our growing consciousness as the human race. When individuals develop their psychic talents, the whole race grows because these abilities feed into the collective unconscious.

I'm in no way a master yet, but I'm farther down the path because I wrote this book. Bach also said in *Illusions*, "You teach best what you most need to learn." I've needed to learn the acceptance I've given to my readers here.

Recently I ran into a teacher on the faculty where I taught for many years. When I told her the title of this book, she chuckled then said, "Toby, I never knew you were in the closet."

I've not been fooling as many people as I thought. Our true nature shows through to those around us. It's there for them to see if they're paying attention. That's as it should be. Maybe other people are on to you more than you think.

PART TWO

IF IT HAPPENED TO YOU

If you've read this far, clearly you want to embrace your true nature. Whether you've denied and repressed psychic experiences or admitted they were happening and worried about your sanity, ask yourself whether you're a fully functioning individual in other aspects of your life—relationships, career, and community. If so, then it's time to start trusting yourself.

You're not crazy. Psychic experiences are a part of life. If you have trouble convincing yourself, maybe this acronym will serve you, as it has served me.

TRUST, the Five Ways Out of the Psychic Closet:

- ◆ Track your dreams
- ◆ Repel ridicule
- ◆ Use it or lose it
- ◆ See your ability as a gift
- ◆ Trust yourself

Part Two of this book can help you with those mental changes. It contains relevant research and other information on a variety of subjects. Read it straight through or skip around to satisfy your curiosity.

The topics covered in this section follow the same order as Part One and have similar titles so you can refer to my experiences if you wish. Resources, lists of books and websites, follow all of the major topics in Part Two. These bibliographies are only representative but should help you get started if you want to do more research in a certain area.

Chapter Seven

Witness to Another World

"This makes no sense and so do I."
Daffy Duck

Ghosts

Thirty-eight percent of the American public believes in ghosts, according to a Gallup Poll conducted in 2001.[1] Add to that twenty-five percent who are uncertain, and you've got a lot of citizens, many who've heard of or thought they've seen a ghost at some time or another.

A follow-up poll conducted in 2007 confirmed the responses in belief with only small changes in the categories. The results of that poll, reported by Bryan Farha and Gary Stewart, Jr. via the *Skeptical Inquirer* are available online at

http://www.livescience.com/strangenews/060121_paranormal_poll.html - belief poll.

Types of Ghosts

Several different kinds of ghosts can make appearances. The ways they act and the effects they have determine the categories.

- Crisis apparition. Someone appears to a loved one at the moment of death or soon after, something that often happens during wartime or with accidental deaths. For example, a soldier appears to his mother in Chicago moments before he dies in battle in Iraq.

- Post-mortem apparition. Someone who has been dead for a while appears to a loved one and gives a message. Occasionally someone returns to tell about a hidden will or other important document. Often those who pass over appear to their loved ones two to three months after death, but it can happen any time.

- Haunting apparition. Someone reenacts behaviors repeatedly without noticing the living who are present, for example, running downstairs and out the door—the kind of repetitive behavior we associate with haunted houses.
- Apparitions of the living. Someone appears to arrive a few moments before he actually does arrive or appears in two places at once, as if he has a double.
- Poltergeists. Ghosts create physical disturbances like throwing objects around a room, starting a fire, or causing a picture to fall off a wall.

Motives of Ghosts

Ghosts often return with a message of love and comfort, such as my friend Marcia gave to me. Perhaps you've not yet experienced the death of someone you love. There's no way out of it. Someday you will. It's better to be prepared with knowledge ahead of time, so you won't have to begin your research while you're in the swell of grief.

Hello from Heaven by Bill and Judy Guggenheim details many encounters with the departed. Here's an example:

Charlotte is a forty-three-year-old nurse in New Jersey. She became a widow when her husband, Glen, died of cancer:

The night Glen died, I needed to talk to someone. So I sat down in the living room and called my girlfriend, Joni, who lived next door.

As I was talking with her on the phone, I saw Glen standing right in front of me, just inches away! He was as solid as a rock, and I couldn't see through him. But he didn't look the way he did when he was sick—he looked absolutely healthy!

Glen leaned down and put his hand on my knee and said, "Charlotte, it's me. I'm okay. Everything's all right. I don't have any more pain. I feel great!"

Well, all I did was scream! He scared the daylights out of me! And the more I screamed, the more he said, "It's okay, Charlotte. It's okay. It's okay. You don't have to worry about me. I'm okay!" That was it, and then Glen just kind of evaporated.[2]

It's logical to assume the essence of people might want to remain near the earth where they have identity or some unfinished business. Patrick Swayze's character in the movie *Ghost* can't leave the earth plane until he exposes his murderer.

It seems ghosts appear in daylight or room light more often than in the dark. Dan and I saw the ghost in his kitchen with the overhead florescent lights on.

Many famous people have seen apparitions or become them. While president, Abraham Lincoln held séances. In later years, Winston Churchill, as well as many visitors to the White House, observed Lincoln's ghost walking around.

Today ghost stories remain popular. Witness the success of such TV shows as *Ghost Whisperer* and *Supernatural* based on fictional characters. By contrast, the documentary style of *Psychic Investigators* gives the use of psychics in crime detection much-deserved credit.

Research

Ghost research has faltered, compared to other psychic phenomena, in part because of the requirement for scientific validation set by Dr. Karlis Osis, Director of Research at the American Society for Psychical Research. His standard is difficult to meet. Two or more people must see the apparition and submit written reports. Another reason is probably that those who see a ghost fear their experience will be called a hallucination and, by implication, they will be considered mentally ill.[3]

There are such cases on record. Dr. Ian Stevenson, a professor at the University of Virginia for over forty years, supervised research on cases involving apparitions, reincarnation claims, and other indicators of the survival of bodily death. Stevenson states: "Among all apparitional experiences collective ones occur in about a third of cases or perhaps in as many as fifty-six percent."[4]

As an example Stevenson tells of a woman who cared for her sick grandfather. While in the hallway outside his bedroom, she heard him call her dead grandmother's name. As the woman walked into the bedroom, she saw the ghost of her grandmother standing at the end of the bed. The grandfather clearly was looking at the ghost also, then he fell back dead. Such cases are hard to explain away.

Fortunately more investigation has recently begun in this area, but poltergeists have been researched much more strenuously. Many incidents of rising furniture, falling pictures, and other physical phenomena become famous because they make good news stories. Some scientists believe poltergeists aren't really ghosts at all but psychic effects created subconsciously by disturbed adolescents. The young people move objects about by the force of mind without conscious awareness through an ability called psychokinesis.

When the Gallup pollsters asked Americans about the ability to communicate with someone who has died, twenty-eight percent said yes, up ten points from 1990, with twenty-six percent uncertain. Women believe somewhat more in this communication and in ghosts than men do.

When you believe in ghosts, the next logical step is to communicate with them. Medical doctor and psychical researcher Raymond Moody has come up with a way to call ghosts of your deceased loved ones to you. He uses a psychomanteum, a semi-darkened room with a mirror positioned so that one can see into the mirror but cannot see one's own reflection. Moody has developed a friendly, supportive environment where people can try to see an apparition. He has had great success, with over half of his subjects actually convinced that they have talked with, seen, or touched their departed loved ones. His book *Reunions: Visionary Encounters with Departed Loved Ones* tells the reader how to do the experiment at home.

Validation

Sighting a ghost doesn't have to induce fear, but it usually prompts a reassessment of our reality. Particularly if we see a departed loved one, we grapple with the idea that perhaps we only saw what we wished. It's natural to want to see our loved ones again and to hope that they continue to live in another place.

If you've ever seen a ghost, you know it's a two-pronged event. First, you have to deal with your own reaction, be it fear, self-doubt, or awe. Second, when you tell others, you may have to counter their negative reactions of derision or disbelief whether you've resolved your own or not. You'll want whatever validation you can obtain.

Validation might involve new information that the ghostly presence gave you, perhaps foreknowledge of some event, such as the death of the person you saw. Another kind of validation happens if more than one person sees the ghost. However, such visitations rarely contain any validation except the emotional quality of the event itself.

Should you think you've seen a ghost, explore your feelings. Did you feel afraid? If so, why? If not, why not? Were you mature at the time of the visit and able to assess its intrinsic value? Or were you a child, dependent on others to interpret the event for you? As a child I felt tremendous excitement in seeing Marcia. In that moment, for me, the chasm between earth and heaven closed. Only the aftermath caused me distress.

Dr. Gary Schwartz, a professor of psychiatry and psychic researcher at the University of Arizona, touches on the subject in *The Afterlife Experiments*:

> Children who report "seeing things" sometimes grow up to be adults who are labeled as psychotic and delusional by mental health professionals. When such experiences are dismissed and labeled as delusions and hallucinations, this rejection often increases dysfunctional behavior. The people having the experiences become fearful of their own consciousness, and they literally feel crazy.[5]

If your child sees a ghost, assess the situation without making him or her feel wrong or incompetent. It's true that you may never know for certain whether the child actually saw a ghost. For that matter, you may not have total confidence even if you, a mature, intelligent adult, see one in clear daylight. And treat yourself with the same kindness with which you would treat your child. Honor the experience whether you can explain it or not.

Resources for Ghosts

Bardens, Dennis. *Ghosts and Hauntings*. New York: Ace Books, 1973.
Guggenheim, Bill and Guggenheim, Judy. *Hello from Heaven*. New York: Bantam, 1997.

MacKenzie, Andrew. *Apparitions and Ghosts*. New York: Popular
    Library, 1971.
Moody, Raymond. *Reunions: Visionary Encounters with Departed
    Loved Ones*. New York: Ivy Books, 1993.
Newport, Frank and Strausberg, Maura. "Americans' Belief in Psychic
    and Paranormal Phenomena Is up Over Last Decade," *The
    Gallup Organization*, June 8, 2001.
Osis, Karlis. "Life After Death," *ASPR Newsletter*, Summer, 1990,
    Volume XVI, Number 3, pp. 25-28.
Stevenson, Ian. "Six Modern Apparitional Experiences," *Journal of
    Scientific Exploration*. Vol. 9, No. 3, Autumn, 1995, 351-366.
Schwartz, G. E. R. with Simon, William L. *The Afterlife Experiments:
    Breakthrough Scientific Evidence of Life After Death*. New
    York: Pocketbooks, 2002.
Stone, Ganga. *Start the Conversation: The Book About Death You
    Were Hoping to Find*. New York: Warner Books, 1996.
adb.online.anu.edu.au/biogs/A040457b.htm — biography of Richard
    Hodgson
afterlife101.com
aspr.com — American Society for Psychical Research
assap.org — a London research group
castleofspirits.com
haunted-places.com — fun sounds
horizonresearch.org — British research on near-death experiences,
    deathbed visions, and out-of-body experiences. You can
    participate.
ghost-hunters.tv — documentary-style show about ghost hunters
ghostresearch.org
ghoststudy.com — has photos of ghosts
spr.ac.uk - British Society for Psychical Research
survivalafterdeath.org

Near-death Experiences (NDEs)

Because of technical medical advances, more and more accident victims and terminally ill people recover after exhibiting all the signs of clinical death, including cessation of breath, of heart beat, of brain waves. Many who've experienced clinical death tell some startling tales like the ones my grandfather and my cousin Judy told.

A minister I once knew found his calling as a result of an NDE. Hurt in an automobile accident and rushed to the hospital, he stopped breathing in the emergency room.

While unconscious, he felt as if he were falling from a great height. With a tremendous force of love, a hand reached out and stopped his fall. Then the hand buoyed him up. He knew a moment of infinite peace, filled with beauty and love.

Then the doctors pulled him into the painful awareness of his injured body. The experience proved so powerful that it confirmed his belief in the afterlife. When he spoke from the pulpit, his face suffused with a glow of joy. His rapt expression more than his words convinced the audience of the reality of his story.

Research—the Experience

The minister's experience, although highly meaningful for him, did not include several of the components possible in an NDE. The subject has been researched at length, and work continues.

Dr. Melvin Morse, a pediatrician, has done important research on NDEs in children. In *Transformed by the Light*, he lists the following components, any or all of which might be present in an NDE.

1. A sense of being dead
2. Peace and painlessness
3. Out-of-body experience
4. Tunnel experience
5. People of light
6. A Being of light
7. Life review
8. Reluctance to return
9. Personality transformation[6]

Morse gives many examples, including this one looking back from an adult perspective:

> When I was eight or nine, I was sick with measles.
> There were no antibiotics in those days and my illness
> became critical. My parents were taking turns sleeping
> with me to keep an eye on me. On this particular night,
> I remember feeling just terrible and waking up. But I

wasn't in my body. I was hovering above it, looking down on my mother and I. My mother was awake and she noticed that I wasn't breathing. She called for my dad who ran into the room and began shaking me. I went up a tunnel at that point. I was headed for a light but at the same time there was a voice in my head that said, *Let her go back. She isn't ready yet.* I went into this beautiful bright light anyway. It was a beautiful feeling that totally took all my fears of death away. Then I came back.[7]

Websites feature NDE stories from Carl Jung to Hollywood actors, from Hindu mystics to Midwestern farmers, even a Baptist minister who says he went to hell. Some of those who've been through an NDE have written books about their experiences, most notably Betty Eadie's *Embraced by the Light* and Dannion Brinkley's *At Peace in the Light.* If you're looking for research updates, a place to record your own experience, or emotional support, there are websites to fill your needs.

Research—the Results

Morse wanted to know what changes, if any, happened in people who had had NDEs as children. He developed a research study with over one hundred fifty subjects plus a control group of people who had not had NDEs. He used tests and interviewing techniques that he described in the book.

His findings revealed that indeed many changes occurred to people who had had NDEs as children:

1. A decreased death anxiety, half the fear of others.
2. An increase in psychic abilities, telepathy or precognition, four times more incidences of psychic events. Only verifiable ones counted; that is, the person had written something down or told another person in advance of an event.
3. A higher zest for living that involves staying very busy but with little stress.
4. A higher intelligence expressed as exercising more, eating more fruits and vegetables, taking fewer medications, missing less time at work, having fewer years of unemployment and fewer symptoms of depression.

Morse also found one fourth of the study group couldn't wear watches because they stopped. He guessed the cause as a very active electromagnetic force field, the one that is measured by various medical imaging machines.

Only the NDEs which included the bright light produce the transformations listed above. The NDE happens in the right temporal lobe of the brain (over the right ear). Morse calls the right temporal lobe the seat of the soul because it modulates spiritual connections with forces outside ourselves, psychic experiences, and NDEs.

Some of Morse's subjects saw Jesus, Buddha, or guardian angels. They also often saw deceased relatives. There were even occasions when one person psychically shared the NDE of a loved one.

Counterpoint

Dr. Karl Jansen of London has experimented with the drug ketamine and induced after-death-like episodes that are identical to the NDE. He argues that NDEs are not proof of the afterlife because all people who have them return to life and thus cannot be properly labeled dead. He tries to steer clear of the philosophical and religious debate by stating that drugs can induce religious experiences.

The scientific jury is still out.

Benefits

Even though shared cases of NDEs are extensively documented, many scientists don't take them seriously. Morse thinks the reason is that to accept them requires a fundamental change in the way we believe the world works.

Changing one's worldview is one of the most difficult things to do. From time to time, I felt content to see myself as crazy to avoid the spiritual work, i.e., thought, prayer, discussion, counseling, and research necessary to encompass my psychic experiences.

As to advantages of NDEs, we can all learn from those of others. We don't have to nearly die to benefit. The NDEs of others can inspire us with faith in our own spirituality, lessen our fear of death, and give us hope about this life and the hereafter.

If you've had an NDE yourself, I doubt you need others to tell you how to judge its accuracy. It may seem impossible for the analytical mind to absorb, but that's because these events happen outside the logical mind.

No matter how our intellect denies it, some part of us keeps on believing in the miraculous and wonderful.

What would happen if scientists proved the Divine existed? What would change if we knew for absolute fact that the Divine was all loving just as It seems to be in the NDE? How would you feel if you knew your departed relatives would be there to meet you when you died to take you to a wonderful place? No ifs, no faith involved, flat-out fact?

Many religions hold up a God that is not all loving, but vengeful and judgmental. NDEs contradict their belief system. To retain their religious beliefs, adherents must ignore scientific evidence proving NDEs and other anomalous events occur.

Whether religious or not, many of us believe that it's impossible to prove that NDEs and other psychical experiences happen, or that they can be verified scientifically. So long as we hold that belief, we prevent ourselves from ever being convinced. We'll always waffle and have to take on faith things we could know as fact.

Neal Grossman says in the *Noetic Sciences Review:*

> As long as religious values are presented as merely religious values, then it is easy for popular culture to ignore them or give them minimal lip service on Sunday mornings. But if these same religious values are presented as empirically verified scientific facts, then everything changes.[8]

NDEs are as proven as science allows. In the last analysis, we must all answer these questions: Do we believe in science? Do we believe in the Divine? Do we believe in our capacity to decide?

Those answers will take us a long way toward accepting ourselves and our experiences. Perhaps we don't have to answer all of the questions at once.

Resources for Near-death Experiences

Brinkley, Dannion. *At Peace in the Light.* New York: Harper, 1996.
Eadie, Betty. *Embraced by the Light.* California: Gold Leaf Press, 1992.

Grossman, Neal. "Who's Afraid of Life and Death?" *Noetic Sciences Review*, Number 61, September-November, 2002.

Jansen, K. L. R. "Using ketamine to induce the near -death experience: mechanism of action and therapeutic potential. *Yearbook for Ethnomedicine and the Study of Consciousness.* Issue 4, 1995 (Eds C. Ratsch; J. R. Baker); Berlin, pp 55-81.

Morse, Melvin. *Closer to the Light: Learning from Children's Near-death Experiences.* New York: Ivy Books, 1990.

---*Parting Visions: Explorations of Pre-death Visions and Spiritual Experiences.* New York: Harper, 1994.

---*Transformed by the Light: The Powerful Effect of Near-Death Experiences on People's Lives.* New York, Villard Books, 1992.

Ring, Kenneth. *Heading Toward Omega: In Search of the Meaning of the Near-Death Experience.* New York: William Morrow & Co., 1985.

San Felippo, David. "Religious Interpretations of Near-Death Experiences," a Doctoral Candidacy Essay, September 17, 1993.

horizonresearch.org – British research on near-death experiences, deathbed visions, and out-of-body experiences – you can participate

iands.org — International Association for Near-Death Studies with support groups

nderf.org — Near Death Experiences Research Foundation. Send your story.

near-death.com — lots of stories

neardeathexperiencers.org — an organization by and for experiencers

Retrocognition, Auras, Remote Viewing

- Retrocognition means perceiving a past event without the use of the senses.
- Auras are the emanations of living things in the space around their bodies. Some psychics can see them.
- Remote viewing involves seeing something in another location or time without the use of the senses. Another name for the ability, clairvoyance, means seeing without the use of the senses.

Retrocognition

Suppose you sat at the kitchen table one evening with your family and suddenly imagined two Union soldiers riding through the backyard on horseback. You might hear their shouts to each other or the clopping of hooves. Although this might sound like an example of a haunting, these soldiers aren't the kind of ghosts referred to previously in the chapter, ghosts, who might see you or try to communicate with you. These soldiers remain in the past and relate to each other, carrying out some activity only they know.

Many theories attempt to account for such an episode. It might be time travel; either you and your family are traveling back to the 1860s or the soldiers are traveling forward into your 2000-something kitchen. Another explanation is reincarnation. You might be remembering a former life, in a sense traveling to the other time or watching scenes from the former time play out. Another camp might call such episodes remote viewing where one travels mentally to another time or place.

An ability to look into the past comes in handy with missing persons cases or violent crimes. Detectives sometimes use psychics to visualize a criminal, a victim, or a crime scene. The psychic then gives descriptions so artists can make sketches. Some difficult crimes have been solved this way, but police departments don't always acknowledge their use of psychics. Obviously the Glendale policeman I encountered when I saw the intruder psychically didn't believe in such abilities at all.

Two psychics who have provided help to police investigators who believed and trusted them are Allison DuBois and Laurie Campbell. Both women have written books about their experiences and maintain excellent websites.

On August 10, 1901 Charlotte Anne Moberly and Elizabeth Jourdain visited Versailles and had a common experience of seeing and interacting with people seemingly from the eighteenth century. Research convinced them they had seen Marie Antoinette on August 10, 1789, the day of her arrest. The two women wrote a book called *The Adventure*, which was published in 1911 to great controversy. Many considered the whole affair a hoax.

Some evidently read the book and believed in the possibility of retrocognition. Two poets, William Butler Yeats of Ireland and the American Ezra Pound, probably read the book. While Pound was in England, he served as secretary to Yeats, and together they experimented with retrocognition. Yeats believed he had viewed his own incarnation in a previous century. He called that incarnation by the name of Leo Africanus and communicated via automatic writing. Yeats considered Leo to be his muse and wrote of the events in his *Autobiography*. Pound valued his remembrances because they contributed to his spiritual development. He wrote about them in *Three Cantos*.

Auras

Perhaps humans or events that are highly charged leave a resonance that sensitive individuals pick up later. That resonance might be remnants of the aura left behind.

Sometimes, if you catch a person in just the right light, you might fancy you see colors dancing around the body or maybe a faint blue glow. Just as quickly the colors disappear. Chances are you've seen an aura. If you have this insightful ability, you can develop it by reading authorities on the subject such as Barbara Ann Brennan and Dolores Kreiger.

Almost every culture throughout history has included the aura as a part of its tradition from the halo around the heads of saints to the energy body defined by Chinese physicians. The life force in the Chinese tradition is called *chi* and in India *prana*. American Indian religions also include references to an aura or life force.

The word aura comes from the occult tradition and comprises various bodies that surround the physical body. The first is the etheric body, which penetrates the physical and extends an inch or so beyond it. Around the etheric body appears the astral body a few inches wider. Next comes the mental body and then the spiritual body. The interplay among these various bodies as they expand, contract, or move in other ways creates the aura. Physical conditions, thoughts, emotions, even deep breathing have an impact on its size, color, and intensity.

This dancing quality of the aura can be seen by psychically sensitive people, who describe it as consisting of changing colors. The yogis base understanding of the aura on a study of the chakras, centers of light that radiate out and disperse color in and through a living body:

Crown chakra, violet, spirit
Brow chakra, indigo, intellect
Throat chakra, light blue or silver, communication
Heart chakra, green, love and healing
Solar plexus chakra, abdomen, yellow, personal power
Adrenal chakra, genitals, orange, sexual identity
Root chakra at base of spine, red, safety, security

When our lives are out of synch, distorted colors show up in the aura. A healer senses or sees the colors, blockages, or discolorations then knows where and how to apply healing energy. The colors of the aura follow a certain symbolism: red for passion or anger, orange for ambition, yellow for intellect, blue for sensitivity, etc. The particular meanings tend to vary with the psychic. One might see purple where another sees mottled blue and gold but both might ascribe the same emotion.

Throughout history, healers have believed in the effectiveness of color to influence people's physical and emotional health. The ancients identified yellow, orange, and red with daylight and vitality; blues and violets with the calm and quiet of night. Early science in Greece attached colors to the seasons and bodily fluids called humors—spring blood red, summer bile yellow, autumn black bile, and winter white phlegm. Such studies went underground because of persecution by Christians and thus became known as occult sciences. Occult means hidden, and these arts were hidden so the practitioners wouldn't end up on the rack or the pyre.

Modern science has rediscovered color through the use of blue light to increase plant growth, rotating classroom colors with students' maturation, painting prison cells calming blues and greens or even pink. Hospitals routinely put jaundiced premature babies under blue light. Red light aids in treatment of migraines and cancer. Both blind people and sighted people wearing blindfolds can discern color.

Studies, whether in light or paint or cloth, continue to reveal the influence colors have on plants, animals, and humans. Some growers have found that red plastic spread under tomato plants hastens ripening of the fruit. Intuitives, especially those who can read auras, use color as a part of healing or emotional therapy, often in combination with herbs and crystals.

Colors are associated with the aura; from top to toe the human form expresses violet faith, dark blue intuition, light blue communication, green health and love, yellow wisdom, orange joy and creativity, red security.

The electromagnetic force fields surrounding the human body can be measured by imaging machines. In addition to radiology, Kirlian cameras can photograph the aura by taking pictures of the gas discharge glow of living things. Research has begun on manipulation of the aura to find possible cures for cancer and to grow new limbs (already done with salamanders).

Other research focuses on the changing emotions visible in Kirlian photographs of people's auras. The changes in the hands of healers during healing can be observed. Some healers have used videotape to capture patients' images then digitally enhance them to see the aura. The aura has been observed to diminish after death.

Many people who have had encounters with unidentified flying objects (UFOs) as well as those who have had NDEs are electrically sensitive. Watches and other electronic equipment sometimes don't work around them.

The electrical fields of both humans and plants can be discerned in the laboratory. Perhaps a person's electromagnetic field becomes more excited as either a cause or effect of psychic activity. Perhaps those who have electrical sensitivities might contribute to further understanding of electronic transmission cases, that is, placing sound onto electronic equipment by an effort of will.

The aura consists of light, electricity, and biochemical components. What else at present we don't know, but doctors are beginning to use the research, a process now called bioholography, for diagnosis.

Remote Viewing

Remote viewing is the easiest and most studied of any type of psi, the name psychic experience goes by in the laboratory. The modern name signifies an ability that's been around forever—clairvoyance, that is, seeing without the aid of the five senses.

The Gallup Poll question of 2001 on clairvoyance netted a response of thirty-three percent believers, up six points from 1990. With twenty-seven percent uncertain, belief in clairvoyance is growing, as it should be. Some heavy hitting laboratory experiments have pretty much proved clairvoyance is a human ability.

Remote viewing in the dream state seems easier for me than waking practice. One night I gave my dreaming self the suggestion to travel to my friend Judith's house in San Diego. I'd been there many times but not in the previous year. In my dream I went to her house and stood in the area where the fireplace was, a dining room/office. Something seemed different about the house. I thought I saw paint cans sitting out and one wall empty of decorations. At first I wondered whether Judith had started to do some art like oil painting, an activity very foreign to her. My next thought? Maybe she planned to paint a wall.

When I emailed Judith, she responded this way: "Hey, I'm definitely planning on painting. The table is empty. I have paint samples in a drawer."

My observation of Judith's room gave me the feeling of redecorating but no precise information. That's often the situation for amateurs like me. Practicing remote viewing increases accuracy.

In 1980 the Mobius Group, about half a dozen practicing psychics, found some treasured artifacts in Egypt through the technique of remote viewing. Judith Orloff, a psychic and author of *Second Sight*, became part of the Mobius Group in 1985. She and several Mobius Group psychics later participated in another experiment during which they discovered the locations of eighteen sunken ships in the Atlantic.

Russell Targ and Hal Putoff did definitive scientific work on remote viewing at Stanford Research Institute during the 1970s and 1980s. Government agencies, including NASA and the CIA, funded much of the research. Some of the results are still secret, but the government released a great deal of information in 1995. Targ has written a fascinating account in *Miracles of the Mind.*

Most of the experiments followed a similar pattern: Experimenter One randomly chose a sealed envelope with an address written on it, a target location within a thirty-minute drive from the institute.

Once in the car, he read the card and drove to the location where he gazed for thirty minutes at the building, park, or whatever had been stipulated.

Back in the institute's office, the researcher doing the remote viewing meditated on the target location and gave impressions as to shape, color, size, or any other perceived information then made written descriptions and/or drawings. Experimenter Two, who did not know the target destination, asked clarifying questions, such as "When you say round, exactly what do you think the object looks like?" That technique elicited as much information as possible.

When Experimenter One returned, independent scientists correlated the drawings with descriptions or photographs of the target locations. The comparisons had a seventy-five to eighty percent accuracy rate.

The research design might lead you to compare remote viewing to telepathy. However, many successful experimenters have used targets that no one knew the appearance of, that they existed, or what they looked like, such as sites behind enemy lines.

Some of the experiments included Russian targets during the Cold War years. At that time United States government agencies could obtain only sparse information about the enemy's capabilities and installations. The remote viewing experiments provided the government with details they needed for defense.

Also, some skilled remote viewers can describe objects or places only revealed at some time in the future. Targ says of his research and that of other scientists who have replicated it, "The true value of remote viewing lies in the fact that it puts us in contact with the part of our consciousness that is unbounded by distance and time. Remote viewing allows us to become aware of our connected and interdependent nature."[9]

The original researchers used only psychics but later discovered they didn't have to. Any interested person can learn to do remote viewing. In fact, Targ and his fellows built a machine to help people improve their skills.

Much of the work strove to understand the faculty people have for remote viewing. The process seems like remembering and can be done in the present, past, or future with equal success.

Well investigated and documented, remote viewing has become the showcase psychic phenomenon. It clearly works. People can tap into information regardless of space or time. It's a matter of focusing attention, effort, and know-how.

It is safe for amateurs to experiment with remote viewing. If you want to try your psychic wings, set up your own experiment similar to the Targ experiments described above. Targ says:

> Although we know that psi is not perfectly reliable, the experimental data show that it is widely distributed in the general population . . . part of . . . a Psychic Internet, the mind-to-mind connections available to all who wish to log on. If the truth be known, we are all already hooked up. We just have to decide to pay attention.[10]

We can discover any place or event. No one can keep a secret from us if we want to know it. Our abilities extend far beyond what some of us have ever dreamed possible.

Resources for Retrocognition, Auras, Remote Viewing

Butler, W. E. *How to Read the Aura.* Wellingborough, Northamptonshire: The Aquarian Press, 1982.

Dalichow, Irene and Booth, Mike. *Aura-Soma: Healing Through Color, Plant, and Crystal Energy.* Carlsbad, CA: Hay House, Inc. 1996.

Ellwood, Gracia Fay. *Psychic Visits to the Past: An Exploration of Retrocognition.* New American Library, 1971.

Graham, Helen. *Color Therapy Then and Now, Parts I and II.* Ulysses Press, 1998. Article Index available at innerself.com

McMoneagle, Joseph. *Remote Viewing Secrets: A Handbook.* Charlottsville, VA: Hampton Roads, 2000.

Schwartz, Stephan A. *Opening to the Infinite.* Buda, TX: Nemoseen Media, 2007.

Targ, Russell and Haray, Keith. *The Mind Race: Understanding and Using Psychic Ability.* New York: Villard Books, 1984.
--- and Katra, Jan. *Miracles of the Mind: Exploring Nonlocal Consciousness and Spiritual Healing.* Novato, CA: New World Library, 1999.

--- *Limitless Mind: A Guide to Remove Viewing and Transformation of Consciousness*. Novato, California: New World Library, 2004.

Ballentine, Brian. "Ezra Pound and the Occult." cwru.edu/artsci/ engl/VSALM/mod/ballentine/resources/occult.html

allisondubois.com

bioholography.org — medical imaging

crystalinks.com — pictures of auras and Kirlian photographs

ebook.lib.hku.hk/CADAL/B31417310/index.html – text of *The Adventure*

espresearch.com — Russell Targ's site

gardening.about.com/od/totallytomatoes/qt/Red_Mulch.htm

innerself.com/Health/Color_Therapy_part_1.htm Korotov, K. G. "Korotkov Research" – a summary of research

irva.org — International Remote Viewing Association

kirlian.org — photography

lauriecampbell.net

mceagle.com/remote-viewing — a blog by the U. S. government remote viewing scientist

organicconsumers.org/corp/tsunami.cfm

sheldrake.org/papers/Animals/animals_tsunami.html

stephanaschwartz.com — author

sri.com — Stanford Research Institute

trvuniversity.com — Psi technology school

Chapter Eight

Fleeting Connections

"I don't think we're in Kansas anymore, Toto."
Dorothy in *The Wizard of Oz*

<u>Dreams</u>

For me dreams have been the connection to my soul. Through them most of my psychic experiences have come.

Prophetic Dreams

My friend Susan, the acupuncturist, had several prophetic dreams over the years. She shared some with me as I worked on this book. In a dream, Susan found herself trapped in an unfamiliar house with a storm raging outside. When debris broke a window and came flying toward her, she screamed and awoke.

The next day she left college for a holiday week at home. Her actor father invited Susan along on an audition so they could visit while he waited. Once at the theater, the director asked if she would like to read for a part, too.

"Why not?" Susan picked up the script. As soon as she began reading, she recognized the character as exactly like the one in her dream, a woman caught inside a house while a storm whirled around her. Susan read convincingly, got the part, and spent her vacation rehearsing.

Dreams that come true have a way of lingering in our minds. My teaching buddy Betty seldom remembers a dream or has a waking psychic experience, but she has premonition dreams when something very bad is about to happen.

One night at the age of five, Betty, her parents, and her grandmother lay asleep in her grandmother's house.

In a dream, Betty's mother went away. Betty searched the house and even tried to tear up the floorboards, to no avail. On awakening,

Betty cried so inconsolably that Grandma awakened Mother for Betty to see that everything was indeed all right.

When Betty's tears subsided, Grandma admonished, "Get back to bed. Next time, don't eat so much popcorn."

Betty's mother died shortly after.

The family dismissed the importance of the dream and made Betty feel unnecessarily foolish for awakening the household. The belief that diet had caused the nightmare threw the entire episode into an inappropriate context. This may seem like a minor point, but Betty remembered the painful comment for sixty-five years.

Negative thoughts work in our consciousness to limit us. In Betty's case, the lifelong mental image of herself messing up psychologically short-circuited the good the warning could have done. It's important to honor children's psychic experiences as legitimate mental events, even if we're not sure we believe in them.

Betty's dream probably came to warn and prepare her for the traumatic experience of her mother's death, even though Betty didn't consider a warning as a positive interpretation of the events at the time. As an adult, however, she learned to trust dreams to help her through crises.

Reminder Dreams

Can we meet the future in our dreams? If we do, will we recognize the dream in the event, caught up in the moment as we are? Does it do any good to know the future?

A problem I've not resolved is how to tell prophetic dreams from all other kinds. Some people seem blessed with that insight because their prophetic dreams have a different quality, an intensity of color or reality of presentation that sets them apart from the others. Precognitive dreams also often awaken the dreamer.

Vijaya, an author of sci-fi romance and a critique-group member, has had several precognitive dreams. She says she always awakens distressed and aware that the dream is very meaningful. She dreamed of her husband's ex-wife, someone she had met only once at a family function. Vijaya described her dream:

A car careened down a road and into a ditch. On top rode a coffin, which tumbled off with the impact. The lid came open, and the ex-wife stepped out, scared and calling for help.

Vijaya awoke, horrified, and got no more sleep the rest of the night. The next morning she recounted the dream to her husband. By noon they had received news that his ex-wife had died in a car wreck in another state around the time the dream occurred.

Prophetic dreams often provide the first brush with our psychic nature. In fact, that's the way I learned of the importance of paying attention to dreams. They taught me that I have psychic abilities. Dreams that come true command attention.

When we discover the miraculous in our lives, the first thing we want to do is share, so we bubble away, telling our spouse, our friend, our student, whoever is around, all the details of the event. Right after that, we're usually treated to the sidelong look that says, "Don't even go there. That kind of thing doesn't exist." The trick is to get through that moment without discounting the experience or, worse, thinking *I must be nuts.*

We don't doubt other functions of the mind. We remember that we called our mother to wish her a happy birthday. We acknowledge the decision to see a movie instead of balancing the checkbook. In my view, psychic thoughts are as valid as memory, decision making, or any other mental activity.

Helpful Dreams

Not many of my dreams are precognitive. More teach me about myself.

Early each August I used to have frustration dreams. I'd dream I was on my way to school but lose my keys or have my purse stolen. I couldn't find the street to turn on and arrive after the bell. Or I'd try to get into the auditorium and find it boarded up or the school burned down. Freud would have had a laugh at my expense about my buried hostilities regarding school revealed in that dream.

After a few years I began to accept frustration dreams as a normal part of my life and harbingers of the opening of school. I learned to laugh at myself for being so uptight. The new semester always turned out all right regardless of whether I worried.

Some dreams show quick and easy solutions to problems. During rehearsals for several different plays at the high school where I taught, I found myself at a loss about how to direct a troublesome scene. Then, not at all astonishingly, in a dream I often *saw* the scene the way it should play. Then I'd go to school and explain to my student actors what to do. Always, these scenes went together effortlessly.

Dreams sometimes track what's going on in our daily lives then weave that information into new connections. Some we remember and some we don't. In one particular instance, my dreaming self taught me a lesson.

Earlier in the day I'd had a conversation with a neighbor named Janie where she complained about having to help care for her semi-invalid mother. Janie spoke in a cold and callous manner as if she didn't care whether her mother lived or died. Janie's manner irritated me and I could barely keep myself from telling her so.

That night I dreamed about her. Here's the dream journal entry followed by notes I made at the time:

> In a dream I carried a five-year-old girl and called her Janie. We went to an estate sale of a huge house with a swimming pool and spa in the upstairs. We swam with other people who were laughing and having a good time. When I got ready to go, I couldn't find Janie. I called her name and she answered but I couldn't find her among a bunch of little girls. I asked a woman in a multi-striped bathing suit if she'd seen Janie. When she shook her head, I thanked the woman and turned away.
>
> As I walked down some steep and slippery stairs, I realized I held the sleeping child, after all. She was so big that, as I carried her on my hip, her head lay against my neck. She murmured, and I realized that I hadn't lost Janie. How ridiculous, I thought, and turned back. I climbed the stairs and explained to the woman how foolish I had been, that I had been holding the child all along. The woman shrugged as if to indicate she hadn't

noticed either. I felt more light-hearted and laughed as
I set off.

Notes made right after the dream: As I came awake
and understood the meaning, I didn't think it funny. I
realized that I'm dealing with the five-year-old Janie
trapped inside the adult, but I expect my neighbor
to behave like an adult all of the time. This dream
humorously reminds me of Janie's inner child. I don't
need to know why her inner child is damaged, just
that it is. I need to accept my neighbor and not judge
her so much. Janie's offensive comments about the in-
convenience of dealing with her semi-invalid mother
probably provoked this dream. In any case, it took me
in a different direction. Despite her childish responses,
she does her part with her mother. I need to let go of
my negative feelings and stop judging Janie. Thanks,
dreaming self, for analyzing this situation for me before
I said something that would hurt Janie for no good
reason.

Dreams bring new perspective to bear on aspects of waking life.
The Janie story proves that dreams play an important role in waking
life. They probably work to some extent even if we don't remember
them but have more impact when we recall and analyze them.

All the dream journal analyses happened after I awoke and had
some coffee to help me think through the experience. I had the
good fortune to remember in detail and improve my attitude toward
Janie.

Dreams are personal to the dreamer, so techniques that help me
analyze my dreams may or may not serve you. There are several individuals working in this field today, giving workshops and writing
books with methods for analyzing dreams for their personal as well
as their social significance. I found Patricia Garfield, Stephen LaBerge,
Robert Moss, and Jeremy Taylor most informative.

Forgotten Dreams

What a wealth of material our dreams present to us each night
whether we remember them or not. We dream about five times per

night. Assuming one sleeps every night, that's more than eighteen hundred dreams per year! Seldom can any of us remember all of them for even one night. I tried for many months and succeeded in remembering about three dreams per night but couldn't maintain that pace and dropped back to one every few nights.

In over thirty years of journal keeping, I have managed to write down approximately one hundred dreams per year. That means probably seventeen hundred went unremembered and unrecorded.

Generally I read back through my dream journals at the end of the year and mark the dreams that have come true. I average about seven precognitive dreams per year, within the standard of four to twelve percent found in research.

Mathematically, that computes to two hundred forty-six precognitive dreams unnoted. If we do indeed dream that much without recall, perhaps that failure to consciously remember helps to explain feelings of intuition or déjà vu.

The Dreaming Self

Imagine your waking self without the responsibility of looking after the physical body and all its needs. That's your dreaming self. There's no reason to fear or to ignore the dreaming self. It's one source of learning and self-understanding, one way of connecting to the higher power, however we define it—God, Goddess, Allah, Brahma, Universal Love, the Life Force. I even knew a minister who called that power Skippy.

Dreaming may be considered not so much a psychic activity as a different framework for the mind. When we're asleep, we suspend many of our mental blocks. Our inner critic sleeps, the one that pesters us with thoughts that we've been stupid or rude or incompetent. In dreams, our creative mind can come out to play.

The dreaming self acts as our gatekeeper to the wider universe. I believe that the knowledge and love of the Higher Power flows through the dreaming self to the waking self. The best attitude is not one of awe but of appreciation. Just as our physical body gets us around in the physical world, our dreaming self gets us around the imaginal realm.

Dreams of the Departed

The openness of the dreaming self allows many different types of experiences to happen besides precognition, problem solving, or personality analysis. Encounters with dead loved ones pepper the literature.

Hello from Heaven by Bill and Judy Guggenheim describes visits from the departed to grieving loved ones. The messages, often in dreams, contain words of comfort, such as "I'm okay, I'm in a beautiful place. Stop grieving and go on with your life. I love you." These are sentiments we all need to hear from those we've lost.

Patricia Garfield has codified many encounters in *The Dream Messenger*. In her view, whether one can prove the actual visit from the other world or not, there's no denying its impact. Dreamers remember details for a long time, and the experience often makes a profound difference in their beliefs. That definitely describes the dream I had about my grandmother and uncle.

Frightening Dreams

On the other hand, many people experience frightening or sad dreams about their departed loved ones. Often the dead seem even sicker, suffer more, or die more horribly. It's normal in the grieving process to initially have such dreams then get past them.

What can we do about nightmares or other troublesome dreams? Turn and face them, fearlessly and with humor. The mind creates nightmarish elements like hands strangling or tigers chasing. We can make the threatening images do whatever we want if we just stand up to them. That takes some work, but it's certainly possible. Dream work becomes more effective if we develop lucidity, conscious awareness while maintaining the dream state.

Lucid Dreaming

My friend Jan, the hypnotherapist and group leader, shared her lucid dream. She knew instinctively as a child how to overcome nightmarish elements, and she did so in a lucid dream. Jan wrote:

> I'm running from my dream terror. Chancing a look over my shoulder I see her, the nightmare witch. She's about five yards behind me, but her long legs carry her

swiftly over the ground. She will catch me at this rate, but then I remember that I can fly.

With this thought I feel a power swelling inside me in the region of my stomach. It's a good feeling. I focus on the feeling and begin to rise above the ground. Soon I am floating several feet above the witch. She jumps and her long, bony fingers strain to grab my clothing. As the dream continues, I notice that I am sinking lower and lower. I will soon be in her grasp if I don't do something. So I focus on my center and the power builds within me, taking me higher and higher until I am looking down on the trees.

Without my continuing concentration, the power wanes and my dreaming self knows the witch will grab me sooner or later. I don't feel fear, though. I have another choice and remind myself that it's just a dream and I can wake up. "Wake up, wake up," I shout.

Jan awakened in the darkened room and snuggled further under the covers, thinking about the dream. The feeling of power lingered within her. She felt good.

Although Jan is far more adept than I at lucid dreams, mine demonstrate some of the facets that alert the dreamer to lucid elements.

I dreamed I was trying to get a hot air balloon to fly over San Diego. In the dream I told somebody that San Diego was the most beautiful spot in the world, incredibly quiet and wonderful to fly above. Then I thought, "Yes, San Diego is beautiful but must take second place to Sedona."

It's this kind of critical thinking within the dream, even though it exposes me as an Arizona chauvinist, that pegs it as a lucid dream, or at least pre-lucid. The dreamer must combine critical thinking with seeming to awaken while continuing to dream, something I had never done.

Complete lucidity allows the dreamer to become aware of the act of dreaming and change the dream in some way as Jan did with the witch. We can become aware in our dreams, change their direction, orchestrate them, travel to other worlds, solve problems, make love, have fun. We can do everything in dreams that we can do awake, even something as mundane as laundry.

Dr. Stephen LaBerge has studied lucid dreaming at Stanford University for many years. His book *Exploring the World of Lucid Dreaming* (written with Howard Rheingold) explains how to become aware that one is dreaming and dictate the content of the dream. LaBerge says, "Lucid dreams can be extraordinarily vivid, intense, pleasurable, and exhilarating. People frequently consider their lucid dreams as among the most wonderful experiences of their lives."[11] He gives many examples and precise instructions for developing skill in lucid dreaming. LaBerge has proved in the laboratory what mystics and primitives have been telling us all along: "dreams are the gateway to infinity," says Carlos Casteneda.[12]

Harnessing Dreams

Many dreams, even precognitive ones, solve dilemmas or seem to bring tidings from another world. Despite the fact that they seem to just happen, we can do much to encourage the kind of dreams we want to have and increase our psychic activity in the process.

Dreams help us deal with emotions. Many universities around the world have researched the way that happens. Our dreaming mind creates metaphors or stories that key off our daily lives and make new connections.

If we dream we're standing on a stage taking a bow, it's easy to see we'd like some applause or other display of approval from others. If we walk naked through our hometown, certainly we're feeling exposed in some area in our lives. We have the intuitive understanding that dreams are important and that they reflect our emotional life in the waking world.

The Internet and the Yellow Pages afford opportunities to learn about dreams, take classes, or find psychics who will analyze dreams. It's big business. A cheaper and more dependable way to put your dreams to work for you, a journal or dream journal will help develop your psychic ability and your self-understanding.

Journal Keeping

The purposes of journal keeping are to serve as a record of your experiences, psychic, dream, and otherwise, and to help increase self-understanding. I've kept a dream journal for many years, but its only difference from any other journal is priority. I record my dreams first thing in the morning, then make notes, then write down anything else that's on my mind or in my heart. Most psychic awareness has come to me as precognitive dreams, but I enter any waking experiences, such as synchronicities or intuitions, as soon after they happen as possible.

To begin, lay a spiral notebook on your bedside table, date the top of the page, and leave the pen. Then, as soon as you awaken, whether during the night or in the morning, pick up the pen and start writing the very first thoughts you think. Don't sit up because the fragile images and ideas often float away the moment you do. Stay lying down in the most comfortable position you can manage. That's the method that has worked for me.

Some researchers disagree with this advice because they've found beginners have a tendency to fall back to sleep instead of recalling the dream. If you have this problem, you'll probably want to sit up or stand up so you can stay awake and focus on remembering the dream before you write it down.

At first you may see nothing but scribbles on your notebook, but within a matter of days you will write out whole dream stories and thoughts. Your handwriting may still appear illegible because of your reclining position, so you may want to transcribe the notes later in longhand or on a computer or typewriter. In fact, it's an excellent idea to recopy your notes to fix the dreams in your conscious memory.

Intensely personal, dream analysis has no set rules. Keep notes of your thoughts and feelings to help you begin. After you have jotted down the dream, write notes on your immediate thoughts about it. You might have additional ones as you transcribe the dream or later when you reread it. Jot those down too. Pay particular attention to the emotions you felt in the dream and add them to your notes.

Next, title the entry to help give it focus and meaning. When rereading, you will find the titles helpful. I put mine in capital letters. If you find three entries in a row with the title AIRPLANE IN THE

DRIVEWAY, you're likely to take a trip, you're in some kind of danger, or you'll soon own a plane.

Learning first to direct and then to influence the dream experience should be private except for one's immediate family. It's probably impossible to keep a spouse, child, or parent from knowing you are keeping a journal. If you can't get the approval of people who live in your household, at least swear them to silence. Tell them you're doing an experiment, and you'll talk about it after a set length of time, like three months. Assuming you can manage to hold off, their curiosity should outweigh any teasing or criticism.

If you don't want to try to remember your dreams, you can still keep the journal. Just begin with waking thoughts. You're still in that border zone between sleeping and waking where the profound can emerge. Your thoughts and imaginings have great congruency in that state.

Journal keeping is not primarily record keeping in the sense that a diary might be. In a journal you make mention of events in your life certainly but as they apply to your emotions, thoughts, and experiences. Your daybook is a good record of daily events, if you want to preserve that kind of personal history. Let the journal express your innermost feelings, fears, thoughts, wants, ideas, hopes, and daydreams along with your night dreams and psychic experiences.

If you have trouble thinking of anything to say, put the pen tip to the paper and write for a length of time, say ten minutes, without lifting the pen. It doesn't matter what you write, even if it's "I can't think of anything to write." Eventually you'll find your feelings and thoughts spilling out almost by accident.

With psychic development as one of your goals, make it a point to record any synchronicity or precognition. Keep dates and circumstances, whether you told anyone in advance, and the outcome. If you're like me, you'll only know a feeling or dream is precognitive in retrospect. Later, when you become more adept, you may have a sense of the precognition.

Here is a sample entry to give you a feel for how to do it:

April 16, 2002   SPIRITUALITY A CLICK AWAY

My dream was interactive. I had three links set up very close together. When I clicked on each one of them, I could go to a fairy tale land of beauty or spiritual loveliness. I tried to recreate the links in another place or web page by selecting all three of them and moving them. I tried several times, but the technique didn't work. I was worried that I would lose the links altogether.

Notes made right away: I worked on my web page a bit before going to bed last night. That obviously provoked the dream. If there's a message here, it may be that spiritual joy isn't just a click away. I have to work for it. Even so, the dream felt fanciful and light-hearted.

9 p.m.   A WAKING HUNCH

Indiana has a large rainfall. While I was growing up there, one rainstorm always refreshed my mind but I became depressed after two or three rainy days in a row. Weather factored into my choice of the Phoenix area as a permanent home since it receives only seven inches per year. Even though I'm susceptible to depression when it rains here, I can ease the severity by lighting candles around the house.

One evening as I sat writing some notes for a chapter in a novel, I got up and went in search of candles even though it didn't look like rain. I'd lived in the house for almost a year, but I had not lit any candles and had to look for where I might have put them away after unpacking. I found two candles and lit them. Not five minutes later, the electricity went off and remained off for forty minutes. It seems my spirit protected me from having to sit in profound darkness alone for such a long time.

An individual entry may not make a big impact on you, but over a period of time you will begin to see themes recurring and ideas taking shape about yourself and the people and places in your life. You will learn from your journal.

You may find you want to expand the scope of the journal into other areas of your life, such as grief or dealing with an illness. For a while, when I was first diagnosed with rheumatoid arthritis, I kept what I called a journal of healing. L. L. Desautels, writing in *Science and Spirit*, said "such scribotherapy is a way of healing and recognizing the importance of self-discovery." Scientific studies on arthritis patients have shown decreased inflammation and perception of pain, but "the writing process must be meaningful and lead to self-discovery for healing to begin."[13]

After recording your dreams for a while you'll discover the method that works best for you. I record my dreams and such other ideas as I want to capture each morning as soon as I arise. Some people write at night the last thing before retiring, as something of a summation of the day. Others like to do their journal over breakfast. Julia Cameron calls that practice morning pages in her book *The Artist's Way*. She makes a strong case for morning pages as very similar to meditation.

In *Freeing Your Creativity: A Writer's Guide*, Marshall J. Cook speaks of the value of keeping a journal, especially on reading it later:

> I encounter a different self, a fellow who sometimes amazes and often embarrasses me. I see recurring themes in my life and in my writing about my life. I note progress so gradual I wasn't aware of it in the day-to-day living of it. I understand my journey better...When I try to put my life into words, I give it new shape and meaning and find out what I'm really thinking.[14]

A journal can serve as a link that helps maintain our sanity. The more we explore our psychic potential, the more we find. A journal can also serve us in a crisis or in our daily life.

Resources for Dreams

Barasch, Marc Ian. *Healing Dreams: Exploring the Dreams That Can Transform Your Life*. New York: Riverhead Books, 2000.

Castaneda, Carlos. *The Art of Dreaming*. New York: HarperCollins Publishers, 1993.

Cook, Marshall J. *Freeing Your Creativity: A Writer's Guide*. Cincinnati: Writer's Digest Books, 1992.

Desautels, L. L. "The Alchemy of Words," *Science & Spirit*, Volume 13 Issue 4, July August, 2002.

Garfield, Patricia. *Creative Dreaming*. New York: Ballantine Books, 1974.

---*The Dream Messenger: How Dreams of the Departed Bring Healing Gifts*. New York: Simon & Schuster, 1997.

---*The Universal Dream Key: The 12 Most Common Dream Themes Around the World.* New York: Cliff Street Books, 2001.

LaBerge, Stephen. *Lucid Dreaming.* Los Angeles: J. P. Tarcher, Inc., 1985.

---and Rheingold, Howard. *Exploring the World of Lucid Dreaming.* New York: Ballantine Books, 1990.

Moss, Robert. *Conscious Dreaming.* New York: Crown Trade Paperbacks, 1996.

Roberts, Jane. *Seth: Dreams and the Projection of Consciousness.* Walpole, New Hampshire: Stillpoint Publishing, 1986.

Varela, Franciso J., Ed. *Sleeping, Dreaming, and Dying: An Exploration of Consciousness with The Dalai Lama.* Boston: Wisdom Publications, 1997.

ions.org — Institute of Noetic Sciences

jeremytaylor.com — excellent source for books and ideas on dream work

lucidity.com — Stephan LaBerge's site

mainportals.com/precog.shtml — Central Premonitions Registry. Send your dreams.

psiarcade.com — Test your psi abilities.

psiarcade.com/gaia — Send your dreams.

mossdreams.com — useful books and articles by Robert Moss

Doubles, Out-of-body Experiences, Astral Projection

The ghost of a living person, a double, appears to travel without the physical body. It is sometimes called the astral image, soul body, or subtle body in English, *doppelgänger* in German, *vardoger* in Swedish, *fetch* in Irish, *ka* in ancient Egypt. The variety of languages that contain a word for the double shows the universality of the concept. This definition expresses the point of view of the witness, much as I saw my son head for the bathroom and my neighbor come out of the apartment building.

The phenomenon of the double carries the names of out-of-body experience (OBE), astral projection, astral travel, or soul travel. There's a great deal of anecdotal literature, from Cicero and Biblical scholars in ancient Rome through modern times, but little scientific proof of their occurrence.

In an OBE, the person seems able to see, hear, smell, and otherwise perceive the world from a focal point outside his or her physical body. With astral projection, the person seems to leave the physical body and travel in an astral or soul body. These are word plays for the same experience.

Both happen spontaneously in sleep or awake and can also be induced through meditation or hypnosis. Danger, grief, or some other disquieting emotions might serve as triggers. Although it's difficult to explain them, doubles, OBEs, and astral projection are a common part of the human condition.

Spontaneous Episodes

Experiencing awareness from a place other than one's mind or brain, especially when unintended and unexplained, may be the most disconcerting of all psychic events. The perplexity on the faces of my acquaintances when they related their OBEs demonstrated how we question our memories. I felt lucky that so many wanted to share even though they weren't wild about having their names in a book, so I'll identify them by their relationships to me.

A student of mine had, at the age of eighteen, purchased her first car. In her excitement to show it off, she jumped out of the car onto her driveway without engaging the parking brake. When the car rolled backward, her foot caught on the door frame, causing her to fall beneath. The front wheel ran over her foot while she lay on the concrete.

Terrified, my student popped out of her body. She felt as if she floated above the driveway, looked down at her injured self, and watched the car edge into the street. Just as suddenly, she found herself back in her body in great pain as people from within the house rushed out to help her.

The OBE thrilled my student, and she talked about it a great deal afterward. A Baptist, she regarded it as proof of her belief that she had a soul.

A secretary acquaintance of mine had an experience very common in hospitals. She had scheduled a complicated surgery. Although her life wasn't in danger, much could go wrong, according to her surgeon.

Worried while the anesthesiologist put her to sleep, the secretary soon found herself comforted because she could watch the whole procedure from a vantage point near the ceiling of the operating room. Not only did she see her surgeon, but she also heard what he and the other medical people were saying.

Later she told her surgeon about hearing what was said, but he denied the possibility, a curious trick of logic on his part.

An unnerving but humorous OBE happened to one of my cousins. He fell asleep in his seat on the aisle of an airplane cabin. Unaware that he had left his body, he awakened to find his head outside the plane, whizzing through the clouds. Shocked, he ducked and returned to normal reality, safe again inside the plane.

My cousin had a mixed reaction. On the one hand, he felt excited at the OBE. On the other, he had great concern that he could endanger himself. Awakening, like my cousin did, seems to be the response to fearful feelings during an OBE.

If you find yourself out of your body, remember that you have control. When you think that you want to reenter your body, you will.

Perspectives

The literature on OBEs seems to contain a number of spontaneous episodes much like those that happened to my friends and me. We discover that our thinking self seems to exist somewhere outside of and away from our bodies. Nothing negative happens, unless we count our sense of surprise at the unusual occurrence.

OBEs often occur without plan or warning and resolve themselves in a few minutes. It seems that, if we can pop out, we can also pop in, with no harm done. However, the aftermath of an OBE can include exhilaration and a sense of wonder that lasts a long time.

One way of describing the phenomenon is as an experience of bi-location, of being in two places at once. Throughout history, stories have been told about a person dying in one location and appearing to a loved one in another place, the crisis apparition. Without knowing, we may have the ability to be in two places at once all our lives but use it seldom or not at all until the hour of our death—if then.

In Dreams or Awake

Near-death experiences, those where a person goes to the medical brink and may even die for a few moments before resuscitation, can include OBEs. In fact, those stories often begin with the person's awareness of leaving his or her body and then going on a journey through a tunnel or into another reality.

Since I became president of Arizona Authors Association in 2006, I've had the opportunity to meet many amazing authors. Because they are so creative they often have psychic tales to tell.

One such author is Cherie Babcock Lee who calls hers an OBE; however, it has many characteristics of a near-death experience, (NDE), and so is doubly interesting. Now she has a husband, children, and grandchildren, but at the time she was only twelve and lived in West Virginia. She speaks for herself:

> I felt cold, sick, and exhausted all the time. When my hair started falling out and I gained a lot of weight in a few weeks, Mom took me to our doctor. He ran tests and prescribed an iodine solution to slow my thyroid. After one month's treatment, I had blisters in my throat and lost whole clumps of hair.
>
> Overhearing Mom tell Dad that she couldn't lose another child, I knew she meant my brother who died at eight months of age. She took me to another doctor in a nearby town. He told her I needed to go to a specialist in Cleveland and made an appointment for us.
>
> My classmates felt sorry for me when I heard them whispering. I bet they thought I'd die like I wanted to do, to escape. Death had to be better than this cold, cold zombie experience with no joy or laughter, just a struggle to breathe and move from place to place. I did not try to read anymore, my favorite treat always.
>
> On the day before the appointment, I felt more tired when I came home from school. I climbed the stairs with pauses between steps. Cold seeped through my whole body even though it was warm outside. I sat on the edge of my bed and pushed against my leg with my index

finger. An indentation appeared. Water dripped out and
ran down my leg. My whole body had retained water, my
eyelids only opened to slits. My weight had gone from
sixty-eight pounds to over one hundred.

I flopped backwards on my bed and gazed at the
ceiling then curled onto my side with blankets pulled up
over me. Still the cold, cold feeling did not go away. "God,
let me die," I cried and fell asleep even though I knew it
was my responsibility to start cooking supper before my
mother came home from work.

I never could figure out how I floated out the top of
my head into the corner of the ceiling. I only remember
a slight pop and wondered why I was up there looking
down at my body. Then I realized I was not cold
anymore. I raised an arm and it did not look swollen. Still
I felt confused and did not understand how I could be in
two places.

Seeming to float to the side window, I looked outside
at the blooming canary tree. There seemed to be no up or
down movements, but I felt surprised when I floated over
the bed and saw my body still there.

The next thing I remember was standing on the slanted
portion of the back roof and could not remember getting
there without a door or open window to pass through. I
wondered if I went through the wall but felt no barrier of
any kind. I did not worry as I looked at the beautiful sky
so rosy pink even though it was still broad daylight.

Some clouds gathered and formed a tunnel. I felt
compelled to enter and knew I had to do it immediately.
I stepped off the roof and was inside the clouds. It was
dark on the sides, but a light beamed ahead of me. Maybe
I walked or floated, I'm not sure. That place felt peaceful
and made me feel contented. There are no words to
describe the peace I felt except that it encircled me. I'd
known some kind of peace when I'd sat beside the Ohio
River on a cracked mud flat bank and watched a bobber
bob in a patch of sunlight.

I kept moving until a white hand punched through
the tunnel. I felt no fear, but sorrow welled up inside
me. The hand was held like a stop sign, and I knew I had
to go back even though I wanted to continue toward a
light in the distance. No one spoke to me, and I never
saw anything in the tunnel besides the hand. Somehow, I
knew I had to stay alive to do some task. I do not know
how I left the tunnel or returned to my room. I only
remember popping back into my still body and wishing
the cold would go away.

My mother shook my shoulder. "Cherie, wake up. You
have to eat something." I wiped hands across my face
and felt moisture below my eyes, but I refused to eat,
just went back to sleep, wishing I could feel that tunnel
warmth again.

When we went to Cleveland the next day, the clinic
doctor said it was a miracle that I had survived. Water
surrounding my heart and lungs should have killed me.
I had a thyroid defect common for adults, but rare for
children. I received a prescription for a thyroid extract in
pill form. Today I take a new form of the medicine.

Later I told Mom about the tunnel. She said it had
happened to her too, but we shouldn't talk about it at
all, so I never mentioned it to Dad. I told a girlfriend, and
her eyes got wider and wider and she backed away from
me saying, "You must have been dreaming." That made
me think what I remembered was not true and could be
a sign of being crazy. Fear of being made fun of caused
me never to talk about this experience, but the peace I
felt was so joyous I often prayed to have it return. The
prayers never were answered, so I finally quit asking to go
back into the tunnel.

With many books and stories about out-of-body
experiences, I know that is what I experienced. However,
I still do not know what task I am supposed to do, but
I try to follow my intuition when I need to make a

decision. A feeling of peace sometimes seeps into my
body from some of my decisions, so I must be doing what
I should even though I feel I am still searching for my
task.

Studies by Lynne Levitan and Steven LaBerge show that people
perceive they are having these experiences while in a dream state as
well as awake or in a reverie state. Some subjects can let researchers
know the OBE is happening while it's in progress. They achieve the
communication by pre-arranged method, such as raising a finger while
remaining asleep. OBEs tend to happen while a dreamer is experiencing sleep paralysis. Thus, the perception of having a body diminishes.

Subjects have not shown increased psychic knowledge during these
OBEs. The psychologist Joe H. Slate, who has done classes in psy-
chic empowerment, lists the following benefits for OBEs in his book,
Astral Projection and Astral Empowerment.

- They are relaxing.
- They are a source of important insight.
- They provide quality solutions to problems.
- They are a source of pleasure.
- They are gratifying and personally fulfilling.
- They add excitement to life.
- They are motivating.
- They stimulate creative thinking.
- They restore physical and mental balance.
- They build self-confidence and self-esteem.
- They promote intellectual efficiency.[15]

Many feel that OBEs contribute to a more cosmic view of themselves and augment their spiritual growth. The experience seems
to prove, at least to the ones having it, their existence outside the
body—the traditional definition of the soul.

Suppose you're lying on the couch on a sunny Sunday afternoon with
nothing particular to do, just enjoying not doing anything. Suppose
you doze and come awake with a vibrating feeling as if your body is
tuning up. Suppose you wave your hand and realize it passes through
the arm of the couch. Then you rise into the air. You look down at

your body. You might have a momentary fear that you've died, but then you see your breath going in and out and realize your body is sleeping although your consciousness remains awake and separate.

You decide to explore, and in the next moment you find yourself soaring above the treetops on your street. Everything looks the same but different from this vantage point. You fly to the ballpark and see a game in progress. By now, you're having fun and feel daring.

You fly toward the sun. Rivers of light billow out, rich reds, vibrant blues, and flickering violets fan toward you. You sense the presence of a loving friend close by although you can see no one. Protective hands lift you up and place you in a golden city, its skyscrapers jeweled with diamonds and rubies. Beautiful light-emitting beings move about, involved in such activities as dancing, playing musical instruments, reading, and painting. You fall in love with the place and think you would enjoy living there too.

With a jolt you return to your body and awaken.

You've just done an astral projection. Many people say they go to other realms, including the astral plane, which is like a dream world. It can look like ours or it can be very fanciful with monsters, fairies, and other dreamlike creatures.

The Experts

Robert Monroe had many experiences with astral projection over a lifetime. At first they were involuntary, but eventually he became able to project out of his body at will. He was so fascinated by the process that he founded the Monroe Institute in Virginia where others may go and try to have similar experiences. The institute also does research.

Some who do astral projection say they travel in a subtle body or astral form. This form looks like their physical body except that it is fairly transparent. In most cases, they exit their physical body through the solar plexus but remain attached to it by a silver cord.

One of the many astral projections Monroe tells about in his book *Journeys Out of the Body* exemplifies the amazing aspect of verification possible in the waking world. Upon hearing that a friend of his was ill and confined to bed, Monroe did an astral projection to visit his friend and find out his progress. After flying over the treetops, Monroe tried to go into the upstairs bedroom but instead saw his friend and the friend's wife getting into their car. Disbelieving, Monroe flew back home. Later, Monroe verified by telephone that indeed the friend had decided some air would help him recover, so he had dressed, gotten into the car with his wife, and gone to the post office. The time of the post office trip coincided with Monroe's OBE.

A religious group, Eckankar, specializes in soul travel. Teachers help students learn the skill of astral projection, which they consider a spiritual practice. *Eckankar: Ancient Wisdom for Today* states the advantages of soul travel:

> When you realize through personal experiences that
> you live beyond the physical body, you are released
> from the fear of death. You worry less. When you realize
> through experience that you are a creative part of a
> loving God, you invite more love into your life. You
> feel less lonely or alienated. When you realize through
> experience that your life has a spiritual purpose, you will
> feel energized.[16]

Possible fears associated with this practice are: severing the silver cord, failing to get back into the body, becoming lost, or encountering negative spirits. Some people might fear that other spirits will enter and take over their body while they are out, preventing their return. In their view, possession could occur, requiring exorcism.

Fears diminish with time and successful practice of astral projection. At least that's true for most people. Unaddressed fears have a way of demonstrating themselves in nightmares or psychological distress. It's important to acknowledge any negative feelings and work through them with guidance.

If you find yourself fearful but still intrigued, read all the books you can find on the subject. After that, pursue experiences under the guidance of a teacher or group with good credentials. If you are able to successfully experience an OBE, you'll have a memorable experience worth the effort.

Resources for Doubles, Out-of-body Experiences, Astral Projection

Cramer, Todd and Munson, Doug. *Eckankar Ancient Wisdom for Today*. Minneapolis, MN: Eckankar, 1995.

Crookall, Robert. *Case-Book of Astral Projection, 545-746*. Secaucus: NJ: Citadel Press, 1972.

Denning, Melita and Phillips, Osborne. *The Llewellyn Practical Guide to Astral Projection*. St. Paul, MN: Llewellyn Publications, 1980.

Levitan, Lynne and LaBerge, Stephen. "Other Worlds: Out-of-Body Experiences and Lucid Dreams," *Nightlight* 3 (2-3), 1991.

Monroe, Robert A. *Journeys Out of the Body*. New York: Anchor Press, 1977.

Slate, Joe. H. *Astral Projection and Psychic Empowerment*. St. Paul, MN: Llewellyn Publications, 1998.

astralvoyage.com

eckankar.org

horizonresearch.org — British research on near-death experiences, deathbed visions, and out-of-body experiences. You can participate.

lucidity.com

monroeinstitute.com

oberf.org — You can share and read others' experiences.

Déjà vu

"It's déjà vu all over again" is a humorous saying attributed to Yogi Berra.

Déjà vu is so common that you've probably already experienced it and only thought it remarkable, not worrisome. Déjà vu, French for already having seen happens when:

- You go to a place for the first time and it seems familiar.
- You meet a person and seem to already know him or her.
- You perform some act for the first time, like play a violin, and feel as though you already know how to do it.

Because of the frequency of déjà vu occurrences, some people think it's not a paranormal event. The fact that most of us have this particular psychic experience means to me that it is as much a part of human nature as hearing or thinking.

Research

Arthur Funkhouser has done research in déjà vu. It's a difficult area to investigate because episodes happen spontaneously and are not likely to happen in a laboratory situation. As a result, Funkhouser describes what people say happens to them. He finds that two-thirds of the people in his research report instances of déjà vu in one form or another.

There's a good deal of disagreement about the origins of déjà vu. Possible causes are a vaguely remembered precognitive dream, a precisely remembered precognitive dream, an OBE, a past life memory, a coincidence, or a temporal lobe excitation. The right temporal lobe, a section of the brain above the ear, has been involved in near-death experiences and confusions regarding time by individuals who suffer from epilepsy.

Some psychologists theorize that fatigue may cause a delay in communication between the eyes or ears and the brain. One has the impression of having seen, heard, or felt something twice when in fact one has not.

This explanation may work for some cases but cannot account for many déjà vu events where verification happens. For example, some cases of reincarnation appear to involve déjà vu where a person claims to remember a former life. In cases researched by Ian Stevenson and others, after naming a particular town that a subject remembers, he or she can guide the research team around, recognizing people and naming streets and buildings. These are facts that the subject could never know in the current lifetime.

Thoughts from Professionals

The famous medium Jane Roberts attributed her many déjà vu experiences to astral projection. She believed that, when we had plans to visit a place we'd never seen before, such as the Chesapeake Bay, we would travel there in sleep to look the place over, perhaps to alleviate anxiety about the trip or simply out of anticipation. The next morning we'd not recall the little outing, and then when we gazed across the splendid waves of the bay, we'd think, *This place looks so familiar. Maybe I lived here in a former life.*

Often when people have déjà vu experiences, they shake their heads and say, "I must have dreamed it." Much of science consists of experimentation that proves the most reasonable explanation, which for déjà vu might be that we have dreamed something that comes true. There is much scientists don't know yet about this tricky subject.

You can be part of the research by going to one of the websites and recording your déjà vu or other precognitive experiences.

- British Society for Psychical Research, spr.ac.uk
- American Society for Psychical Research, aspr.com — the oldest and most broad-sweeping. Click on Online Research to enter your experiences in the database.
- Institute of Noetic Sciences, ions.org. psiarcade.com/gaia, a goal "to correlate collective dreams with world events, including natural and unnatural disasters, to see if collective dreams are predictive"
- mainportals.com/precog.shtml — a site that has been in operation for several years with the same goal
- theintentionexperiment.com — a new site with "a series of scientifically controlled, web-based experiments testing the power of intention to change the physical world."

Déjà vu experiences are the least fear-inducing of any paranormal events. If you're feeling nervous about having them, know that no bad can come from them. The psychic Judith Orloff gives some rather poetic advice in her book *Second Sight*:

> ...enchanted moments that sparkle with ethereal light. These are déjà vu...Don't let these possibilities pass you by. Take notice, rely on your instincts, and investigate. There's no way of predicting where one of them might lead or what it will teach you. Identifying the psychic is only the first step. Summoning the courage to take a chance and act

on it, to have faith in what is not yet visible, will make the experience your own.[17]

Resources for Déjà vu

Funkhauser, Arthur. "Dreams and Déjà vu," *Perspectives*, Vol. 6, No. 1.
--- "Three Types of Déjà vu." home.cc.umanitoba.ca/~mdlee/
     dejavu.htm.
Orloff, Judith. *Second Sight*. New York: Warner Books, 1996.
judithorloff.com
livescience.com — articles on déjà vu
pni.org — summary of research
web.mit.edu/newsoffice/2007/deja-vu-0607.html — article on
research

Visions, Angels

Defining Visions

A vision is a scene played out before one's eyes in an illusory sense. As the person sees the scene, he or she believes the events are actually happening, a moment later realizing they have not happened in exterior reality, only in mind. However, the vision carries truth often borne out soon after.

Visions elude scientific research because they happen spontaneously, sometimes as reactions to situations. They are similar to hearing voices or acting on a hunch. Perhaps they happen more to people who learn visually. Visions seem more dramatic, however, and often occur when there is danger to the percipient or a loved one. Maybe at such times, the façade of disbelief fades, and subtle perceptions, like an inner knowing or gut feeling, can penetrate our conscious mind more easily.

I thank the Divine Intelligence for the next story. When I wrote the notes for this chapter, I felt comfortable with everything in it except that I had no example of a vision. The next time I went to the dentist for my regular check up, the dentist asked me what book I was working on. When I told him, he confided his experience of an angelic visitation. Some might call it a coincidence, but for me it's the synchronicity of the universe working.

Dr. Jack, a pseudonym, sat on a bench with his wife as they watched their nine-year-old son and seven year-old daughter ski on the bunny slope at the Snow Bowl near Flagstaff. The children had skied down several times without incident.

Dr. Jack felt a very strong presence, maybe an angel but nothing with wings or anything. Then he saw a vision: his son skied down the slope, lost control, bounced against one rock, flipped, and landed on another rock.

Frantic, Dr. Jack jumped up and called out to his son, but the boy took off without listening. Dr. Jack hurried to the second rock and sat down. Just the way it happened in the vision, his son skied down the slope, lost control, bounced against the first rock, and flipped. But the boy landed uninjured in his father's arms.

The son complained, "Why are you stopping me?"

With a hearty laugh, Dr. Jack hugged his son, giving thanks for the vision.

As a child, Dr. Jack heard a voice that told him of future events. When he shared this information with his parents, they chided him and told him he was wrong. He thought he was crazy and tried to ignore his inner promptings. As an adult, though, he began to experiment with listening to the voice, which in his mind is the same thing as the presence. Sometimes he sees a fleeting glimpse of it; sometimes he only hears its voice in his head.

Early in his marriage, he had a very successful medical practice, but he made some investments that turned sour. Dr. Jack feared losing all of his money. At Christmas he wanted to buy a gift for his wife even though he couldn't afford to spend much money.

The voice in his head told him to go to Goldwater's Department Store. Dr. Jack went. The voice said, "Go to the furs collection." Dr. Jack began to argue mentally, but the voice insisted and guided him to a beautiful mink coat marked twenty-seven hundred dollars then said, "This is the one." He knew his wife would love it.

While the clerk dealt with another customer, Dr. Jack sat beside an older man who had two fur coats on his lap. The two men got to talking, and the older man mentioned bargaining for the price. Dr. Jack hadn't known that would be possible in a department store. He thought the price was the price. Take it or leave it.

When the clerk returned, Dr. Jack offered nine hundred dollars for the coat. To his surprise, the clerk asked him to wait while she made a phone call. When she returned, she agreed to the amount to his even greater surprise. Dr. Jack sucked up his courage, trusting the voice, and put the coat on his credit card. By February, when the credit card payment came due, Dr. Jack's financial affairs had made a complete turnaround. He could pay for the coat with no trouble. He thanked God for sending him the voice.

Dr. Jack admitted that honoring the presence helps him to live his life fully and richly and to feel authentic. It pleased him that I wanted to use his stories. On the other hand, he didn't want his name mentioned in the book because it might be bad for business. People might avoid his practice. The same old fear of rejection has dogged him from childhood.

His conflict has a familiarity to mine. Dr. Jack is, like me, a work in process. Even though his fear of losing business is valid, how authentic in his relationships with himself and with others can he be if he hides behind the persona of a man who doesn't have visions?

We must eventually open ourselves to these experiences when we have them. Visions, like precognitive dreams or hunches, can serve as spears to spiritual growth. They must be dealt with in a way that facilitates growth or they will disappear.

Types of Angels

Dr. Jack's experience has the feel of an angel intervention. Generally, angels bring messages from God and aid humans in trouble. Historically, we do not worship or pray to angels but honor them. Angels respond to individual requests for help. Some people consider this the method by which God operates in the world.

The Gallup Poll quoted in the first footnote in Chapter Seven did not include a question about angels, but obviously many people believe in them. Forty-one percent of Americans accept the possibility of devil possession. By extension they must believe in the devil, who was after all the fallen angel, Lucifer.

References to angels abound in the Bible of the Judeo-Christian tradition. An angel came to Adam, to Daniel in the lion's den, and to many others in the Old Testament. An angel announced the coming of Jesus to Mary, then one heralded His birth. Revelations predicts the coming of Jesus with a host of angels.

Angels take different forms. *The Apocryphal Book of Enoch,* a religious treatise of the time of Jesus not included in the official Bible, lists the names of the archangels as Uriel, Raphael, Raguel, Michael, Sarakiel, Gabriel, and Phanuel.

Guardian angels belong to each of us and protect us or pique our conscience.

Angels are beings with wings or with light around them. They also can pose as human beings. A line in Hebrews 13:2 *New American Standard* alludes to angels in disguise. "Do not neglect to show hospitality to strangers, for thereby some have entertained angels unawares." In biblical times, angels appeared both in human garb and in their beautiful, dazzling aspect.

Islam came into being because Mohammed received a visitation from the archangel Gabriel.

Angels continue to be a part of the language of our culture. Some of the most beautiful websites on the Internet contain drawings and paintings of angels, stories about angel interventions, and angel paraphernalia for sale. Type in the word "angel" on a search engine, and enjoy the great variety of art, touching stories, and angel lore.

Popular television programs feature angels from a variety of perspectives: *It's a Miracle* shows amazement and appreciation that anomalous events occur in our lives; *Touched by an Angel* has the angels helping and sometimes interfering in human affairs for the people's good; *Quantum Leap* features two angels, one orchestrating miraculous events from on high, the other a human who has great impact on people's lives. Many movies show the actions of angels in our lives, often in delightful ways, for example, *City of Angels, Michael, It's a Wonderful Life, Heaven Can Wait,* and *Angels in the Outfield.*

Doreen Virtue, the New Age popularizer of angel communications, says we all have two guardian angels and as many more as we call in, including archangels, deceased relatives, spirit guides, and ascended masters. She has a sweet message: the goal of the angels is "peace on earth one person at a time."[18] Whatever you need to make your life more peaceful they will try to provide. All you have to do is ask.

According to Virtue, angels might look like glowing lights, shimmering colors, clouds or mists. You might see whole angels with wings or a being who looks human. Angels can appear as lights in photographs. Also, you might see a sign such as a stopped clock or a falling picture. Or you might see a mental movie, as Dr. Jack did.

Virtue in her book *Messages from your Angels: What Your Angels Want You to Know* delineates the types of angels:

- Guardian angels that remain with us individually.
- Archangels (fifteen of them) that are universal and come to everyone who calls upon them. Sometimes they intercede on their own in dangerous situations like Dr. Jack's.
- Ascended masters such as Jesus, Buddha, Moses, Quan Yin, Mary, Yogananda, saints, and yogis.
- Nature angels such as fairies, elementals, divas that guard the earth.
- Spirit guides who might be relatives deceased before we were born or incorporeal spirits that we perceive as angels.

Ancestors as Spirit Guides

Although not a part of the Christian religious tradition, ancestor worship is an important component of a number of religions: Chinese Confucianism and Buddhism, Japanese Shintoism, Kwanzaa in American and traditional African faiths, some American Indian faiths, particularly Hopi, and remnants of the Incan tradition visible in Mexico and Central and South America. In fact, the strength of this particular belief greatly hinders Christian missionaries from converting citizens of other countries.

In Kwanzaa, the supplicant lights a candle seven days in a row with a request for protection in remembrance of his ancestors. Many Asians build altars in their homes to honor their ancestors, light candles for their souls, and ask them to intercede in human situations.

On the Day of the Dead, November 1 and 2, Mexicans traditionally take gifts of food to the graveyard and pray to their ancestors for intercession, perhaps to heal a sick child, find lost articles, or help solve a problem. Such practices might indicate simply an adoption of Western culture from Spain; however, the Spanish explorers found the Aztecs already celebrating the Feast of the Dead with flowers, altars, and prayers for intercession.

It might be blasphemous to suggest but praying to the saints seems hardly different. You might pray to St. Anthony to help you find your lost car keys. Even though he's not your ancestor, he could be somebody's ancestor.

Modern observations of Halloween and All Saints Day result from the mesh of ancient Celtic beliefs with Christianity. From about 44 BC to about 475 AD, Rome ruled Europe and Britain. The leader Constantine became a Christian. Soon, Roman soldiers and priests began to repress or absorb the Celts, the Druid intelligentsia, and other indigenous people of the local communities, particularly in France and England.

Much like the Indians of Mexico, the Pre-Christian religions of Europe celebrated the Celtic New Year, Samhain, October 31 to November 2, as the interface between summer and winter that belonged to neither. They believed the veil between the world of the living and the world of the dead grew thin. They built fires to prevent discarnate spirits from possessing humans. They said prayers to their ancestors, deified heroes, fairies, their gods, and their goddesses.

The custom of honoring and praying to ancestors spanned the ancient world and finds many devotees in modern times. If the Gallup Poll of 2001 asked Americans whether they believed in spirit guides, they'd probably say no. If it asked if they believed their ancestors lived on in another spiritual dimension, the majority would probably say yes.

Miracles

An angel intervention is one type of *miracle*, which carries an aura of unreality. A miracle is only a miracle because it violates natural law. That can't happen, says a reasonable, thinking mind; however, miraculous events do occur. Perhaps we think they can't because we assume that we know all of the laws of nature. Likely something we label a miracle is a natural event we just haven't figured out the rules for yet.

Such a stance doesn't preclude the sacred nature of the event or the holy nature of any angel or god. Perhaps such divine beings are aspects of a nature too grand for us to understand with our limited intellect. The Catholic Church defines a miracle as an event provoked by God or His angels, as contrasted to magic, which occurs through humans as paranormal phenomena.

Inviting Guidance

Dealing with fears is the same whether one uses the terms angels, spirit guides, or departed loved ones. Virtue has several ideas. I found one particularly helpful. She said the ghosts in movies were far scarier than real ghosts.

We can apply that same assertion to all psychic phenomena. They seem far more forbidding and esoteric than they really are.

At one time, only psychics could see auras around people. Scientists scoffed, but now they photograph the aura for use in medical diagnosis. Until recently many considered telepathy a part of the realm of fantasy, but scientific studies have verified that people can read the minds of others. Years of positive results in the Ganzfeld experiments are described in the section on telepathy in Chapter Ten.

Sometimes it seems far-fetched to believe there are angels or spirit guides that we can't discern around us. And more so that they help us out when we ask them to or stay around us for protection. Someday scientists may also prove the existence of these spirit essences. In the meantime, acting on spirit guide energy or angel energy helps to make it work. If we believe it works, it's much more likely to work.

Ephemeral emanations, angel and spirit guide communications take us into the nether regions of our own psyche and beyond. If you want such communion, begin by protecting yourself. Surround yourself with white light, say a prayer of protection, whatever feels right. Then,

- Call on them
- Listen for them
- Find them through the techniques of journal keeping, affirmation, hypnotherapy
- Reread your dreams for clues
- Ask a medium or psychic to interpret for you

To pursue the experiences, you might want to put yourself under the tutelage of a reputable teacher until you feel comfortable. You don't have to commit to the New Age or occult life style of its practitioners to learn from them. We are all free spirits on both sides of the veil.

Peak Experiences

"Suddenly, totally unexpectedly, I had this incredible revelation. It was so indescribably beautiful; it was so simple and so elegant. I just stared in disbelief for twenty minutes."[19]

You might think that statement came from an artist or poet, but it was actually a mathematician, Andrew Wiles, alluding to the breakthrough moment in solving Fermat's Last Theorem, a problem that had stumped mathematicians for three hundred years. Wiles spoke those words on television during a program on the BBC, documenting his accomplishment.

Bruce Charlton, a psychology professor at Newcastle upon Tyne in England, describes this and other peak experiences from a variety of fields: the discovery of the concept for the atomic bomb, Einstein's daydream of riding a beam of light that forecast relativity theory, a dream of snakes biting their own tails that led to the discovery of benzene; the poetry of Samuel Taylor Coleridge, the historical novels of Robert Graves that seem far more realistic than historical sources.

A peak experience is the sudden realization of unity and truth accompanied by feelings of happiness. It often happens to people who invest great effort in solving a problem of any kind. Suddenly, the whole answer appears as if by magic in a moment of delight. A lot of work may remain to complete the foreseen development, but the peak experience lays the groundwork for success. After I saw the two images of myself in the mirror, I felt calmer than I had for weeks. It took quite a bit more work to come to a peaceful place in my life, but the experience gave me hope and direction.

A second type of peak experience happens without the presence of a problem, catapulting the percipient into a state of bliss, of oneness with all life and intense satisfaction. Not only can people attain this state of grace, also called cosmic consciousness, but some can remain there all the time.

Abraham Maslow, an American psychologist, did pioneering work on peak experiences in the 1960s. He studied them in part through interviewing people who'd had them spontaneously, and he also used psychedelic drugs to induce them in research subjects. Maslow came to believe that many people are capable of achieving peak experiences and that it is beneficial to teach them how.

Peak experiences have been documented throughout history in most cultures as part of a religious experience. A comparison of those reports yields nine universals:

1. Unity, a sense of cosmic oneness
2. Transcendence of time and space
3. Deeply felt positive mood
4. Sense of sacredness
5. Feeling of illumination, of knowing the truth
6. Sense that opposites can be entertained
7. Feeling that the experience is beyond words
8. Transiency, or diminishing intensity
9. Positive changes in attitudes and behavior [20]

Not only are these characteristics of religious conversion, but they are also the qualities of some drug-induced experiences and bear resemblance to NDEs, as well as featuring in reports by Buddhist yogis, Christian mystics, Hindu holy people, Zen masters, and Sufi monks. In other words, peak experiences happen all over the world in all times. People who have them describe them with ecstasy, and people who don't have them want to.

Attempts to create peak experiences abound. Although drugs are illegal, many people try to use them for that purpose. Legal methods have also been devised. One is the use of acupressure points on the face. The runner's high is a popular introduction to inducing peak experiences. Whether intentionally or not, athletes often report entering a blissful state during training or competition, probably an alpha state they call peak performance.

Another approach uses devices with headsets where electronic sounds induce the brain states of alpha and theta where peak experiences tend to manifest. Some expensive training programs boast the use of this equipment, including the Monroe Institute, which teaches astral projection, and Psi Tech, which teaches remote viewing.

If you're on a budget, you can meditate on what you find beautiful, perhaps something in nature, a person you love or admire, a burning candle. Or contemplate what it would be like to be a cat or a child or an ant. Daydream. Wonder. Imagine. In those realms, you short circuit your left-brain beta mind and gain access to the right brain with its unity and mystery.

Why encourage peak experiences? As a shortcut to work, they can't be beaten. They speed up the creative process and make it more effective. On the playful side, the percipient has an intense feeling of well being and happiness along with a sense that the world is in right and perfect order. No wonder there are attempts to manufacture those feelings through drugs. Some projections of the future include artificially incorporating the feelings produced by peak experiences through such means as genetic programming, that is, our DNA would be modified so that we would enjoy a constant experience of bliss or happiness. These are obviously experiences humans enjoy and want to encourage.

At the moment I had a peak experience, I did not step back psychologically and think, *Ah ha, I'm having a peak experience. This will ultimately be good even though I'm upset now.*

I had to learn the implicit value. Later I experienced more minor peak experiences. For example, occasionally when I was directing a play, I found moments where everything fit and I felt exhilarated by the process. That has happened from time to time with writing as well. Or when I'm hanging out with my kids or grandkids. Maslow calls such times plateau-experiences. I look forward to those moments because they tell me I'm doing what I'm supposed to be doing, satisfying my soul.

Resources for Angels, Visions

Charlton, Bruce G. "Peak experiences, creativity and the Colonel
          Flastratus phenomenon." *Abraxis* 1998 Volume 14, 10-19.
Fry, Gill. "Encounters with Angels: Interview with Emma
          Heathcote." netowne.com/angels-christian/angels/
          encounters.htm.
          (not a relative of mine)

Maslow, Abraham. *Religions, Values, and Peak Experiences.* The
  Viking Press, 1970.

---*Future Visions: The Unpublished Papers of Abraham Maslow,*
  edited by Hoffman, Edward. Thousand Oaks, CA: Sage
  Publications, 1996.

Pahnke, Walter N. "The Psychedelic Mystical Experience in the
  Human Encounter with Death," *Psychedelic Review,*
  Number 11, 1971.

Pearce, David. "The Hedonistic Imperative," *Hedweb,* www.hedweb.
  com

Virtue, Doreen. *Messages from Your Angels: What Your Angels Want
  You to Know.* Carlsbad, CA: Hay House, 2002.

Webster, Richard. *Spirit Guides and Angel Guardians: Contact Your
  Invisible Helpers.* St. Paul, MN: Llewellyn Publications, 2001.

angeltherapy.com — Doreen Virtue's site

angels-online.com — stories of angel encounters

angelshop.com/encounters

catholic.org/saintsmonroeinstitute.org

psychedelic-library.org

Chapter Nine

Speaking and Listening

"A box without hinges, key, or a lid,
yet golden treasure inside is hid."

Bilbo Baggins in *The Hobbit*

Glossolalia, Electronic Transmissions, Stigmata, Xenoglossy

This chapter includes a variety of ways to experience psychic communication between beings, in or out of a human body. I've no first-hand knowledge of the first set but have witnessed or researched them. Experiences listed later have been very much a part of my own journey.

Glossolalia

If you attend a religious function and become swept away with emotion, you may experience glossolalia, speaking in tongues. You enter an altered state like self-hypnosis and begin to speak unintelligible words that have the rhythm of speech.

Those who experience glossolalia are often called charismatic. Pentecostal churches have nurtured the practice, but it also occurs in other Christian churches and elsewhere in the world in organizations that are not Christian.

The speech sounds like a foreign language with an underlying structure. Practitioners do it in large groups and believe they are speaking to God or speaking the language of angels. Others in the church often translate the messages for the rest of the congregation. Authority for this practice in the Christian religion comes from First Corinthians, which enumerates the gifts that God gives mankind, one being the gift of speaking in tongues, another the ability to interpret the language.

The Institute for First Amendment Rights reports that linguists have studied the phenomenon but have been unable to find enough corollaries to say that glossolalia is a system of speech that would classify as a language, that is, with words that have agreed-upon meanings cast in grammatical structures.

This is not to say that glossolalia doesn't have significance for those who perform it, those who listen to it, or those who attempt to decipher it. It has a similar effect to music. Generally those who perform it and those who interpret it have the sanction and approval of their peers within a church context.

If you have experienced glossolalia and have concerns about it, read the research and discuss the process with a minister or a psychologist.

Electronic Transmissions

With the advent of telephones and electronic recording devices came a new spirit phenomenon in the twentieth century. Thomas Edison, inventor of the light bulb, the phonograph, and the moving picture camera, tinkered with a telephone for communication with the dead. Although unsuccessful, he predicted that departed spirits would take advantage of electronic media to contact the living.

There have been many instances informally reported about an individual's answering the ring of a telephone then hearing a message from a deceased loved one. The messages often are meant as a good-bye. Sometimes they offer a warning or needed information. There is a rumor that the actress Ida Lupino received a phone call from her deceased father, who told her where to locate needed legal papers to settle his estate. Several websites give D. Scott Rogo as the source in his book *Phone Calls from the Dead*.

This kind of experience is not very surprising and really no different from traditional ghost sightings. If the departed can manifest their images well enough for their loved ones to see them sitting in a chair, why would it be any more difficult to manifest the ringing of a telephone and the sound of a voice?

Some highly controversial attempts have been made to record spirit voices on tape. The first started innocently enough in the 1950s by a Swedish man named Fredrich Jurgenson, who intended to record bird songs at night, so he left a tape recorder running in the woods. On playback he discovered voices discussing bird songs. On later tries he recorded voices that addressed him personally. If you're interested, you can download Jurgenson's book, *Voice Transmissions from the Deceased*, free on the Internet at fargfabriken.se/fjf.

In the 1960s and 1970s a researcher from Latvia named Konstantin Raudive conducted many experiments in which he recorded voices saying phrases, in Latvian, of course. You can read about his work on worlditc.org/h_11_raudive_0.htm.

The British Society for Psychical Research did an investigation of the phenomenon but found no support for the idea of discarnate causes.

No matter how one addresses the subject, there seems to be little doubt that something gets recorded on tape. The question is, what? Assorted explanations include extraterrestrials, Akashic records, spirits of the departed, unconscious recording by the researcher, and electronic interference.

Despite lack of proof, some people find comfort in electronic phenomena. The psychologist Dr. Elizabeth Fiore suggests leaving a tape recording on overnight if you suspect you have a ghost or a haunting spirit.

Sometimes people hear things they aren't supposed to be able to hear on electronic devices. My friend Judith had such an experience. As we sipped margaritas on her patio overlooking Fiesta Bay in San Diego, we talked about strange events.

Judith said, "I heard a radio broadcast while I was driving to work in Maryland in about 1970. The guy on the car radio was talking about info from the Forties. The commercials and all were from that era. It was so creepy but neat. Was broad daylight. Sunny and warm. I'd been noticing car colors and suppose I was open to psychic impressions."

I sat, attentively, not wanting to influence her responses. "How do you explain what happened?"

She crunched a tortilla chip. "I think my story means I was letting myself be open to whatever came through from anywhere. It didn't have to be the radio. I was noticing the color of cars, red and white, just noticing everything. Anyone I questioned about the broadcast denied hearing it, in a sideways glance, corner-of-the-eye way. Like, here-she-goes-again attitude."

"I have a tough time coping with that kind of criticism," I responded.

"Not me." Judith shrugged. "During that time in Maryland, I was living alone, meditating, and generally able to go inside myself. I think that's why I could see and hear things other people didn't always notice. The indifference or skepticism of others never bothered me. I felt sorry for them. I knew I'd added another dimension to my surroundings."

Judith's healthy, life-giving attitude allows her to remain open to new experiences and to accept them as an interesting part of life. I consider her auditory experience the same as retrocognitive sightings such as seeing the soldiers march through the kitchen. They are harmless unless you forget you're driving. Should you have such an experience, investigate the theories and research about auras, remote viewing, clairvoyance, and intuition.

Stigmata

Of all the unsolicited psychic phenomena that happen to people, stigmata is probably the most disturbing. Wounds on the hands, feet, side, or brow of a victim mirror the wounds of Jesus of Nazareth during his crucifixion. These wounds often do not smell like blood but give off perfume. Sometimes there are no abrasions, only blood.

Several movies have portrayed the experience in a horrific way, *The Stigmata* in 1995 and *Stigmata* in 1999. Even though movies tend to involve non-Catholics in the stories, most actual experiences of stigmata have happened to Catholics, many of them in convents or monasteries.

The Catholic Church recognizes sixty-two people, beginning with St. Francis of Assisi, as saints because they displayed stigmata. Church people believe the phenomenon to be a manifestation of piety. Although religious authorities have documented over three hundred cases, episodes appear to be diminishing with only a few reported in the twentieth century.

Psychologists offer autosuggestion as an explanation for the phenomenon, basically that people talk themselves into displaying the symptoms. Individuals can cause bruises or warts to appear or disappear through auto-suggestion, often with the aid of hypnosis.

Of course, another explanation is fraud, and some stigmatics have later confessed to perpetrating hoaxes. Some may unconsciously self-inflict wounds and never become aware of creating them. The Church offers a counter argument that no one has successfully produced the wounds at will. So far my research has shown the Church is correct on this point. The fact that some or all of these negative explanations may be involved doesn't necessarily make the phenomenon false. William James's white crow theory works here. "In an oft-quoted lecture in 1890 Prof James declared: 'To upset the conclusion that all crows are black, there is no need to seek demonstration that no crow is black; it is sufficient to produce one white crow; a single one is sufficient.'"[21] One genuine stigmatic constitutes proof.

As with the truth of scientific studies, it comes down to a question of whose authority to believe. We tend to believe the results of scientific studies because we believe in science, scientists, or the scientific method. Should you experience stigmata, decide who you believe—scientific studies resulting in treatments performed by psychologists or prayer by Catholic priests based on hundreds of years of experience with this phenomenon.

Xenoglossy

Rare but mystifying, xenoglossy means speaking an unlearned language. For example, while hypnotized, an Englishman might begin speaking fluent Italian or ancient Hebrew even though he had never been exposed to the language or learned it in school. Hypnotists have occasionally happened onto those with such a gift while doing past life regressions. An Australian lawyer, Victor Zammit, gives many examples from anecdotal and scientific literature. He concludes:

> There are literally thousands of xenoglossic cases, many
> hundreds of which have been documented. They involve
> modern and ancient languages from all over the world.
> Psychic investigators... used scientific method to illustrate
> xenoglossy and claim that there are only two possible
> explanations—either spirit contact or past life memory.[22]

Experiences are controllable. You don't have to submit to hypnosis or any other altered state where you suspect you might produce xenoglossy. On the other hand, should you want to investigate your ability, you could work with a hypnotist. If you are able to speak another language under hypnosis, I suggest you read the literature available on the phenomenon and on the country of origin of the language.

Resources for Glossolalia, Electronic Transmissions, Stigmata, Xenoglossy

Rogo, D. Scott and Bayless, Raymond. *Phone Calls from the Dead.* Prentice Hall, 1979.
Voice Transmissions from the Deceased, by Fredrich Jurgenson at fargfabriken.se/fjf.
Zammit, Victor. "Xenoglosssy," *A Lawyer Presents the Case for the Afterlife.* Available on line: victorzammit.com/book/chapter22.html.
firstamendmentcenter.org
newadvent.org — Catholic Church
religioustolerance.org — explanations of practices
skepdic.com — arguments against
themystica.com — explanations
worlditc.org — World ITC, the New Technology of Spiritual Contact

Voices

An episode of xenoglossy, fascinating as it might be, is far less disconcerting than a voice inside your head.

Inner voices speak aloud or silently within your mind. In my case, my first questions were: Where did the voice come from? And, Am I crazy?

Where Do the Voices Come From?

According to whom you ask, these are the possible places from which an inner voice or inner voices can originate:

1. Sub-personalities, such as the mother self talking to the teacher self or the adventurer self talking to the home decorator self
2. Non-vocal speech, going over words in one's mind like practicing a speech without verbalizing
3. Inner self, talking to oneself as opposed to thinking, depending on past programming from parents and teachers, relying on internal conclusions one has made about life

4. Conscience, the sense of right and wrong
5. Higher self, that part of the individual connected to the collective unconscious
6. Discarnate entities—deceased relatives, spirit guides, or other people who live in the astral world or some other non-earthly place and maintain a personality structure
7. God, Goddess, Jesus, Buddha, Mohammed, an angel or other Divine source
8. Other humans or organizations

Numbers one through five from the above list represent fairly safe ground because they're self-contained experiences. Numbers six and seven require leaps into areas of belief science can't support, at least not at the present time.

As to Numbers six, seven, and eight some people who commit murders or other crimes say God told them to do so. One of my former students, several years after graduation, murdered a man and gave the defense that God had commanded him. Because he said he heard the destructive voice inside his head, psychologists diagnosed him with schizophrenia. His family was undone by this event.

On the other hand, many people who do wonderful, philanthropic acts also say they are responding to God's direction. This is a dangerous area and requires caution.

Obviously, if voices seem to come from other people or organizations such as the CIA, the advice below is relevant.

Am I Crazy?

The Frequently Asked Questions section at the website for Consciousness Research Laboratory answered the question this way:

> The vast majority of people who complain that others are listening to their thoughts, or believe that others' thoughts are intruding into their minds, are suffering from mental illness. This may not be true all of the time, but it is true often enough to provide a very strong recommendation: If the thoughts of other people are disturbing you, please see a psychologist or psychiatrist. The likelihood that the FBI or the CIA are conducting mind-control experiments on

you is extremely small. And if your doctor or psychiatrist has given you medication, you should take it to see if the voices go away. If they do, then you were probably experiencing a chemical or neurological imbalance, which can be adjusted. If the voices do not go away, even after taking medications prescribed by a doctor, then you *may* be acutely sensitive to psychic impressions and may benefit from long-term meditative practice to quiet your mind. Please note that exceptional levels of natural psychic sensitivity are exceedingly rare, but it is not unknown. If you are disturbed about your experiences, we strongly recommend that you check first with your doctor on these matters. [23]

Unfortunately this quote no longer appears on the website since it has been updated to include other very good information by Dean Radin, the former head of consciousness research at Princeton and now senior researcher at the Institute for Noetic Sciences.

Despite what psychologists think or research agencies recommend, I had to grapple with the voice in my head in my own way and come to terms with it when it told me to go to the Bible study. I've never heard the voice again with that particular clarity, that insistently or loudly. However, I've heard smaller voices, almost like sentences that march across the area over my right ear. That voice came to warn me and keep me out of a repressive religious situation. It had my best interest at heart. The smaller voices have given me useful or interesting information but nothing like the Bible study voice.

At that time my marriage had just ended, and I was emotionally distraught. Some counseling helped me adjust to life after marriage. At the suggestion of the counselor, I began to use affirmations to change my beliefs about myself. Affirmations work because our minds are pliable and open, particularly to our own thoughts. It takes some work, but we can change our beliefs.

Affirmations

An affirmation is a statement of a belief we would like to hold about ourselves. For example, *I am psychic. I am content with my psychic ability. Being psychic is wonderful. I love being psychic.*

Simple but effective, affirmations take us a step closer to becoming what we want to be. They work in any area of life—simple statements that we tell our unconscious mind, either aloud or silently. In other words, we are our own voice in our head.

Affirmations may take other forms besides statements that we repeat to ourselves. They might also be images of ourselves that we consciously choose to hold in our minds, such as imagining ourselves smiling, looking directly into our coworker's eyes, and confidently sharing a precognitive feeling to warn him to check his brakes. It helps to remember another situation that produced a feeling of calm and confidence then imagine carrying that feeling over to the new one.

It's important to phrase affirmations positively. *I am psychic* rather than *I will stop limiting my psychic ability*. Also, the affirmation is in the present, not in the future. For example, *I am confident* rather than *I will be confident*.

All ranges of possibilities are operating within us at this moment; therefore, we can act as if the thing is true and it will become so. We can only control our own behavior through affirmation. We cannot control the behavior of another person by concocting something like *"my boss will treat me nicer."* You could say to yourself *"I am happy and confident at work."*

Once you have framed your affirmations, quietly relax, close your eyes. Repeat the affirmations several times to yourself. Then, invoke the images of the scene you have created to visualize the affirmations as accomplished. Do this for a few minutes every day until you see the changes occurring in your life.

My favorite times to repeat affirmations are while I'm driving or exercising. In both cases, my mind relaxes and feels open to new beliefs. Any time works, of course. Saying affirmations often seems pointless, repetitive, boring, and ineffective, but then one day I'm surprised to find that I actually do believe what I wanted to believe. While I doubted my ability to write, I used simple affirmations, which have become a part of my beliefs about myself: *I am an author. I write well.* The time I blessed affirmations the most was when I fell ill. Such thoughts as *I am healthy and happy, I am well and whole* helped me get well, not alone but in tandem with other practices.

Inspiration with an Attitude

It doesn't matter whether the creative outlet is painting, gardening, or rebuilding engines—the source of inspiration is the same, guidance from beyond everyday mentality.

Writers tend to call the source of their inspiration a muse. In Greek and Roman mythology, the muses are goddesses who inspire creativity in the arts. Maybe because writers create stories, their muses tend to have personalities separate from the writer. They often use their muses as models for characters.

Muses fulfill different roles in people's lives, no matter what their careers or hobbies.

William Butler Yeats considered his muse, the one he met through retrocognition, as an anti-self.

The psychologist Carl Jung had a muse named Philemon and considered his mental conversations with his muse essential to his intellectual life.

Napoleon, the leader of France, had a muse in the form of a dwarf dressed in red who warned of personal danger.

The ancient Greeks thought that everyone had a *daimon*, a spirit guide from birth. These guides gave inner inspiration and also could manifest in the physical world as visions. Socrates had a daimon who cautioned him when he was about to do something foolish.

The Buddhists have a similar concept in *yidam*, an internal spiritual guide. Many Native American religions and other indigenous religions profess belief in the same phenomenon.

Inner companions sometimes advise, sometimes warn of danger. They can serve as conscience or guide. Or get us into trouble if we act on the wrong message. These are such well-known aspects of people's inner lives that we all understand the caricature of the angel and the devil on our shoulders.

Inspiration doesn't have to manifest as a personality such as the daimon or yidam. One author I know speaks of writing from an altered state when she creates original copy, not editing, a task most writers consider less inventive. That altered state isn't out of this world; it's one we all know and have exhibited ever since we were kids.

Suppose you're a teenager engrossed in a good book, not doing homework. Your mother asks you to take out the trash, but you don't hear her. She finally has to shout to get your attention. Then you come out of your trance or wherever you've been mentally and jump, surprised that she's angry with you.

My guess is that you've entered this altered state many times when you were doing something that engaged your creativity.

The medium Doreen Virtue believes her inner messages come from angels. In her workshops, she gives the following advice on discerning which inspiration or message from a higher source to credit. She says that emotional responses like fear or excitement indicate that past programming, the voices of our inner parents and inner critics, is involved. Make sure the advice is a "dispassionate, emotionless response." Then you can trust that it comes from a higher source even if the message is negative.

Trying to see only the positive can get us in trouble. When a voice in our head says no, it's important to weigh the consequences before deciding whether or not to follow the advice.

Resources for Voices

Assagioli, Roberto. *Psychosynthesis: A Collection of Basic Writings.*
        The Synthesis Center, 2000.
deanradin.com – psi research
livescience.com/health/060915_hearing_voices.html
mentalhealth.org.uk/information/mental-health-a-z/hearing-voices
nli.ie/yeats – National Library of Ireland – Yeats Exhibit

Precognition

Whenever we try to capture time, control time, even understand time, we end up sliding off the mark. That of course doesn't keep us from occasionally veering off the forward progression of time in contemplation, meditation, or dreams when we get a glimpse of the future. Our response to these glimpses into the future is our choice. We can ignore the events, fear them, explore them, accept them, or reject them. Knowing we're not alone, that others have similar experiences, is one good palliative to fear and a spur to exploration.

The Gallup Poll on ESP

Extrasensory perception means knowing something without the use of the five senses—smell, touch, sight, hearing, taste. Names given to ESP abilities include telepathy, clairvoyance, precognition, déjà vu, and retrocognition.

Fifty percent of the Poll's respondents said they believed in ESP and another twenty percent answered as uncertain. Americans who believe in the paranormal or are uncertain constitute the majority. However, what they will tell a pollster and what they will admit to a spouse, parent, or close friend are two entirely different things.

If you've had an episode of ESP, you've got a lot of company. Assuming you are willing to talk openly about your experience, you need to remember others may not respond in a supportive way. That doesn't make you wrong. It's important to get past the feeling that others will disapprove. If someone ridicules or disbelieves you, explain the poll results and trust that you have truth behind you.

Use It or Lose It

You can rid yourself of precognitive experiences by repressing them in one way or another. Be sure that's what you want to do. I didn't think about consequences when I began to repress my dreams and later regretted my decision. I was simply responding to my fear and not thinking clearly. Now I know precognition can be helpful either to avert disaster or to prepare one to deal with the unavoidable.

Another way to repress psychic abilities is to analyze them away. When confronted with a precognitive experience, Ted Moore, an engineer, inventor, and writer, analyzed it logically and controlled it through the scientific method with very interesting results. I knew Ted as a fellow writer in a critique group. We had in common the fact that we were Indiana transplants to Arizona. I asked him to write his experience for this book.

Here is Ted's story in his own words:

> My fiancée and I strolled through the Indiana State
> Fair grounds. Summer's humidity had released its grip
> and, with the maples and oaks showing red and yellow,
> sweater weather had arrived. The smell of the cattle pens
> almost overwhelmed me.

My mind drifted to the odd things I'd been increasingly experiencing in recent months—multi-word precognitions without context or background knowledge. They began with short episodes like meeting a girl and asking, "What's your favorite sport?" and knowing only as I spoke the words that she would answer, "Table tennis."

At first it didn't happen more than two to four times a year. As time passed, these events came more and more often and the number of words increased. Still, this forecasting ability seemed normal enough that I felt nothing paranormal.

The first time I thought *whoa* was in a three-way conversation at work. When two coworkers approached me, I knew he would ask, "Do you have the Western Electric samples?" and she would say, "I need you in plating." I would say, "Just a minute." Afterward, I wondered whether I really had foreseen the exchange or just imagined it.

Then another happened at a friend's house party. I approached a trio, which included a young woman I didn't know. I suddenly knew she would look at me and say, "Do you believe in ghosts?" I would reply, "Not really." She would then say, "I've always thought it would be neat to know one." And so it went.

Later I considered altering my response and discussed the idea with my friend Bob. We had taken some statistics and probabilities courses at the university and calculated the odds of my experience happening by random chance. The very high number of possibilities in the English language exceeded our math skills. Such odds must be very large.

Bob and I wondered what my experience might imply about the true nature of reality. In the worst-case scenario, reality is pre-ordained and life is a movie played on a screen with no such thing as free will. Bummer. Or maybe reality is like concrete, liquid and moldable until it sets, but fixed once it does—perhaps the reason why my foresight never preceded the event by more than a few seconds. Bob thought our liquid theory might explain how some people are unusually lucky. They may often see the outcome of a roll of dice or draw of a card just early enough to adjust their bet. Anyone who could see five minutes into the future would be an unstoppable handicapper.

Unable to quantify by equation, we agreed that one thing I could do was experiment. The next time I fore-saw an exchange in which I played a role, I would try to change my words. It shouldn't matter what I said, just anything except what I was *supposed* to say. My speaking different words would prove reality is not completely predestined. Even if it is but remains fluid a few seconds prior to events, my experiment would prove the human mind has the power to crack the concrete and change the foreordained.

My reverie broke when I saw my fiancée's older brother and his wife waiting for us in front of the swine exhibit. Then, it happened again. I knew before he spoke that he would look at his watch and say, "Where and when can we meet if separated?" My fiancée would ask, "How about the floral exhibit?" I would ask, "Then make it four?" Her brother would say, "Done."

My chance had come.

"It's two. Where and when can we meet if separated?"

"How about the floral exhibit?"

I was prepared, yet it seemed to take an immense ef-fort to push my lips together and form words. "Inside or out?"

For a full ten seconds, no one spoke. At last my fiancée said, "Maybe... maybe..."

Her brother made the decision. "Inside at four."

We all walked into the swine exhibit with almost no conversation. My fiancée leaned toward me. "Are you okay?"

"Yeah.." I didn't know if that was true.

I have felt ever since that a point was proven. We live in a free will, not a foreordained, reality. Oddly, however, I occasionally predict a word or two from someone whose habits I know well, but I have never again had foreknowledge of whole conversations. And almost half a century has passed.

Precognitive knowledge has a delicate nature. We can encourage or discourage its presence in our experience. Ted might have used a more scientific approach than some of us, but the impulses to understand and control are common. The fact that he ended, or at least drastically curtailed, his precognitive ability shows that we can consciously direct our experiences.

Psi Research

Researchers use the word *psi*, the twenty-third letter of the Greek alphabet, as a group word to denote a variety of paranormal episodes. Besides precognition, psi can mean telepathy, clairvoyance, psychokinesis, and other unusual episodes. It's an abbreviation for psychic phenomena. Labs also use the common word *anomalous* to denote episodes that don't fit ordinary definitions of experience.

Many organizations are currently doing psi research with an emphasis on precognition. In the United Kingdom alone, there are half a dozen universities which pursue these studies.

Some facts about precognition verified in research and summarized by paranormal researcher Dr. Arthur T. Funkhouser in his essay "Dreams and Déjà vu" are:

1. Most precognition happens in dreams rather than in waking life.
2. The subject matter is usually of the "every day" variety.
3. People who record their dreams tend to find somewhere between four and twelve percent have precognitive elements in them.
4. The playing out of the future scenarios can take several years; however, over half occur within the first twenty-four hours after the dream.
5. Precognitive dreams are of two types, realistic and detailed or metaphorical and symbolic.

6. Precognitive dreams can be induced through intention.
7. Situations fraught with emotion tend to precipitate precognition.[24]

That's quite a lot of information known about a phenomenon the skeptics say doesn't exist.

A popular television show based on precognition, *Medium,* has a main character who honors her gift. She often knows what will happen to a victim based on her precognitive dreams or feelings then acts to prevent the disaster. The show is based on the life of a practicing medium, Allison DuBois, who once worked for the Maricopa County Prosecutor in Arizona. Her husband, her employer, and others in her circle supported her efforts—a perfect situation both for the real life Allison and for the character in the TV show; art imitated life for her. We who experience precognition without a supportive environment can hope that one day life will imitate art for us as well.

Premonitions

The scientific literature and popular writing on foreknowledge seldom differentiate between precognition and premonition. They both mean knowledge of an event before it takes place without the use of the five senses. In common parlance, however, we tend to use the word premonition to denote precognitive knowledge of an unsettling nature, about which we often feel anxiety or dread.

A premonition warned my friend Betty of the death of her mother. During her second pregnancy, she had another premonition, that something had gone wrong with the fetus. The symptoms were very unlike those in her first pregnancy, but she chided herself that probably all pregnancies differed. She tried to talk herself out of worrying but couldn't ignore a recurring nightmare.

Betty dreamed she stood in a barren room that contained only an empty bassinet. She walked around it with horror.

The message became clear when her child was born with severe physical problems and died young.

Some premonitions are so vague they're called intuition or gut feelings. We've all heard stories of people who canceled their ticket or lost it at the last minute then learned the plane had crashed or the train had wrecked. Or, our stomach might roll over when the phone rings. Then, when we answer, we receive bad news.

One reason they are called gut feelings is because they happen in the area of the stomach, in the solar plexus. I sometimes receive warnings that are less dramatic than the rolling-over effect: more like little thoughts arising in the area of my stomach and my heart. These thoughts are so vague as to be easily ignored, as I did with the premonition about the makeup that caused blisters.

I've always struggled with the issue of what is intuition and what is thought. They're probably different sorts of thoughts. The one from the belly seems to have my best interest at heart, but of course I say that in retrospect. The trick is to know that real intuition is kindly and to trust its delicate voice. We encourage it by honoring it. Then it gets stronger.

Animals

Animals have premonitions so often that we take them for granted. Peaches, an overweight, grouchy Chihuahua, goes crazy, barking and running to the garage door at least five minutes before my son's car pulls into the driveway. How does she know he's coming when he's still half a mile away? Does she hear the car? Does it sound different from other cars?

Rupert Sheldrake suggests in *Dogs That Know When Their Owners Are Coming Home* that animals are displaying telepathy when they act like Peaches does. He posits that animals have premonitions about earthquakes and other natural disasters. That's why they become restless or fly away. We are so accustomed to stories about animals who find their way home over many miles that we take that ability to be a part of their nature. Sheldrake would call it their *morphic field* instead. By that he means a mental connection to others of one's species, either a field including all dogs or only one dog and its master.

In January, 2005, just after the tsunami hit Sri Lanka and India, some unusual behavior indicated that the animals had advance knowledge of the disaster, whether through sensitive hearing, vibration, or another unknown sense. Although the human devastation was huge, rescue workers found few dead animals. Some elephants and flamingoes ran for higher ground. A man reported that his dog refused to go for a walk, and some animals in a zoo remained in their shelters. Animals appear to be highly sensitive to the earth and to humans.

A wonderful story about a horse came my way as I wrote this chapter. A former teacher who now owns a ranch wrote:

> I went to a psychic fair a couple of months ago. About thirty people were seated at six tables, and various psychics spent about thirty minutes at each table. The last one at our table was a man named Jamie who communicated with the other side. He was talking to a girl at the other end of the table when he said he had to stop because he had a beautiful horse that wanted to come through. The horse wanted me to know that he was sorry his death was so hard on me. (I actually miss this animal more than any of my relatives.) Then the psychic described how this horse died. He had a blood clot in his iliac artery which caused a hind leg to produce debilitating granular tissue. If you talked to twenty large animal vets, you probably would not find one that had seen that condition. Then the horse told him that he was with me for fifteen years and that he had a great life and we traveled a lot. All of this was factual and, needless to say, I was stunned. I could tell that the psychic knew very little about horses just from his conversation, but I also knew that he could never have come up with any of this information on his own. It was bizarre.

Bizarre, the rancher says, but very comforting to know that animals, too, retain consciousness and can communicate with us both here and from the other side.

Resources for Precognition

Cohen, Sherry Suib. *Looking for the Other Side.* New York: Berkley Books, 1997.

Funkhauser, Arthur. "Dreams and Déjà vu," *Perspectives*, Vol. 6, No. 1.

--- "Three Types of Déjà vu." www.home.cc.umanitoba.ca/~mdlee/dejavu.htm

Guiley, Rosemary Ellen. *Harper's Encyclopedia of Mystical and Paranormal Experiences.* HarperSanFrancisco, 1991.

Hansen, George P. *The Trickster and the Paranormal.* Xlibris, 2001.

Mitchell, Edgar D and White, John, Ed. *Psychic Exploration: A Challenge for Science.* New York: A Perigee Book, 1974.
Ostrander, Sheila and Schroder, Lynn. *Psychic Discoveries Behind the Iron Curtain.* Englewood Cliffs, NJ: Prentice-Hall, Inc., 1970.
Rhine, Louise E. *ESP in Life and Lab: Tracing Hidden Channels.* New York: The Macmillan Company, 1967.
Schmicker, Michael. *Best Evidence: An Investigative Reporter's Three-Year Quest to Uncover the Best Scientific Evidence for ESP, Psychokinesis, Mental Healing, Ghosts and Poltergeists, Dowsing, Mediums, Near Death Experiences, Reincarnation, and Other Impossible Phenomena That Refuse to Disappear.* Second Edition. San Jose: Writer's Club Press, 2002.
Talbot, Michael. *The Holographic Universe.* New York: Harper, 1991.
aspr.com - American Society for Psychical Research - the oldest and most broad -sweeping. Click on Online Research to enter your experiences into the database.
boundaryinstitute.org
dailygalaxy.com/my_weblog/2007/06/cetacea-mind-be.html
ehe.org — Exceptional Human Experiences
espresearch.com
mainportals.com/precog.shtml Central Premonitions Registry a site that tracks premonitions. You can contribute.
paranormal.about.com
parapsi.com
parapsychology.org
pni.org — Pacific Neuropsychiatric Institute
psiarcade.com — Noetic.org ESP tests
psiarcade.com/gaia - the goal is "to correlate collective dreams with world events, including natural and unnatural disasters, to see if collective dreams are predictive" — You can contribute.
psychicscience.org — articles on topics can be downloaded in pdf
rhine.org
spr.ac.uk — British Society for Psychical Research
victorzammit.com — online free book on psychic phenomena

Channeling, Mediums

These terms are interchangeable, the first being of more recent coinage. They involve communications between the spiritual side and the physical side of life. Channeling is a modern term, which means to receive spiritual ideas from a source seemingly outside the self.

Historical Perspectives

References to mediums go back as far as recorded history. Examples include the Oracle at Delphi and many religions which have been founded on channeled material. According to Arthur Hastings in his descriptive research work, *With the Tongues of Men and Angels: A Study of Channeling*, Mohammed channeled the Koran. And he thinks certain books of the Christian Bible appear to have been channeled by the saints.

Channeling the word of God or the angels involved a good deal of risk in certain epochs. With the Inquisition came much repression of revelatory material. Think of Joan of Arc, executed by the Catholic Church for saying she heard the voices of angels. Later the same church that burned her at the stake proclaimed her a saint. Many others were also burned at the stake for their beliefs.

Interest in the occult waned with the rise of democracies and a reliance on logic and reason during the eighteenth century. The mid-nineteenth century brought the popularity of Spiritualists, séances, and the beginnings of modern scientific interest in mediumship. Many scientists tried to debunk mediums by showing they used trickery. Many charlatans gave good cause for suspicion.

In the late nineteenth and early twentieth centuries, scientists began seriously to study mediums. The British Society for Psychical Research investigated several and concluded that they gave good evidence for life after death.

The American psychologist William James investigated Leonora Piper in Boston and ended up believing that mediums could do what they profess to do despite the number of charlatans, primarily because Mrs. Piper's work was so sincere and accurate.

For James, Mrs. Piper was the white crow. She proved the authenticity of mediumship, according to a biography of William James on spr.ac.uk, the website of the Society for Psychical Research in London,

England. He served as one of the early presidents and introduced it to one of its best mediums in Mrs. Piper.

On the other hand, the Australian Richard Hodgson, one of the founders of the Society investigated the famous medium Madame Blavatsky, the founder of the Theosophy movement, and called her a fake. I reference Hodgson's biography on the website of the Australian National University. He debunked other mediums as well but came to believe in Mrs. Piper, just as James had.

An amazing aftermath of these studies was that three of the Society of Psychical Research founders died and began to deliver messages to Mrs. Piper and other mediums in several different countries. The former president, F. W. H. Myers appeared to send messages to several mediums over several years. These communications were called cross correspondences and involved over two thousand references to the Greek classics, material for the most part unknown to the mediums. However, the deceased researchers, who were classical scholars, had plenty of expertise to send the messages. These cross correspondences provide some of the best proof for the survival of human personality.

The Society has published many books on the cross correspondences, as have other researchers since the end of the transmissions around 1930. Their website includes an excellent list of recommended books: survivalafterdeath.org.uk/books.htm

Some Problems Regarding Mediums

Sincere mediums, more than any others involved in psychic activity, bear the brunt of ridicule and character assassination. Be that as it may, there is fraud in this occupation. A charlatan can solicit information through questioning the sitter in subtle ways, using a technique called cold reading. Magicians who supposedly do telepathy often employ cold reading. Through clever questioning, a fraudulent medium can fool a too-trusting sitter.

You have less chance of encountering a charlatan if you consult a medium with membership in a spiritual community. Some mediums are very popular today in TV, radio, and books—John Edward, James Van Praagh, and Sylvia Browne, for example. Reports of their accuracy vary considerably. The public often sees them as frauds or freaks.

From time to time, a medium with a good reputation has found his or her powers fading and has resorted to fraud.

It's impossible to calculate the number of people who hope to contact dead relatives or to talk with someone who can. John Edward has a waiting list backed up for years, and that's just to get into the lottery for his audience with the hope of getting a message. The dead will incarnate again before the living relatives can get tickets!

One of the reasons for the popularity of mediums and channels is that they offer solace, the hope that the dead are not lost forever and that we might be able to communicate with them. Mediums, at least the reputable ones, insist that we all have psychic ability and can make our own contacts with the departed. John Edward makes a big point of this in his shows.

To me, there's no difference—professional mediums are communicating with the beyond in the place of the bereaved. When the bereaved see the ghost of a loved one, aren't they communicating directly with the spirit world?

It's more rewarding to see an apparition or hear the voice of someone who has passed on than to pay a medium to enable communication, but if you don't have any luck communicating with your loved ones yourself, then you might engage the services of a medium. If you do, be sure to check credentials. Generally, the best recommendations of mediums are made personally. Someone who has actually sat with the medium often can tell you whether or not he or she seems reputable. The proof is in the number of correct statements the medium makes as well as in his or her personal integrity.

Windbridge Institute, a new research organization, has recently begun testing mediums for accuracy and certifying them. Their requirements and standards are quoted from their website, windbridge.org:

> Before participating in research at the Windbridge
> Institute, each prospective research medium is screened
> over several months using an intensive 8-step screening
> and training procedure:
> Step 1: Written Questionnaire
> Step 2: Personality/Psychological Tests
> Step 3: Phone Interview (with an existing WCRM)
> Step 4: Phone Interview (with a Windbridge Investigator)

Step 5: Two Blinded Phone Readings
Step 6: Mediumship Research Training
Step 7: Human Research Subjects Training
Step 8: Grief Training

Upon successful completion of the eight steps, the medium becomes a Level 1 Windbridge Certified Research Medium (WCRM-1). The mediums' certification levels increase over time, from Level 1 to Level 5, as they participate in additional research studies.

Each WCRM agrees to donate a minimum of four hours per month to assist in various aspects of the research, to uphold a code of spiritual ethics, to embrace a strong commitment to the values of scientific mediumship research, and to abide by specific Windbridge standards of conduct.

If the Windbridge program is as successful as they have envisioned, theirs will be an outstanding contribution to legitimatizing mediumship in the eyes of the public. You can read about their mediums on their website and probably find a reputable one.

Modern Channels

A famous American medium, Eileen Garrett, founded the Parapsychology Foundation and devoted her life to facilitating the study of her gift. Scientists measured her brain wave patterns during trances. She had four different controls, and the tests revealed five discrete sets of brain wave patterns.

Ira Progoff, the Jungian analyst, interviewed Garrett and each of her spirit guides. Progoff concluded they were not separate entities but "a very deep part of Eileen Garrett connecting with an archetypal energy, and then being personified."[25] Dr. Arthur Hastings reported this finding in his study of channeling done as a research project for the Institute of Noetic Sciences. I interpret his meaning this way: the spirit guide represents the medium's link to the collective unconscious.

Other mediums have been studied, including Edgar Cayce, Arthur Ford, and Jane Roberts, whose control dictated the Seth books. The

Seth books contributed more than any others to my own development and worldview. The discourse is logical, direct, and sweeping, the attitude humanistic and believable. Seth's essays spring from a profound belief in the divinity of all life without religious overtones. That approach speaks to me.

Those with a more religious bent often respond to the *Course in Miracles,* channeled material co-authored by Helen Schucman and William Thetford, both Professors of Medical Psychology at Columbia University's College of Physicians and Surgeons in New York City. The material purports to come from Jesus and addresses psychological and spiritual attitudes toward life. It became popular in the 1970s but many churches still offer study groups on the *Course in Miracles* today.

Looking for White Crows

Gary Schwartz and Linda Russek, research scientists at the University of Arizona, studied after-death communications through five accomplished mediums, George Anderson, John Edward, Anne Gehman, Suzane Northrop, and Laurie Campbell. Their research question: After eliminating fraud, cold reading, and human error, could mediums produce accurate information under laboratory conditions?

In the first study, two Arizona women who had each lost six or more relatives and close friends in the past ten years served as the sitters. They sat on one side of a divider while the mediums sat one at a time on the other and received impressions, names, and other references. The experiment was videotaped and later served as the subject of an HBO documentary.

Statements by the mediums sounded like this example I made up:

> Something's coming through like an older man above
> you, like a father, who tells me he died of lung cancer. He
> has an H name, maybe Harold or Harry. He says to wish
> you a happy birthday in October. He has an older woman
> named Ellen with him.

In the research study, both the sitters and a control group of students evaluated the statements with a rating of +3 to −3 for truth or falsity.

If that reading had been for me, I would have given +3 for a father who died of lung cancer, +1 for an H name (my father's name was Howard, not Harold or Harry), and +3 because my birthday is in October, and −3 because I know no older woman named Ellen in the afterlife. I would have scored the medium at +4.

Say you were a student control, you would answer the questions with ratings as if the reading applied to you. −3 if your father did not die of lung cancer, +3 if his name was Harry, and −3 if your birthday is in May. You would have given the medium a score of −3.

The mediums in the research study achieved high accuracy between seventy-seven and eighty-three percent for statements similar to the example, average scores of +2 or higher. The control group of sixty-eight college students attained thirty-six percent accuracy or a score of about −1.

Another finding of the study showed that the mediums' hearts beat out of rhythm with the sitter's, not in synchrony, as the scientists thought would happen on the assumption that telepathy might be taking place.

With less than one in ten million odds that the results happened by chance, the researchers concluded:

> Highly skilled mediums are able to obtain accurate and replicable information… Since factors of fraud, error and statistical coincidence cannot explain the present findings, other possible mechanisms should be considered in future research. These include telepathy, super psi, and survival of consciousness after death. [26]

This particular study received harsh criticism for weak design, and subsequent studies refined the procedure to less and less contact between the medium and the sitter, such as complete silence on telephone mute rather than mediums and sitters in the same building. These later studies replicated the original findings, probably because the mediums had been honest all along. The details of the various studies appear in Schwartz's book, *The Afterlife Experiments.*

The study helped to establish the credibility of high profile mediums, often described as frauds by the public and by skeptics. Studies in other fields, like those to prove the efficacy of drugs we take, stand with results of one in a thousand. When a scientist gets results like

Schwartz does—one in ten million—it's hypocritical and intellectually dishonest not to accept them as valid.

Despite stringent standards and repeatedly valid results, some critics still attack Schwartz's work. They often refuse to accept any possibility that psi experiments could actually reveal new truth.

Skeptics need to revisit their assertions, which might verge on libel. In evaluating the arguments of skeptics, it's important to remember that they often make their livelihood from debunking.

Either consciously or not, they have a vested interest in finding fault with the studies. I wonder what it would take to convince them.

What's Really Going On?

Often, the messages mediums communicate contain information the sitter already knows. However, sometimes the sitter has to do research, such as discovering from an aunt that a certain great-grandfather, unbeknownst to the sitter, had three wives. Or, as in the most thrilling type of case, when a sitter discovers a lost cache socked away by the deceased, its location revealed through the medium.

If one rules out communications with the dead, one explanation for the medium's good results could be a combination of telepathy, as in reading the mind of the sitter, and clairvoyance, as in remote viewing of sources such as objects or documents. This is known as the Super Psi hypothesis.

However, no studies have ever proven mediums can practice that high a degree of telepathy and clairvoyance. We need more research before we can actually say how mediums know what they know. Clearly, some process is at work that cannot be explained by current knowledge.

Despite the successful research, eighty-five percent of Americans don't believe it's possible to receive psychic messages from the beyond through a living person, so any help a professional medium can give them is limited. Most contacts that people actually recognize as such communication come in the form of visitations from departed loved ones. Those events happen to bereaved individuals with emotional involvement. They need ways to process their own psychic activity, if they find themselves, for instance, hearing the persistent voice of dead Aunt Maude.

It's not easy to deal with the fear of ridicule, concerns about one's sanity, and the rampant self-distrust that often follows. A part of learning to cope is to try to determine where the material comes from and what its value is. Opinions vary on the answers.

Hastings, referenced earlier, the author of *With the Tongues of Men and Angels: A Study of Channeling*, alludes to metaphysical issues as discussed in the Seth material and the *Course in Miracles*, health issues as channeled by Edgar Cayce, literary work channeled through Pearl Curran, paintings through Luiz Gasparetto and mathematical formulas channeled by Srinivasa Ramanujan. Hastings concludes that even though we can't be certain whether channeled material comes from spiritual beings or from the higher self or soul of the channels, "there are many channeled teachings that are worth listening to, that you can learn from, and that are a real contribution to our culture and society." [27]

Some churches frown on the practice of mediumship, maybe with good reason. There are citations in scriptures warning against it. One modern writer, Joe Fisher, found himself caught up with some channeled material that he found to be mischievous, if not malevolent. His book, *The Siren Call of Hungry Ghosts*, tells the story of his failed search for verification of channeled material. He draws the positive conclusion that mediums are in touch with the departed but the negative one that these beings are earthbound spirits who have little to share in the way of spirit growth. Fisher warns:

> Channelers, then, are clearly asking for trouble—both for themselves and for those who are attracted by their "gift" of mediumship. In subjecting themselves body and soul to the whim of undesirable influences, they are also relinquishing their priceless faculties of personal will and self-responsibility. [28]

Fisher's conclusion that all discarnate speakers are earthbound spirits seems an unwarranted generalization; however, I think his cautionary tale should be heeded. Perhaps the truth lies somewhere in between.

Certain channels get fixated on their messages and listen to their own voice too much. Many people adore and revere them although that's probably not appropriate. It's easy to see that dealing with pride and self-centeredness presents a problem for many mediums. Those who regard their abilities as a divine gift maintain humility. They are the ones to seek out.

Inviting channeled material or launching a career as a medium without a reputable teacher could lead to misinterpretations and disappointments. If messages come uninvited, as happened to me, a good medium, a psychic, or other spiritual teacher can help you understand and develop your gift. If you don't want it, there are ways to suppress it. In fact, my fear drove my gift away.

Automatic Writing

Automatic writing can be thought of as a divining tool. You can use the technique to achieve a state of detachment. Words drop onto the page without the writer having any awareness of a thought process to produce them. There is a sense of another mind conceptualizing thoughts. Explanations of whose mind vary. Some say it's the alter ego or subconscious mind of the person doing the automatic writing. Others say it's a being from an alternate reality, perhaps an angel or spirit that has never lived on earth. Often the messages purport to come from deceased relatives, friends, or strangers. Some say beings from outer space speak through the process. The fact is that no one knows for certain; perhaps any of the above could apply.

Automatic writing is simple; all you need is pen and paper. Or, if you prefer, use the computer or a typewriter. One of my spirit guides, Emmons, taught me in my sleep. Later after I began the practice, he said he impressed ideas on me. All I had to do was relax, listen, and write down the words that occurred to my mind. It's important not to criticize the material intellectually until after the automatic writing session ends. The material is nearly inexhaustible. It is ours to decide how much we wish to receive. The Emmons experience happened to me because I allowed it.

To produce automatic writing, the practitioner must maintain a willing and open state of mind, producing alpha waves rather than beta. No doubt, this method of touching in with the spirit world can produce fraudulent material. Or, as often happens, the practitioner may engage in self-delusion. As a result, information received through automatic writing must produce verifiable results.

The British Society for Psychical Research studied automatic writing and concluded that some, but not all, such communications had to originate outside the practitioner. However, the Society also asserts that in some instances automatic writing provides some of the best evidence available for the continuation of intelligent life after death. The website survivalafterdeath.org.uk contains many pertinent writings. The specific link for this article is survivalafterdeath.org.uk/articles/barrett/identity.htm

The practicing medium Bob Olson published his personal experience with automatic writing on his website, bestpsychicmediums.com. Reading his account will be encouraging, should you wish to try this tool.

Channeling is a fairly new term that indicates substantially the same process as automatic writing except that the words are generally spoken rather than written down. Because of this difference, a channel or medium appears to take on the personality of the spirit essence being channeled. Often there are changes in physiognomy and posture that might indicate the presence of a different personality. Research done on mediums, particularly on Eileen Garrett, indicates that major brain wave changes do happen while the other personality is being channeled.

Because of the special nature of this technique, I suggest participating in it only under the tutelage of a practicing medium or other member of a spiritual community. It's better to be safe. In some cases, emotional instability might result or some physical harm.

Dana Corby, a British Traditional Witch/Wiccan for over thirty years, and a Druid for over twenty, related the following negative incident that happened to her personally:

> Personal harm can occur in a mediumistic trance: One night in about 1968 or '69, at the Vedanta Fellowship in Los Angeles, I was serving as the "ground" for a medium who was being beset by a very nasty entity. I was socked in the jaw by some invisible entity hard enough to snap my neck around to the left with a loud pop. It felt exactly like a corporeal fist socking me in the jaw.

Dana now lives on an island in Puget Sound. You can read about her online at the links provided below.

If you find yourself drawn to explore mediumship, I suggest before you continue that you read books by or about some famous mediums who present other personalities, such as Eileen Garrett, Jane Roberts, or the still-living Lee Carroll, who channels Kryon.

Edgar Cayce worked in a somewhat different way. Although he entered trance, no other being or personality presented itself. Cayce said that he could read the Akashic records of people, that is, the book that contained the story of their past lives. Curiously, Cayce, a practicing fundamentalist Christian, struggled with the idea of reincarnation, but his subconscious personality asserted its truth.

By studying the biographies of people who have devoted their lives to mediumship, you will know what to expect and how to avoid the mistakes they made.

Consider seriously before following this path. Mediumship requires commitment, time, and energy. It's not something to enter into on a whim or out of curiosity. If you have the psychic ability that would allow you to become a medium, you may want to put the energy into mediumship or you may want to put that energy into ancillary activities, such as I am doing in writing about the processes. Whatever you decide, Spirit will honor you because we are all free, here and beyond.

Resources for Channeling, Mediums

Berger, Ruth. *They Don't See What I See*. Red Wheel/Weiser, 2002.

DuBois, Allison. *We Are Their Heaven*. New York: Simon & Schuster, 2006

Edward, John. *Developing Your Own Psychic Powers*. Carlsbad, CA: Hay House Audio, 2000.

Hastings, Arthur interviewed by Jeffrey Mishlove. "What Is Channeling?" *Thinking Allowed Series*, 1995.

Hastings, Arthur. *With the Tongues of Men and Angels: A Study of Channeling*. New York: Holt, Rinehart, and Winston, 1991.

Kautz, William H. and Branon, Melanie. *Channeling: The Intuitive Connection*. San Francisco: Harper and Row, 1987.

Lautz, William H. and Brandon, Melanie. *Channeling*, San Francisco: Harper and Row, 1987.

Roberts, Jane. *The Nature of Personal Reality*. Englewood Cliffs, NJ: Prentice-Hall, Inc., 1978.

Schwartz, G. E. R. and others. "Accuracy and Replicability of Anomalous After-Death Communication Across Highly Skilled Mediums." *Journal of the Society for Psychical Research*, Volume 65.1, January, 2001.

---with Simon, William L. *The Afterlife Experiments: Breakthrough Scientific Evidence of Life After Death*. New York: Pocketbooks, 2002.

Wiseman, Richard and O'Keeffe, Ciaran. "A Critic of Schwartz et al.'s After-Death Communication Studies, *Skeptical Inquirer*, November, 2001. csicop.org/si/2001-11/mediums.html.

dailygalaxy.com/my_weblog/2007/06/cetacea-mind-be.html

Corby, Dana. "Harry Potter and the Cuckoo's Egg" witchvox.com/words/words_2003/e_harry01.html

---"In the Big Rock Candy Coven" at newwiccanchurch.net/redgarters/rg_itbrcc.htm

---"The Mohsian Tradition" at witchvox.com/trads/trad_mohsian.html

aspr.com — American Society for Psychical Research

des.emory.edu/mfp/james.html

edgarcayce.com

fst.org — a spiritualism site with some good advice

intuition.org

jeffreymishlove.com

johnedward.net

kryon.org — Lee Carroll's website

parapsychology.org — founded by Eileen Garrett

bestpsychicmediums.com — Bob Olson's story and a list of mediums

spr.ac.uk — British Society for Psychical Research

survivalafterdeath.org.uk/articles/rogo/crosscorrespondences.htm

survivalafterdeath.org.uk/researchers/james.htm

windbridge.org – research and certification for mediums

Chapter Ten

The Presence of Power

"Yesterday upon the stair, I saw a man who wasn't there,
He wasn't there again today. Oh how I wish he'd go away!"

John Hugh Means

Telepathy

Telepathy happens when thoughts, ideas, or pictures from one person occur in another person's mind without the assistance of such methods as speaking, writing, or drawing. Some might see that as one mind speaking into the other mind, much like what psychologists consider schizophrenia, hearing voices in one's head—except that in telepathy the voice in one's head is not manufactured by one's own mind.

Telepathy is one of the most highly researched and verified of all psi phenomena. We've got a long way to go before we understand our inner selves, however, because the Gallup poll showed only thirty-six percent of respondents believe in telepathy, with twenty-six percent uncertain.

Telepathy about phone calls occurs commonly in modern times probably because we depend on the phone to conduct so much of our business and social life. Frequently, people pick up the phone to call someone and find that person on the end of the line because the two dialed at the same time, engaging the line. Telepathic emails are probably already burning up the Internet.

The Wiccan Dana Corby, whom I quoted earlier, gave a humorous example:

I used to have a friend I needed to talk to frequently
but whose phone number was a toll call I couldn't afford.

I began to notice, though, that every darn time I got in the bathtub, he seemed to call me. So I decided to test it out, and for the rest of our acquaintanceship whenever I wanted to talk to him I'd take a bath – and it worked!

Research Proves Telepathy

For over twenty years, psi laboratories have run the Ganzfeld experiment. Researchers place halves of ping pong balls over the eyes of the Receiver. White noise is piped through earphones. The Sender has a set of four images, photo or painting or video, unknown to the Experimenter, who is running the Ganzfeld. The Sender visualizes, thinks, or otherwise tries to send images to the Receiver. The Receiver describes what he is thinking to the Experimenter, who records the words. Then the Experimenter shows the four target pictures to the Sender, who must pick one as the target.

With only chance involved, the Sender would pick the correct target one out of four times. However, over the twenty-year span the Senders have picked the correct target one out of three times. If you believe in the efficacy of the scientific tests as I do, this huge difference, statistically highly significant, shows telepathy works.

I also believe these experiments indicate that all people have some ESP. However, both the scientists and we ordinary folk have a way to go before we develop our full potentials. There's no time like now to start. Here's how you can start.

Do It Yourself

The skins of experimental subjects, when tested with galvanic skin response machines, indicate that the body receives information that never reaches the conscious mind. To bring telepathic communications to the conscious mind, it's necessary to eliminate distractions and enter a relaxed state; otherwise, their whisperings get lost in the unconscious.

In other words, we know and don't even know we know. For example, when someone is staring at us, we turn toward that person. Studies show that, even if subjects are being videotaped while an unknown person stares at the video screen, the subjects turn to see who is staring. You can find a summary of research on sheldrake.org/papers/Staring/JCSpaper1.pdf.

As Director of the Dream Laboratory at Maimonides Hospital in New York, Stanley Krippner researched telepathy in dreams during the 1960s and 1970s. He found direct correlations between the dreams of Subjects and the pictures Senders concentrated on. Sometimes the Subjects' statements were literally the same like describing a dream about "going to Madison Square Garden to buy tickets to a boxing match." On that same night, a psychologist in a distant room had been focusing his attention on a painting of a boxing match. Sometimes the correlations "... were symbolic as when the randomly selected picture was a dead gangster in a coffin and the dream focused on a dead rat in a cigar box."[29]

Perhaps telepathy is a latent ability that our ancestors developed, one we've submerged with the advance of the ego's dominance over our affairs. Maybe it's a use-it-or-lose-it deal. In moments of great emotional stress, we seem able to transmit a strong enough message to break through the ego layer of others, especially when family members far away are in danger.

Many studies support the fact that about fifty percent of people have had some kind of psychic experience. In addition, scientists know that these events tend to happen in the right temporal lobe of the brain. Further, psi may happen when the geomagnetic field of the earth is calm, that is, when sunspot activity and electrical storms hit a low point. This conclusion comes from the Spottiswoode Library. You can read summaries of ongoing research on the subject at jsasoc.com/library.html.

Thus we can assume that we all have the ability to receive telepathic and other psychic communications. We are receiving information all the time, but probably we fail to register it on the conscious mind because of disturbances on the earth and within our own thoughts.

Our lives would change in positive ways if we could bring our telepathic abilities under conscious control. Crime might diminish because victims would have advance warning. Human relationships might become more honest because we could tell when someone lied to us. Whenever we felt lonely we could tap into the minds of others.

Then we'd have new issues, like finding ways to block telepathic communications to protect our privacy. We may have a Star Trek future ahead, living among telepaths.

Resources for Telepathy

Bem, Daryl J. "Ganzfeld Phenomena." In G. Stein (Ed), *Encyclopedia of the Paranormal* (pp. 291-196). Buffalo, NY: Prometheus Books, 1996.

Krippner, Stanley. "Psi Research and the Human Brain's 'Reserve Capacities," *Dynamic Psychology*, Online Magazine, 1996.

aspr.com — American Society for Psychical Research

boundaryinstitute.org

ehe.org Exceptional Human Experiences

espresearch.com

jsasoc.com/library.html

mainportals.com/precog.shtml — Central Premonitions Registry

paranormal.about.com

parapsi.com

parapsychology.org

pni.org — Pacific Neuropsychiatric Institute

psiresearch.org

rhine.org

spr.ac.uk British Society for Psychical Research

sheldrake.org — information and opportunity to participate in experiments

victorzammit.com — online book on psychic phenomena

<u>Spirit Guides</u>

New Age wisdom says we all have one or two spirit guides, who are often family members who died many generations before we were born. They may have more recently crossed over but still have common cause with us. For example, say Aunt Minnie died without getting to fulfill her desire to paint with watercolors. She might become a spirit guide to a niece who had some undeveloped talent in that area.

Perhaps my great-grandmother, Alice Prudence, is my spirit guide. I've always felt a fondness for her even though she died long before my birth. A psychic told me Alice didn't want to reincarnate again but instead wished to oversee her brood on earth. I can understand why she might not want to have a body since she bore nine children in the last one. Becoming a spirit guide might serve her in more than one way. I wish I had a sense of my great-grandmother as a presence in my mind like I had a sense of the two spirit guides named Richard and Emmons of whom I spoke in Part One.

Carl Jung is often quoted as saying, "I shall not commit the fashionable stupidity of regarding everything I cannot explain as a fraud." I now know that what came to me in the Emmons transmissions included some psychic material, some good advice, and some interesting ideas about the nature of reincarnation.

Control Personalities

Many mediums, channels, and oracles say they speak for God, the gods, the angels, or spirit guides and masters from on high, sometimes even from outer space. They often have what they call control personalities to interface between the world of the living and the world beyond.

Maybe controls are mediums in the spiritual dimension and interface with the mediums on this side to create the communication link between the worlds. Mediums develop important relationships with their controls: Rosemary Althea and her American Indian man, Jane Roberts and Seth, Eileen Garrett and four different personalities. Then there's the marvel of Dr. Peebles, who lived a long life as a medical doctor and Spiritualist. He has become the control for many mediums in different countries over the years since his death in 1922.

The concern is the same agony my writer friends suffer while trying to come up with an original plot. There's no such thing. All stories have been told. Some authorities say there are only thirty-eight possible plots. The freshness a writer can bring is his or her particular twist of personality or style.

At some level, that quality is true also of spirit guides. Emmons spoke through me and gave some particular twist on the eternal spiritual truths that could only come from him through me.

Not all experiences with spirit guides turn out to be positive. In fact, many require counseling.

Exorcism, Possession

Devil possession is the only area of the paranormal where belief went down in the Gallup Poll, from forty-nine percent in 1990 to forty-one percent in 2001 with sixteen percent uncertain. Education levels went up as belief went down. The tendency to express religious belief also contributed to belief in the devil.

In *The Unquiet Dead: A Psychologist Treats Spirit Possession*, Dr. Edith Fiore wrote about five patients who appeared to be possessed by deceased spirits. She marks a difference between possession by demons and by the dead and does not handle the former. *Sometimes the former disguise themselves as the latter in order to prey on the living, and it's hard to tell which is which.* All the patients she has helped suffer from seeming possession by the departed, including loved ones, acquaintances, or strangers.

The possessing spirit usually enters after surgery or some physical trauma, which leaves the patient unconscious or with psychological defenses low. Reasons for possession have to do with the possessing spirit, not with the host. The possessing spirit may fear going to the light because of bad deeds done in life. If drug or alcohol abuse is involved, the spirit may not want to give up the substance and will choose a host who is already addicted or one whose energies are low. *Sometimes the possessing spirits are just plain malicious.*

The person possessed tends to take on the attributes, personality, and behaviors of the entering spirit. People who never have abused drugs may begin to do so immediately after possession.

Common symptoms of spirit possession are:

- Low energy level
- Character shifts or mood swings
- Inner voices
- Abuse of drugs (including alcohol)
- Impulsive behavior
- Memory problems
- Poor concentration
- Sudden onset of anxiety or depression
- Sudden onset of physical problems with no obvious cause
- Emotional and/or physical reactions to reading her book[30]

Dr. Fiore doesn't insist that spirit possession exists or try to present any theological arguments for or against. She approaches her patients pragmatically and found that what she calls *depossession* works in practice. Once the possessing spirit is identified, usually through hypnosis, the doctor asks him or her to leave by suggesting that loved ones have arrived to serve as escort to the light. After the depossession exercise, symptoms clear up immediately.

Dr. Fiore's ways to prevent possession include surrounding yourself with white light on a daily basis, abstaining from drugs or alcohol, and praying. She has spoken to other psychologists, many of whom also encountered spirit possession. Evidently, the symptoms are common, and she suggests that many hospitalized schizophrenics probably suffer from possession.

Should you be a counselor, psychologist, or psychiatrist, or have an interest in becoming one, you may want to investigate including exorcism and possession as a part of your repertoire.

Possession by demons is a matter the Catholic Church confronts. Some charismatics do likewise. There are no resources outside that framework that I could recommend.

Resources for Spirit Guides

Altea, Rosemary. *The Eagle and the Rose*. New York: Time Warner, 1995.

Dane, Christopher, *Possession*. New York: Popular Library, 1973.

Fiore, Edith. *The Unquiet Dead: A Psychologist Treats Spirit Possession*. New York: Ballantine Books, 1987.

Fisher, Joe. *The Siren Call of Hungry Ghosts: A Riveting Investigation into Channeling and Spirit Guides*. New York: Paraview Press, 2001.

Knight, J. Z. *A State of Mind, My Story: Ramtha: The Adventure Begins*. New York: Warner Books, 1987.

Roberts, Jane. *The Unknown Reality: Volume One of a Seth Book*. Englewood Cliffs, NJ: Prentice-Hall, Inc., 1977.

--- *The Unknown Reality: Volume Two of a Seth Book*. Englewood Cliffs, NJ: Prentice-Hall, Inc., 1979.

Roman, Sanaya and Packer, Duane. *Opening to Channel: How to Connect with Your Guide*. Tiburon, CA: H. J. Kramer, Inc., 1987.

Ryerson, Kevin. *Spirit Communication: The Soul's Path*. New York: Bantam Books, 1989.

afterlife101.com — a medium's message and free online book

catholic.net
kryon.org
near-death.com
newadvent.net
nsac.org/spiritualism.htm — National Spiritualist Association of
    Churches
sethcenter.com
survivalafterdeath.org.uk
themystica.com — online encyclopedia of the paranormal
todancewithangels.com/contacts.html – Dr. Peebles channels

Magic and Shamanism

Magic means both tricks done by stage magicians and the spiritual craft of creating desired changes through one's will, sometimes with incantations, rituals and tools such as wands. Practitioners of the second definition sometimes use the spelling magik or magick to differentiate themselves from entertainers. The work, often known as the Craft or witchcraft, contains both low and high magic.

Low magic, properly called *thaumaturgy*, is magic for practical purposes including healing, spell work, and shamanism. To perform these functions, witches often use a wand. According to an English witch named Anna Franklin, a wand is a "tool that joins the physical and the spiritual realms and transmits energy from one to the other. It focuses and directs the magical will to make it manifest in the world." [31]

High magic, *theurgy*, is magic for spiritual purposes alone and includes most of the workings of such magical orders as the Golden Dawn and the Theosophical Society.

Practitioners of both kinds of magic often work in a solitary manner or in secret societies and with good reason. In the history of European and Anglo peoples, many worshipped the Goddess and the Horned God, who is a different deity from the Christian devil. Even if they simply channeled messages, as in automatic writing, these practitioners were often convicted of witchcraft and executed by hanging or burning.

Not all accused of witchcraft channeled, of course. Some offered healing potions to the sick or told fortunes. Estimates of the murders of witches are astounding, numbering in the thousands in Great

Britain, Europe, and the American colonies as late as the 1700s, when killing witches was finally outlawed.

Reader, beware. Most of the techniques espoused in this book could have gotten you hanged. Once in a meditation I had a sense of myself hiding while watching someone I loved hanged as a witch. The images weren't clear enough for any conclusions. But if we reincarnate at all, the chances are pretty good that some of us have seen that particular scene reenacted or died in that way ourselves. With no proof whatsoever, I'll just guess that having such an experience in a past life may account for some of our fears surrounding psychic phenomena in general and witchcraft in particular.

I'm not advocating religion. It's not my purpose to set you on the path of Christianity or any other religion. Be aware that treading into magic and the occult mysteries will lead you to people who are sincerely practicing religions. If that is your path, blessings on you. No doubt participation in those religions increases psychic ability, but that's not a reason to join them.

One religious form of witchcraft is called Wicca. Its core beliefs include worship of a Goddess and God as the Divine Mother and Father. Their sacred power flows through the believer, who can learn to use it, along with the power raised, to do magick. Other forms of witchcraft, as most folk magic is termed, may or may not have a religious component.

In the same Gallup poll previously quoted, twenty-six percent of Americans believe in witches, with fifteen percent uncertain. Young people are more likely than older people to believe in them. It seems to me that asking the question in the Gallup poll "Do you believe in witches?" is like asking if you believe in Buddhists or Christians. Of course, there are witches, just as there are Buddhists and Christians. The question should more properly be "Do you believe witches can cast spells, do magic, or heal the sick?"

Much of what we consider magic today comes from the Kabbalah, a religious text of Judaism, which filtered through the lens of Christianity to form the magickal lodge orders of the Renaissance and later.

Earlier religions were often tribal with a shaman as spiritual leader. Many South American countries still have such religious leadership.

> Every society has different strata of practitioners of magical arts … witch doctor, wizard, diviner, wise woman, witch… sorcerer and magician. Magic also may be the province of a priest or religious leader. Some specialize, such as in healing, divining, prophesying, and cursing … Such individuals are likely to possess psychic skills. [32]

Resources for Magic, Shamanism

Castaneda, Carlos. *The Art of Dreaming*. New York: HarperCollins Publishers, 1993.

Conway, D. J. *Advanced Celtic Shamanism*. Freedom, CA: The Crossing Press, 2000.

Crowley, Vivianne. *Phoenix from the Flame*. London: The Aquarian Press, 1994.

Ellis, Pete Berresford. *The Druids*. Grand Rapids, MI: Wm. B. Eerdmans Publishing Co., 1995.

Franklin, Ann. "Midsummer Magic," *New Worlds*, NW022.

Guiley, Rosemary Ellen. *Harper's Encyclopedia of Mystical and Paranormal Experiences*. HarperSanFrancisco, 1991.

Kalweit, Holger. *Dreamtime and Inner Space: The World of the Shaman*. Boston: Shambhala, 1988.

Karlsen, Carol F. *The Devil in the Shape of a Woman*. New York: W. W. Norton & Co., 1987.

Kraig, Donald Michael. "The World of Magick," *New Worlds* NW023.

Ross, Anne. *Pagan Celtic* Britain. Anne Hutchison Radius, 1997.

Summers, Montague. *The History of Witchcraft*. New York: Carol Publishing Group, 1984.

celticcrow.com
huna.com
newwiccanchurch.net
oraclegatherings.com
shamaniccircles.org
shamanism.org
sunnyway.com
witchvox.com

Earth Mysteries

Ley Lines, Power Points, and Crop Circles

Ley lines are places of intersection, power points where humans can most easily discern the earth's energy. For example, Glastonbury in England, Sedona in Arizona, Devil's Tower in Wyoming, Mt. Shasta in Oregon, and Machu Pichu in Peru. Some believe the electromagnetic energy of the earth is greater in these spots, and that their power can be utilized by humans.

> Ley lines, or Leys, are alignments of ancient sites stretching across the landscape. Ancient sites or holy places may be situated in a straight line ranging from one or two to several miles in length. A ley may be identified simply by an aligned placing of marker sites, or it might be visible on the ground for all or part of its length by the remnants of an old straight track.

This definition came from the website of Dr. Christopher L. C. E. Witcombe, witcombe.sbc.edu. A professor in Virginia, Witcombe is actively seeking research projects on the subjects of ley lines and other earth mysteries. His is a website to watch.

Similar to ley lines and power points, crop circles are designs created on the earth, often in wheat or barley but also in other crops or even in grass or snow. The characteristic shape is a circle, arc, or some combination of shapes that appears to have been applied from above. The stalks are bent but not broken in a progressive fashion around the shape.

Sherry and I grew up together in Indiana, but I had lost touch with her over the years. When she began to winter in Arizona, we renewed our friendship. She told me of a trip to England and Ireland. The highlight for her was getting to walk around a crop circle that had been formed the previous day. Sherry said the pattern appeared so intricate and the stalks so finely bent that no human agency could possibly have done the work. She's unwilling to venture an explanation but considers the idea of a hoax ridiculous.

Often one must discern the pattern from the air because the crop circles cover several acres. The patterns are truly astonishing and have to be seen to be believed. A British website, cropcircleconnector.com, displays excellent photos. Crop circles may remain for days, weeks, sometimes longer. There's a cottage industry in taking visitors on buses to see them in England.

Many theories circulate about what causes crop circles, but nobody really knows. Hoaxes have accounted for some but not most. Some people believe they are created by the electromagnetic behavior of the earth, influenced by the ley lines. Others believe UFOs create them.

Whatever their origin may be, crop circles have appeared all over the world. A very high concentration of them occurs near Stonehenge, in Wiltshire, England.

The idea that some sort of consciousness amplifies the energy of power points and heals the earth is possible. Such a consciousness does not have to belong to aliens. It might be a cosmic, natural intelligence that heeds Earth's calls for help. Perhaps we're speaking here of the same natural intelligence in our bodies that heals a cut finger by regenerating skin tissue. When we have an infection within our bodies, our immune system begins producing antibodies. Cut a gouge in a tree and a similar process works as healing cells isolate or minimize the damaged cells in the tree. If a mountain is damaged, for example by strip mining, repair takes longer, maybe generations, however to overlay the rock with new vegetation. Consciousness is present on the earth and in the stars and planets of the cosmos.

Consciousness is unified and self regenerating, according to Dr. Ervin Laszlo, professor of philosophy, systems theory, and futures studies. He founded the international think tank, The Club of Budapest, and has been nominated twice for the Nobel Peace Prize. Laszlo says in *Science and the Reenchantment of the Cosmos*:

> Space and time do not *separate* things. They *connect* things, for information is conserved and conveyed in nature at all scales of magnitude and in all domains… a whole-system universe that builds on the information it has itself generated. The world is more like a living organism than a machine. It evolves from the present toward the future on the basis of its evolution from the past to the present. Its logic is the logic of life itself: evolution toward coherence and wholeness, through interconnection and interaction.[33]

Strange Sightings

Reports of sightings of unusual beings and events are varied and seemingly endless. In some cases, witnesses have been people of good character and normal intelligence. Researchers have tried to give explanations within the bounds of science. That works sometimes and other times not. There is little agreement on whether these sightings are true or false.

In any event, reports of sightings continue. Here's a partial listing:

- Mermaids and mermen
- Fairies, little people, dwarves, wood sprites
- Sea serpents, mountain monsters
- Sky monsters, cloud aliens
- Ape-like beings, reptile-like men
- Space aliens, men in black
- Werewolves, vampires

About all we know for certain is we don't know why people keep seeing things that other people say "aren't there." We just know that they do.

It's not easy to live with the unknown. Anomalous experiences "remind us what a mystery this world is, and what mysteries we ourselves are," says Jerome Clark in *Encyclopedia of Strange and Unexplained Physical Phenomena.* [34]

If you've had a sighting, know you're not crazy and you have a lot of company. Read all you can about the subject. Accept living with the unknown. And, keep your eyes open for another encounter. If you never have another, at least you've lived through one marvelous event.

Unidentified Flying Objects, Alien Abductions

UFO researchers and enthusiasts agree on the classification originally devised by the founder of the Center for UFO Studies, Dr. J. Allen Hynek.

- Close encounters of the first kind—a UFO appears to be within five hundred feet of the witness.

- Close encounters of the second kind—a UFO leaves effects such as burn marks on the ground, broken trees, cuts and scrapes on witnesses.
- Close encounters of the third kind—humanoid occupants visible within or around the UFO.
- Close encounters of the fourth kind—abduction to a UFO with rape-like examination by humanoid aliens, often leaving the victim with memory lapse and post-traumatic stress syndrome.
- Close encounters of the fifth kind—communication between humans and aliens.

After angels and near-death experiences, you might think it's a trip from the lofty to the low to explore alien abduction. Not so, says Dr. Kenneth Ring. In a revealing study called the Omega Project, he compared the people who have had NDEs with those who claim to have been abducted by extraterrestrials, and he has found astounding parallels.

The Gallup Poll indicates thirty-three percent of Americans believe "that extraterrestrial beings have visited Earth at some time in the past," and twenty-seven percent are uncertain. That number represents an increase since 1990. Younger Americans are more likely to believe than are older people, men more than women. Additionally, religious people tend not to believe in alien abduction.

The book *The Omega Project: Near-Death Experiences, UFO Encounters, and Mind at Large* describes Ring's study. His object was to build a psychological profile of the people he called extraordinary experiencers, those who claimed to have had near-death experiences (NDEers) or those who claimed to have been abducted by extraterrestrials (UFOers). He wanted to see what effects these claims had on their personalities, beliefs, and attitudes. Also, he tried to find out the differences between NDEers and UFOers. He used two control groups: one group had not experienced NDEs but had an interest in them, and one had not experienced UFOs but had an interest.

Both types of experiences involve a similar narrative of the experience:

- The NDEer leaves the body, goes through a tunnel, sees a loving light and possibly deceased loved one, angel, guide, or a religious figure, such as Jesus or Mary, who tells the experiencer he or she must return to life.

- The UFOer sees or is pulled to a space ship where there are often lights that fascinate and humanoids who dispassionately perform rape-like experiments, impart knowledge or opinions often about ecology, then return the experiencer to his or her bed or other point of origin.

Of course, there's a good deal of variety in the individual narratives, but they follow similar outlines. Both stories trace the path of a traditional hero as outlined in *A Hero with a Thousand Faces* by Joseph Campbell. The path is called the hero's journey: it includes three basic steps — separation, ordeal, and return. The hero leaves life as he has always known it, goes through some struggles, and returns to tell those he left behind what he has learned. That's the same pattern for most narrative arcs in book, film, or oral history, likewise for the heroes of the NDE and UFO narratives.

The two groups of experiencers go through different ordeals. The NDEer tends to have a positive experience, returning to tell of love and peace, while the UFOer may have either a positive or negative one and returns to tell of ecological or other problems on Earth.

Even though the two experiences have different details, the people who experience them are similar. They are not fantasy-prone, something skeptics often charge. Both groups have experienced alternate realities and are psychically sensitive. They have often been neglected or abused as children. They are often sensitive to electricity. They can feel energy in their bodies.

According to Ring, both experiences seem to happen with electromagnetic stimulation in the temporal lobe of the brain. Some UFOers exhibit physical symptoms like scratches, bruises, and punctures from the probing of the aliens. Even though there are sometimes physical symptoms, the experiences happen in an imaginal realm inhabited by God, angels, deceased loved ones, guides, or alien beings.

Afterward, the experiencers in both groups tend to:

- Appreciate life more
- Have more concern for others
- Be less materialistic

- Be more spiritual but not more religious
- Have high concern for the welfare and ecology of the planet
- Believe their experience is part of an evolutionary unfolding of humanity

One major difference is that UFOers tend to believe there are extra-terrestrials experimenting with humans and that those extra-terrestrials have a concern for the welfare of Earth. NDEers are less inclined to believe in aliens.

Ring asserts that alien abductions and near-death experiences are dreams of Mind at Large, a sort of collective unconscious that can impact our reality. Some experiences are like nightmares but others point to a more idyllic, loving environment.

"Extraordinary experiencers appear to be the gateway to a radical, biologically based transformation of the human personality."[35] They might serve as shamans for the modern age, our visionaries, leading human evolution. Perhaps when we are transformed as a species, we will one day live in the imaginal realm visited first by them.

As you might expect from knowing that psychically sensitive people tend to remember alien abductions, two members of my psychic development group have such memories.

My friend Vijaya, who grew up in France, tells of having climbed the Pyrenees Mountains with three other people and seeing lights—one orange, one blue in the sky above their heads. The lights remained overhead for quite some time then shot off in different directions. Her companions saw the lights as well.

One night she awoke and saw an orange light glowing outside her window. A courageous and adventurous girl, she threw on some clothes, went outside, and walked toward the light where she could distinguish what looked like tripod legs extending down from a spaceship.

"A voice in my head said, 'don't go,'" Vijaya told me. "Don't ask me how I knew. I just knew, if I went toward the glowing orange light, I'd see people who weren't human, and I was afraid of what they would do to me. I ran back home as fast as I could."

Another member of my psychic development group feels as if she'd had an alien companion since childhood. She drew its head, elongated with big eyes, and later saw the similarity with UFO stories. She also remembers when the little guy took her onto a space ship and put her on a table. She felt angry at her loss of control so he put a patch on her neck. She fell asleep and doesn't remember what he did to her. At a later date, the alien took her up and put something in her cervix to keep her from getting pregnant. She has never had children although she's been married for many years.

Overall, her attitude about the experiences is positive except for the anger she felt while on the table. She sensed that the little guy cared for her, and she never felt afraid. Even now she feels calm when talking about the encounters, which seem to have stopped when she hit her forties.

Neither woman can explain what happened with certainty, but both accept the UFO encounter as a part of that imaginal realm they enter from time to time. Despite some fearful moments, most experiences there have been good for my two friends.

However, abductees often suffer from post-traumatic stress syndrome after remembering encounters with aliens. Psychiatrist John Mack tells of treating his patients in *Abduction: Encounters with Aliens,* including detailed accounts of individual experiences.

The abduction experience is unpredictable, often begins in childhood, and causes great stress. However, the patients Mack has treated do not display symptoms of psychiatric illness. If you don't count the tales of the abductions themselves, these people are psychologically normal.

Sometimes abductees have positive feelings about their experience, considering it an honor to be sought out or, more often, a responsibility to inform others of the need to end destruction of the planet. They sympathize with the aliens' message and often feel love for the primary abductor, regarding him as a lifelong friend.

The most stressful part of the experience is the lack of control about going to the ship and/or being forced to lie on the table and undergo rape-like procedures. Mack thinks this loss of control may be designed to make the experiencer believe that humans are not the smartest beings on this planet or the most powerful.

Such feelings of powerlessness contribute to a process called ego death. The ego is the portion of our psyche that negotiates in the world and takes care of us. When the ego cannot perform these functions, we must rely on another aspect of our psyche, perhaps a deeper layer, that is, soul or spirit.

When we are operating from a place in ourselves that is closer to spirit, we have transcended ego. Ultimately, a new worldview must emerge to accommodate the experience of transcendence. Many abductees emerge from psychological treatment having attained that transcendence.

Mack says: "Abductions profoundly affect the lives of those who experience them. These effects are traumatic and disturbing, but they can also be transforming, leading to significant personal change and spiritual growth." [36]

The above observation mirrors those of Ring when he compares NDEs to alien abductions. Ring's six-part breakdown for growth includes: appreciating life, more concern for others, less materialistic, more spiritual, concern for ecology, and belief in evolution of humans.

It's difficult to conceive of alien abductions as being actual events. Even the people who have the experiences often deny them later out of fear or concerns for their sanity.

Even without a definitive understanding, we can as a society gain value from the message—for the abductions seem to involve the conveying of a message to us. Mack says: "Virtually every abductee receives information about the destruction of the earth's ecosystem and feels compelled to do something about it."[37]

Aliens seem not to accept our aggressiveness toward our planet, and appear to intend to prevent us from harming our home. That aliens who do the abductions are said by the abductees to worry about our ecology is rather touching. Whether they are real beings from another planet, beings from the imaginal realm, or dreams of our group consciousness, they are drawing our attention to problems that confront us—global warming, the ozone layer, deforestation.

The Dalai Lama and many thinkers believe that the destruction of our ecosystem has an impact both in our universe and in the spiritual realm. Ring, says of alien abduction, something that could be said as well of crop circles and many other strange sightings:

Mind at Large has given humanity a cosmic koan to
dwell upon, for we are all disciples in the mystery school
that life itself represents ... the fate of the earth and our
future evolution as a species depend on our unflinching
and dedicated determination to open ourselves up to
their healing energies.[38]

In what reality do alien abductions take place? Is it a merging of
dimensions? A bridge between the physical and the spiritual? There
are no answers to these questions at the moment. The best we can all
do, whether experiencer or not, is to admit we don't know what's going on, treat the abductees with respect, and remain open to greater
understanding in the future.

Resources for Earth Mysteries

Alien Encounters: Mysteries of the Unknown. Alexandria, VA: Time-
　　Life Books, 1992.
Campbell, Joseph. *The Hero with a Thousand Faces* , 3rd Ed. Novato,
　　California:New World Library, 2008.
Clark, Jerome. *Encyclopedia of Strange and Unexplained Physical
　　Phenomena.* Detroit: Gale Research, Inc., 1993.
Hamilton, William F. III. *Alien Magic: UFO Crashes, Abductions,
　　Underground Bases.* New Brunswick, NJ: Global
　　Communications, 1996.
Kitel, Lynne D. *The Phoenix Lights.* Charlottesville, VA: Hampton
　　Roads, 2004.
Korff, Kal K. *The Roswell UFO Crash: What They Don't Want You to
　　Know.* New York: Prometheus Books, 1997.
Laszlo, Ervin. *Science and the Reenchantment of the Cosmos.*
　　Rochester, Vermont: Inner Traditions, 2006.
Mack. John E. *Abduction: Encounters with Aliens.* New York:
　　Scribner's Sons, 1994.
Ring, Kenneth. *The Omega Project: Near-Death Experiences, UFO
　　Encounters, and Mind at Large.* New York: William Morrow
　　and Co., 1992.
ancient-wisdom.co.uk
cropcircleconnector.com
cropcircleresearch.com

cufos.org — Center for UFO Studies
mysteriousplaces.com
nuforc.org — National UFO Reporting Center
ufoevidence.org
seti.org — SETI Institute's mission is to search for extra-terrestrial
        life and further understanding of our place in the universe.
        You can participate.
witcombe.sbc.edu/earthmysteries/EMIntro.html

Chapter Eleven

Exploring the Knowledge

"To die is different from what any one supposed, and luckier."

Walt Whitman

Past Life Memories

A memory of a past lifetime doesn't usually come to a person all in one download with name, time and place of birth, parents' names, and important events noted. Alan Jay Lerner and Burton Lane named their Broadway show about reincarnation *On a Clear Day You Can See Forever*. Such clear seeing of a past incarnation is probably romantic fantasy. Instead, memory creeps up, sometimes in subtle ways.

Perhaps you've met a person at one time or another and taken an instant, unaccountable dislike. Try as you will to overcome your distaste, it continues. Or, you might find yourself unusually drawn to a person you meet. Perhaps that person is not your ideal mate in appearance and characteristics, but you fall in love anyway. In both of these instances, you might recognize a person from a former lifetime you shared. What you do with this instant recognition is, of course, up to you.

As travelers we sometimes have a similar experience. We take an interest in a certain country, say Spain, and read a great deal about it. Yet we arrive unprepared for the poignant familiarity Spain evokes, as if we've always known it. The reverse happens too. We can abhor a country and not be able to get to the airport fast enough. Even though we don't have a conscious memory of, say, being tortured during the Inquisition, we won't enjoy visiting Spain one bit.

Dreams can be a source of past life memories. A particularly vivid dream of yourself dressed in the garb of another time can give you a hint.

A gentleman I know couldn't understand his fascination with a certain good-looking woman who kept refusing to date him. He asked his dreaming self to show him the connection. He then dreamed of driving a Conestoga wagon in the Old West. As an itinerant worker, he went from farm to farm, entertaining the lonely frontier ladies. And who was the good-looking woman? None other than the wife he'd left behind. He then understood the lady's reluctance and patiently awaited her timing. Now they are happily married, and he's faithful.

A dream scenario that keeps repeating over a series of weeks, months, or even years can be a tip off about a past life memory trying to work its way to consciousness.

In *The Search for Grace*, Bruce Goldberg tells of a patient who came for therapy because of a recurring dream of being choked to death. Regression to her former lives helped her understand the circumstances behind the nightmares and eventually end them. The patient remembered many details of a lifetime when she was murdered in 1927. Goldberg hired a researcher who found documentation in newspapers and other public records. This excellent case of reincarnation became a CBS documentary.

Past life memories can spontaneously arise as a result of activities with unrelated goals. For example, suppose you have trouble dealing with stress at work and you try to establish a practice of meditating every evening as soon as you return home. Once you relax and empty your mind, you might find random thoughts arising. Or see random pictures of yourself in another body or in another house or in another century. Just let the material come in any way it presents itself. Later, you can begin to piece together bits of information in the same way you analyze dreams.

The most profound past life recall happens during past life regressions where a hypnotist or hypnotherapist, a counselor who uses hypnosis as a tool, directs the retrieval of information.

Popular Culture from the Past

Our heritage from thinkers and authors in previous centuries includes ideas about reincarnation. Many believed in it; others wondered about it. The German philosopher Johann Wolfgang von Goethe said: "I am certain that I have been here as I am now a thousand times before, and

I hope to return a thousand times."

The Transcendental movement in New England during the nineteenth century had a great impact on American thought and democracy. The major tenets were:

- Each individual can know the divine through individual action.
- Intuition provides the way of learning truth.
- Nature and spirit are one.

Although reincarnation was not a stated tenet, many of the Transcendentalists accepted it through their own inner knowing of divine truth. Their influence remains a part of New Age religions to the present day. "New" is a misnomer for such traditional American theology.

The leader of the Transcendentalist movement, Ralph Waldo Emerson, said somewhat humorously: "Nothing is dead: men feign themselves dead, and endure mock funerals and mournful obituaries, and there they stand looking out of the window, sound and well, in some new and strange disguise."

Transcendentalists included Henry David Thoreau, Nathaniel Hawthorne, John Greenleaf Whittier, Henry Wadsworth Longfellow, and Bronson Alcott. Later in the century Mark Twain, Walt Whitman, Emily Dickson, and the abolitionists Frederick Douglas and Harriet Beecher Stowe carried on the tradition in literature and politics.

Alcott's daughter, Louisa M. Alcott, the author of *Little Women* and *Little Men*, summed up the belief:

Immortality is the passing of a soul through many lives or experiences: and such as are truly lived, used, and learned, help on to the next, each growing richer, happier and higher, carrying with it only the real memories of what has gone before.

At the turn of the twentieth century, the popular novelist Jack London said:

I did not begin when I was born, nor when I was conceived. I have been growing, developing, through incalculable myriads of millenniums. All my previous selves have their voices, echoes, promptings in me. Oh, incalculable times again shall I be born.

In the Present

The trend has continued today. Twenty-five percent of Americans profess a belief in reincarnation, with twenty percent uncertain.

Doubtless many more wonder about it. Otherwise, there wouldn't be so many books and films on the market about the subject. Carol Bowman writes stories about children who profess to remember former lives. Many hypnotists write about their subjects, from Morey Bernstein's *Bridey Murphy* in the 1950s to Bruce Goldberg, Brian Weiss, Jess Stearn, and many others today. Two other popular writers address the subject from a personal level, Richard Bach and Shirley MacLaine. I've barely tapped the surface of reincarnation literature and refer you to your local bookstore.

How Reincarnation Works

Reincarnation has a simple mode of operating: After one dies, one's spirit returns to earth in another body. Understanding the ramifications of that rule becomes complex indeed. All sorts of questions arise. What is death? How does the past life affect the present? Why can't most people remember past lives? What part of us reincarnates? What is the soul? How does evolution figure in? What is the purpose of life? Why are we here in this particular body in this particular time? If we survive death, what determines where we go or what becomes of us?

Religions in the Past

Many of the world's religions, whether in the present or the past, involve a belief in reincarnation.

- The iconography of the Celts included an image of people lining up for rebirth as a decorative motif on swords, cauldrons, and jewelry. They believed in it so strongly that repayment of debts could be arranged for the next life.
- The pre-Christian Greeks had many proponents, including Pythagoras, Plato, and Socrates, who said "I am confident that there truly is such a thing as living again, that the living spring from the dead, and that the souls of the dead are in existence."

Current Religions

- Islam remains divided on the issue. A passage in the Koran reads: "God generates beings, and sends them back over and over again till they return to him." COW 2:28 Although all sects of Islam do not embrace reincarnation, the mystical branch, Sufism, includes it as a part of their belief in the transmigration of souls. The Sufi poet Jalalu'ddin Rumi wrote: "I died as a mineral and became a plant, I died as a plant and rose to animal, I died as animal and I was man. Why should I fear? When was I less by dying?"

- Hinduism contains a belief that we, as conscious souls, are aware of ourselves. We incarnate in order to come into full self-realization. The way we live one life sets up the next for good or ill. Whatever the shape of the mind when the body dies, the soul carries that state into the next incarnation. If we ignore the process of self-realization, we may be born as, say, a dog or insect, the doctrine again of transmigration of souls. Our goal is to become completely self-realized and leave the cycle of birth and death. In the *Bhagavad-Gita* II:22, one of the Hindu holy books, the prophet Krishna tells his pupil: "As a man casts off worn out clothes and takes on other new ones in their place, So does the embodied soul cast off his worn out bodies and enters others new." In *Bhagavad-Gita* IV:5, Krishna says: "Many a birth have I passed through, And (many a birth) hast thou. I know them all, Thou knowest not."

- Buddhism includes many ideas about the best way to live one's present life. Its ideas on reincarnation are similar to those in Hinduism except that returning as an animal has been eliminated. The founder, Buddha, is often quoted as explaining this way: "What we are today comes from our thoughts of yesterday, and our present thoughts build our life of tomorrow. Our life is the creation of our mind." Karma is a dynamic force in the religion: the thoughts and acts of one life determine the next. Therefore, it behooves us to do as well as possible in this lifetime to create a better life next time.

- Theosophy teaches reincarnation largely according to the Buddhist model.

- Wicca contains belief in reincarnation along with other beliefs from the pre-Christian religions of Europe. However, the Wiccan view does not necessarily include the idea of progression or spiritual evolution, focusing instead on the idea of being reborn within the fold of Wicca and with loved ones.

- Christianity does not formally include reincarnation in its teachings although its New Age branches such as Unity and Religious Science sometimes accept it. The Catholic Church and many Protestant denominations oppose reincarnation. Some scholars argue that the early church originally embraced the doctrine but excised it in the year 553; however, the Catholic Church today denies the claim. In any case, Jesus made many statements recorded in the Bible and often interpreted to assert that He accepted reincarnation. He told the disciples that John the Baptist was Elijah reborn. According to the *New American Standard Bible*, Jesus said in John 3:3: "Unless one is born again, he cannot see the kingdom of God." Also, Jesus healed a man who had been blind from birth. Afterward, someone asked who sinned, the blind man or his parents? The blind man could not have sinned had he not lived before. The Bible offers other examples, which indicate that reincarnation was an accepted part of the religious framework during the lifetime of Jesus. Many Christian denominations interpret these references to reincarnation metaphorically as a spiritual rebirth only.

- Judaism. The Torah does not specifically mention reincarnation although some of the other holy books do. As a result, some Jews believe in it and some don't. Tradition says that all Jews were present at Mt. Sinai when Moses made the pact with God. If so, they might have reincarnated down through history in order to be surviving today. In addition, many young Jews today carry past life memories from the Holocaust of World War II. I have spoken with two who described their memories. Rabbi Yonassan has written a book on the subject, *Beyond the Ashes: Cases of Reincarnation from the Holocaust.*

Research

Investigating past life memories primarily involves attempts to verify details that people recall of their former lives. Jenny Corkell, an English woman, remembered a recent life in Ireland when she had died leaving several children. Jenny searched in both church and public records until she found her family. Some of the children accept her as their lost mother, although she is many years their junior now. She details the experience in *Across Time and Death: A Mother's Search for her Past Life Children*. I saw her and several of her children interviewed on a TV talk show. The love Jenny felt for her children and theirs for her showed through. Love provoked her search and sustains them throughout time and change from one body to another and through the aging process.

A group of people in California pieced together a lifetime they shared in a pre-Civil War Virginia town. The hypnotherapist Marge Rieder regressed them and subsequently traveled to Virginia with several group members. They found verification of their memories in places and public records. Rieder's book *Mission to Millboro* describes the episode.

This kind of research makes sense because, if reincarnation happens at all, it's likely we return with others, maybe not a whole town together as a rule but certainly in close relationships with family and friends. Such research can provide new insights into family dynamics as well as patterns in history and human development.

Dr. Ian Stevenson has done incredibly persuasive work on reincarnation, written in a scholarly style. His most famous work entitled *Twenty Cases Suggestive of Reincarnation* details many of the cases he has investigated. Over a lifetime, there were thousands of cases of children who claimed to remember former lives. Much of his work in later years centered on those that also included a birthmark or birth defect.

An example comes from his book, *Where Reincarnation and Biology Intersect*. A boy was born in British Columbia with two small birthmarks, one on his left palm and one on his left wrist. When he began to talk he said that his gun discharged and hit him in those two spots. Actually, one of the boy's relatives had died three years before of such an accident, not from the bullet wounds themselves but from gangrene that developed in them. Stevenson verified the relative's medical records.

Chester A. Carlson, the man who invented the process we call Xerox, endowed Stevenson's chair at the University of Virginia to fund research on reincarnation. Here's an example of philanthropy by an inventor who strove to understand his creative gift and sustained the work of the world's most influential research on reincarnation described above. Both men have passed on, but they left a great legacy for us.

Channeled Information

Several popular channels or mediums include reincarnation in their subject matter—Jane Roberts, *The Course in Miracles*, and Patience Worth, among others. That's probably why reincarnation is so much a part of the New Age movement.

The concept of reincarnation might be too much for some people to swallow. After all, we live in a society predominantly opposed to it. The two greatest influences on western culture are Judaism and Christianity, both of which formally deny reincarnation as a tenet of belief. However according to both opinion polls cited previously, about twenty-five percent of Americans believe in the idea, making it a minority belief.

In that case, what can you do with your own memories that seem to relate to a former life?

- Don't think you're crazy. Many people have such memories.
- Respect the workings of your inner self. It has much to teach you.
- Think of the memories as a metaphor for your life today.
- Look for fresh insights the past life story can bring to your present life.
- Believe the messages from your subconscious mind.

I keep a sign on my desk. It's been there for many years lest I ever forget. In the words of Emerson, one of my favorite writers, "Nothing is at last sacred but the integrity of your own mind." That focus on integrity can help us honor past life memories whether they are culturally supported or not.

Resources for Past Life Memories

Bernstein, Morey. *The Search for Bridey Murphy*. Garden City, New
    York: Doubleday & Co., Inc., 1956.
Bhaktivedanta, A. C. Swami Prabhupada. *Coming Back: The Science
    of Reincarnation*. Los Angeles: The Bhaktivedanta Book
    Trust, 1982.
Bowman, Carol. *Children's Past Lives: How Past Life Memories Affect
    Your Child*. New York: Bantam Books, 1998.
Cheetham, J. H. and Piper, John. *A Shell Guide to Wiltshire*. London,
    Faber & Faber, 1968.
Cockell, Jenny. *Across Time and Death: A Mother's Search for her
    Past Life Children*. Fireside, 1994.
Cole, G. D. H. and Postgate, Raymond. *The British Common People:
    1746-1946*. London: Methuen, 1961.
Falkus, Malcolm and Gillingham, John, Editors. *Historical Atlas of
    Britain*. New York: Continuum, 1981.
Fisher, Joe. *The Case for Reincarnation*. New York: Bantam, 1985.
Greshom, Yonassan. *Beyond the Ashes: Cases of Reincarnation from
    the Holocaust*. Virginia Beach, VA: A. R. E. Press, 1992.
Goldberg, Bruce. *The Search for Grace*. St. Paul, MN: Llewellyn
    Publications, 1997.
Head, Joseph and Cranston, S. L. Ed. *Reincarnation: An East-West
    Anthology*. Wheaton, IL: The Theosophical Society, 1962.
Higham, Charles. *Charles Laughton: An Intimate Biography*. New
    York: Doubleday & Co., 1976.
McTaggart, Lynne. *The Intention Experiment*. New York: Simon &
    Schuster, 2007.
Newton, Michael. *Destiny of Souls: New Case Studies of Life Between
    Lives..* St. Paul, MN: Llewellyn Publications, 2000.
--*Journey of Souls: Case Studies of Life Between Lives Between Lives*.
    St. Paul, MN: Llewellyn Publications, 1994.
Noetic Sciences Review, 1986 to Present, Institute of Noetic Sciences,
    101 San Antonio Road, Petaluma, CA 94952
Rieder, Marge. *Mission to Millboro*. Grass Valley, CA: Blue Dolphin
    Publishing, Inc., 1993.
Sherk, Warren. *Agnes Moorehead A Very Private Person*. Philadelphia:
    Dorrance & Company, 1976.

Shroder, Tom. *Old Souls: The Scientific Evidence for Past Lives*. New York: Simon & Schuster, 1999.

Stearn, Jess. *The Search for a Soul: Taylor Caldwell's Psychic Lives*. New York: Doubleday, 1973.

Steiner, Rudolf. *Reincarnation and Karma: Two Fundamental Truths of Human Existence*. USA: Anthroposophic Press, 1992.

Stevenson, Ian. *Children Who Remember Former Lives: A Question of Reincarnation*. Revised Edition. MacFarland and Company, 2000.

---*Twenty Cases Suggestive of Reincarnation*. New York: American Society for Psychical Research, 1966.

---*Where Reincarnation and Biology Intersect*. Westport, Connecticut, Praeger, 1997.

Whitton, Joel L. and Fisher, Joe. *Life Between Life*. New York: Time Warner, 1986.

blavatsky.net

crystalinks.com/reincarnation.html

Healthsystem.virginia.edu/internet/personalitystudies — Ian Stevenson's site

themystica.com

krishna.com

livescience.com/strangenews/060121_paranormal_poll.html - belief poll

livescience.com/strangenews/070406_past_lives.html - memory errors

whatismetaphysics.com/reincarnation.html

Many of the authors have websites with articles and other interesting content.

Intuition, Impulses, Synchronicities
===

Random House Webster's Dictionary defines an impulse as "a sudden, involuntary prompting to action" and intuition as "direct perception of truth ... independent of any reasoning process."

Roget's Thesaurus further illuminates the comparison, listing as synonyms of impulse "urge, drive, instinct, itch, spur, goad." And for intuition it lists "sense, sixth sense, hunch, insight." The words "feeling and instinct" are used as synonyms for both processes.

Intuition and impulse appear to be much the same except for the underlying intent to take action, implicit in the word impulse. You can't act on an impulse without having a provoking intuition. However, you can have an intuition that you should do nothing. That's often a viable alternative.

Or, it's possible to have an intuition and deny it. Later, you might be sorry.

For several years, my family and I have gone to the same hairdresser, Joan. As she combed my hair in preparation for cutting it one afternoon, she asked about my current writing project. I told her about the idea for this book and asked her if she'd ever had an intuition.

Joan frowned. "Every time I decide not to follow my intuition, I regret it."

"Really? I'm always looking for good material. Can you give me an example?"

"Oh, yeah." Joan slapped the comb along her jeans-clad thigh. "One time I went to see a psychic. The first thing she told me was that I'd be going on a short trip to Laughlin or Las Vegas within a month. She really had my attention because I already had the trip planned."

"What else did she tell you?

"The psychic described three diamond machines sitting in a row and said, if I played them, I would win a lot of money with very little investment. At the end of the session she told me to always follow my intuition." Joan paused and gazed at me in the mirror, her dark eyes hooded.

I couldn't stand the suspense. "Well, did you win?"

"I looked for the diamond machines and found several in a row. The stools were empty at two of them. I asked myself which one to sit down at. This one on the left. That was my gut response. Then, I thought better of it and decided to sit at the one on the right." Joan sighed. "I fed a lot of money into that machine. A lady sat down at the other, put in two quarters, and won over $10,000."

"Oh, no."

Joan brandished the scissors above her head. "If I'd followed my intuition, that money would have been mine."

"Always go with the first impulse."

Joan nodded with a forlorn look.

Intuition can involve such a minor occurrence as deciding to sit at one slot machine instead of another or turning on one street contrary to customary practice, as I did when I avoided a car accident. On the other hand, intuition can precipitate a major event that changes the lives of many people, results in a personal fortune, or builds a professional reputation.

Albert Einstein credited intuition with his development of the theory of relativity. That doesn't mean to say that just anyone could have come up with the theory. A great amount of knowledge and thought preceded the final intuition.

Much the same thing happened with Elias Howe in nineteenth-century America. Many inventors in Germany, England, and France had taken out patents on sewing machines, but none worked well enough for the inventors to secure financial backing.

Howe's work on his invention stagnated until he had a dream of being boiled for dinner by cannibals. Every time he tried to climb out of the pot, a cannibal would force him back with a spear.

On awakening Howe realized all of the spears had holes in the tips, the idea he put to successful use to give us the sewing machine we all know today. He got a U. S. patent and died wealthy, but not at the hands of cannibals.

As a direct result of listening to his intuition, a man named Lynn L. Charlson invented the hydraulic power steering unit in cars. Since most cars have such a unit today, he made a great deal of money. Charlson decided the world should know more about such little-understood processes, so he funded research studies on intuition.

Developing Intuition

It's difficult for me to tell when a message is coming from my intuition, from intellectual thought, or from emotions provoked by past programming. What I've learned from others can disguise itself as intuition. For example, when I sort laundry, I get a twinge every time I fold washcloths inside out. That's not intuition. It's my mother's voice in my head, admonishing me to fold them correctly. Much of the basis for our actions consists of such programming from our parents, teachers, or our own conclusions about how we should act. There's plenty of static to drown the tiny voice of intuition.

A practicing psychic, Echo Bodine, gives good advice for distinguishing programming from intuition:

> Ask yourself if there's an emotion attached to it. When the inner voice speaks, no matter what it has to tell us, it's always calm and without emotion. Even when a message appears to be negative... you'll sense the calmness in the voice and know that your intuition is speaking. [39]

A part of our response to intuition has to do with the assumptions we make about it. Do we assume it's an ability reserved for psychics or mediums? Often it has been denigrated as *only* women's intuition. Or relegated to behavior like dogs that find their way home as *only* animal instinct. It's my belief that everyone has intuition. There's nothing esoteric about it. Not only do we all have intuition, but we can all nurture it.

An obstacle to developing intuition is that the messages are so faint. They can get lost in a sea of processes going on in our bodies and minds.

Just think about the multitude of images our eyes have to sort, discern, and react to. The number of noises our ears hear at all times, from the air conditioner's hum to the cat's meowing to get out.

Add to that smells and sensations. Although we may not think consciously about how tight our belt is, our waist is aware of the constriction. What's more there's a babbler that rattles on in our heads with random emotions like residual anger toward a cranky store clerk or idle thoughts like what time *Survivor* will come on after Daylight Savings Times goes into effect.

With all of this competition, it's a wonder any hunches make it through. We can increase our chances of bringing intuition into conscious awareness by paying attention to it. Meditation and contemplation help us focus and strain out competing messages. The simple technique of sitting in a chair, closing your eyes, and directing your attention to your solar plexus will help your hunches come into your conscious awareness. The solar plexus is the area from which people often receive intuitive knowledge. In fact we've built that location into our language with phrases like "I feel it in my gut" or "it's a gut-level feeling." The quieting and attention help; but, even more so, the statement to your subconscious that you're ready to pay attention validates the process.

A little impromptu survey of ten of my friends revealed that only two think intuitions come from their heads. Another eight say they have a feeling in their solar plexus, ergo, a gut feeling or gut reaction. The big news? All ten of my friends acknowledge having had a hunch at one time or another.

Kathlyn Rhea, a psychic who works with police on missing persons cases in Washington, D. C., must rely on her intuition for her livelihood. When Jeffrey Mishlove interviewed her on the TV show *Thinking Allowed,* she said: "My biggest goal is to make people realize they're all intuitive. It is not a separate thing. It is part of every human being, and they can use it as a very practical tool."[40]

If you faithfully pay attention to your hunches and act in accordance with them, one day they'll become like second nature. You won't have to meditate, contemplate, or focus. Your intuition will know it's an equal player in your life, and you'll be able to access it whenever and wherever you want to.

I honor my intuition. I honor my intuition. I honor my intuition. After the episode of avoiding a car wreck, I repeated that affirmation as the weeks went by until I thought I believed it. Sometimes I get tripped up by the resurfacing of old thinking patterns. There's not much else to do except start over on the affirmations.

Signs

There's a circular quality to the subjects of synchronicity, impulses, and intuition. Many use synchronicities as ways to validate their impulses, proof that their intuition is working. Meg Lundstrom says of such people: "They follow an inner urge or message and watch for the results: if a meaningful coincidence results, it is a sign to them that they are on the right track and that they can trust that voice in the future."[41]

You can use synchronicities to validate your intuition. Say you've got a hunch you should change jobs even though there's nothing particularly wrong with the one you have. You decide to honor the intuition and plan to check the want ads in the Sunday newspaper.

A few days later, your rich uncle arrives for a visit and says he's looking for someone to run a new business he's just bought. Would you be interested? At twice the salary you're now making? Now that's a synchronicity anyone could enjoy. And it would prove beyond a doubt that following your intuition is a happy path.

Significance

It's important to pay attention to tiny impulses. They can save your life or someone else's. They can also help you get to work on time.

Freud and many of the psychologists who followed him did us a great disservice by teaching that our inner self is evil and capricious. If we believe ourselves to be basically bad and in need of policing, how can we learn to trust ourselves and our intuition? All of us have issues from time to time, perhaps low self-esteem or self-sabotage. However, believing that our subconscious is good and kind provides a far better outcome for intuition.

You can listen to promptings from within more confidently. When you follow an impulse and it pans out, you build self-trust and self-esteem. Your inner self has your best interest at heart.

Honoring your intuition means allowing a certain vulnerability. A current teacher and writer on this subject, psychiatrist Judith Orloff recommends using our intuition in life and work rather than just seeing it as a special thing or something to be hidden. To make it a part of our daily lives, we must protect ourselves emotionally at the same time. This advice comes from her book *Emotional Freedom*, but several of her books are useful if you want to explore this aspect of your psychic gifts.

Jane Roberts makes assumptions about impulses, a word she uses with the same meaning as intuition. In *The God of Jane*, she says:

- Impulses are meant to be constructive.
- They can be trusted.
- They don't operate contrary to one's conscious intent.
  "Impulses emerge from the deepest sources of the psyche... they're meant to help us follow the paths of our greatest development and to interwork with the impulses of others so that the entire species is benefited."[42]

What better purpose could we have?

The Uncanny Coincidence

If someone mentioned synchronicities to you, you might remember the wonderful songs of The Police sung by Sting, *Message in a Bottle* or *Walking on the Moon.* In psychological terms, however, synchronicities are "the uncanny coincidence, the unlikely conjunction of events, the startling serendipity."[43]

You understand synchronicity if you've ever picked up the phone to call someone, only to find that person on the other end having just called you. When I've had this experience, it seems a technological miracle that the phone has not rung. Or, you're trying to remember the name of the actor who played in an old movie when he appears on the TV screen, narrating a documentary. This is an unlikely conjunction of events where cause and effect do not seem to operate.

Over the years, some coincidences are bound to happen by the law of averages. Synchronicities differ because they hold special meaning.

Carl Jung's Theory

What causes events to happen? One explanation is cause and effect where one event causes the next, which causes the next, and so on.

Another method of reasoning asserts that we cause events to happen by the meaning we give them, by projecting our hopes. For example, we want to become a realtor, so we go to real estate school, study hard, and pass the test.

A Swiss psychologist practicing in the first half of the twentieth century, Carl Jung agreed with these explanations but also believed a third cause played a part, synchronicity. He defined it as meaningful coincidence.

Jung said each living being was part of what he called the collective unconscious, a vast mind to which each of our unconscious minds remains connected. We can dip into the collective unconscious to obtain information or create events. In fact, we can't escape that mind because it shapes our beliefs and dreams from the moment of our birth. In Jung's view, synchronicities prove our connection to the collective unconscious.

Jung thought synchronicities happen in response to a person's strong need. There are three major types:

- An event in outer reality occurs at the same time one feels an inner need, such as the example of trying to remember the actor's name.
- A dream, vision, or premonition comes true.
- A dream or vision happens at the same time as some distant event, such as the death of a loved one.

As a kid I sat in the back seat of the 1953 Chevy, a pink and white beauty, beside my fidgety sister. I read a book, the title long since forgotten, unlike the synchronicity about to happen.

An announcer on the radio said "cabbage" just as I read the word "cabbage" in my book.

I yelled out what had happened. My parents exchanged a shrug of shoulders in the front seat. They had long since grown used to my oddity, I suppose. But the amazing occurrence enchanted me, enough to lodge it permanently in my memory.

Deepak Chopra in *How to Know God* says, "All coincidences are messages from the unmanifest—they are all like angels without wings, so to speak, sudden interruptions of superficial life by a deeper layer."[44] Synchronicities remind you that you are in the flow of life. Such instances build faith that there is a higher order expressing in our world.

Resources for Intuition, Impulses, Synchronicities

Bach, Richard. *Illusions*. USA: Delacorte Press, 1980.
Barron, Frank, Alfonso, Montuori, and Barron, Anthea, Ed. *Creators on Creating: Awakening and Cultivating the Imaginative Mind*. New York: Putnam Book, 1997.
Bodine, Echo. *A Still, Small Voice: A Psychic's Guide to Awakening Intuition*. Novato, CA: New World Library, 2001.
Boeree, C. George. "Carl Jung," ship.edu/~cgboeree/jung.html.
Cameron, Julia. *The Artist's Way: A Spiritual Path to Higher Creativity*. New York: Putnam's Sons, 1992.
Chopra, Deepak. How to Know God: The Soul's Journey into the Mystery of Mysteries. New York: Harmony Books, 2000.
Emerson, Ralph Waldo. *The Complete Essays and Other Writings of Ralph Waldo Emerson*. New York: Random House, 1950.

Lundstrom, Meg. "A Wink from the Cosmos," *Intuition Magazine*, May, 1996.

Orloff, Judith. *Emotional Freedom: Liberate Yourself from Negative Emotions and Transform Your Life.* New York: Harmony Books, 2009

--- *Positive Energy.* New York: Three Rivers Press, 2005.

--- *Second Sight.* New York: Warner Books, 1996.

Rhea, Kathlyn, interviewed by Jeffrey Mishlove. "Training Psychic Intuition," *Thinking Allowed Series*, 1998.

Roberts, Jane. *The God of Jane: A Psychic Manifesto.* Englewood Cliffs, NJ: Prentice-Hall, Inc., 1981.

Sheldrake, Rupert. *Dogs that Know When Their Owners Are Coming Home.* New York: Three Rivers Press, 1999.

awakening-intuition.com

crystalinks.com/synchronicity.html

innerself.com

intuition.org

webspace.ship.edu/cgboer/jung.html

<u>Psychic Development Tools</u>

If you're convinced that psychic abilities are a part of our true nature, you might want to try to develop yours with some tools. They have little power in themselves. The practitioner's focus allows psychic intuitions to flow.

What we believe comes to pass. Playfulness leads to psychic information. You'll have more success if you choose a tool that's fun.

No matter which tool you decide on, know that its purpose is to allow your Higher Self to come through with the great knowledge.

Hypnosis

When you stare out the window and lose track of your location in space and time, you are in a hypnotic trance. It's a normal state, which we often enter unknowingly. We can also choose to enter the state through focused attention. Some techniques to hasten the transition include relaxing music, imagining a lovely environment, staring at a candle flame, or counting slowly down from thirty to one. We can hypnotize ourselves this way or have a hypnotist do it for us.

Generally, if we trust the hypnotist, we can go deeper with help and allow the hypnotist to give us suggestions. Our minds accept the suggestions more easily with conscious resistance minimized. The hypnotist may also give a post-hypnotic suggestion, a suggestion made during hypnosis that we will do a certain action after we come out of the trance. Generally, people do respond to such suggestions. Stage hypnotists like to give mildly embarrassing post-hypnotic suggestions, such as, "You will pretend to fly around the room when you hear the word giraffe." However, the post-hypnotic suggestion to stop smoking or have confidence in your work can create powerful change in your life.

There's nothing scary about hypnosis, and the subject is always literally in control. It's generally believed that people never do anything under hypnosis that they wouldn't ordinarily do. They might embarrass themselves a bit, but they'll never do anything illegal or immoral if they wouldn't do it in waking consciousness, despite what any hypnotist may suggest. There is room for some doubt about this belief, so if you have concerns and intend to employ a hypnotist or hypnotherapist, be sure to check his or her credentials. You also may want to read a summary of the research done on hypnosis and mind control at Psych Web, psywww.com/asc/hyp/faq5.html.

Once in the hypnotic state, we can

- Change our behaviors in order to lose weight or stop smoking
- Change our attitudes to relieve anxiety about a test or relationship
- Allow a dentist to work on our mouths
- Go back in time to resolve emotional issues
- Remember details of some event in the past, say as a witness to a crime
- Go back to former lives and remember details

The first hypnotists in the 1700s called the process mesmerism after Franz Mesmer, a German doctor who discovered he could affect his patient's mental state by making passes with his hands over parts of their bodies and staring into their eyes. He believed that he passed his own animal magnetism to his patients and thus helped effect recoveries from illness.

Hypnosis was little understood until the 1900s when doctors began to use it for practical ends. Today many dentists and doctors use the tool in their practices. Hypnotherapists are licensed to practice counseling as well.

Modern research has shown the safety and efficacy of hypnosis. A recent study at Ohio State University gave some interesting results. One hundred twelve students took a test to determine their susceptibility to hypnosis. The ones with the lowest scores were asked to act as if they were highly hypnotizable. A practitioner hypnotized all of the students and told them that when they awoke they would write down with one hand certain numbers he gave them while they performed a different task with the other hand.

> The researchers found that those students less susceptible to hypnosis—but acting as if they were highly susceptible to it—were six times more likely to complete the automatic writing task correctly than were the more hypnotizable students.[45]

The study concluded that, if someone sincerely wants hypnotherapy to work, it probably will, much like affirmations.

Hypnotherapy, hypnosis, and self-hypnosis, are gateways to past life memories and can assist in spiritual development. I've been hypnotized several times and remembered past life memories. It's a refreshing and amazing experience with no downside, unless you remember a particularly objectionable lifetime. You can give yourself a suggestion to remain calm and relaxed, no matter what memories come up. Should you decide to explore past life memories, begin with a hypnotherapist to guide you. Perhaps later you'll feel confident and knowledgeable enough to go on your own.

Resources for Hypnosis

Kershner, Kelly McConoghy. "Success in Hypnosis Depends on Motivation, Study Suggests." Ohio State University - researchnews.osu.edu/archive/hypno1.htm
Newton, Michael. *Destiny of Souls: New Case Studies of Life Between Lives.*. St. Paul, MN: Llewellyn Publications, 2000.
--*Journey of Souls: Case Studies of Life Between Lives Between Lives.* St. Paul, MN: Llewellyn Publications, 1994.

hypnosis.org — a commercial site with good definitions
hypnosis.com
iarrt.org — International Association for Regression Research and
    Therapies
ngh.net — National Guild of Hypnotists
psiexplorer.com
psywww.com/asc/hyp/faq5.html - hypnosis and mind control

Psychometry

Once I gave a talk on psychometry before seventy-five people at
my local library. I told them about some of my psychic experiences
and then had them count off by fifteens, a process that divided them
into groups of five. My teacher training came in handy there. While
they moved about the room, I shouted that, if they didn't want to try
something psychic, now was their chance to escape. Six or eight left,
exercising their free will.

After forming into the groups, participants followed my instructions to make certain they didn't know anyone. Some moved to other
groups to avoid friends or acquaintances.

Then I said, "Take out some small, personal item and hold it tightly
in your hand to make sure it has your cooties on it." I waited while
they did so. "Now pass your item to the person on your left. Just allow ideas to come in. The key to success is to relax and trust yourself. Trust that you can do it. Trust the images or sounds or feelings,
whatever comes to you." A vibrant silence held sway. "Go around the
circle and allow each person to give impressions to the person on his
or her right."

Ten minutes later the participants were laughing and talking. They
had "known" amazing things about the others—like the color of their
living room, the kind of car they drove, a recent event in their lives.
Two discovered they had had similar dreams the night before. Others
discovered that they had grown up in the same city back east.

I felt superfluous, a wonderful response for a teacher. Psychometry
is an icebreaker. It gets people acquainted quickly. It takes only a few
minutes for them to become aware of their connection to each other
at an experiential level.

Actually, psychometry is so easy and so revelatory that it has a party game feel to it. Perhaps that's its strength. The jolly atmosphere allays fears of failure. People just play the game and find miraculous connections.

Resources for Psychometry

innerself.com
paralumun.com
paranormal.about.com/cs/espinformation/a/aa063003.htm
powerful-psychic-reading.com/psychometry.html — tips on doing psychometry

Astrology

Astrology is a system of divination based on the positions of the stars and planets and their influences at the moment of one's birth and at the present time. A complicated system of calculation includes the twelve signs of the zodiac. Astronomy and mathematics play a major role in creating the astrological chart of any person.

Based on the chart, astrologers predict the future and consider also the actions of karma or soul influence. Most assume that we came into this life with issues to resolve from past lives. We have plans for goals and accomplishments in the present lifetime. Despite the many rules governing chart readings, a practitioner often uses the chart as a spur for intuition, particularly in assessing personality dynamics and the interplay of outside forces on the person whose chart is being read.

Records mentioning astrology in Egypt and India go back as far as eight thousand years, and in many cultures the astrologer has served as priest or counselor. The Greco-Roman tradition depended on astrology to forecast events in personal life and public life.

About one fourth of the population of the United States believes in astrology with eighteen percent uncertain. An interesting finding is that as education goes down belief in astrology goes up. The Russians use astrology a great deal. Also it is very popular in India.

You can find thousands of books on astrology—exactly 4,250 appear on the Amazon.com search engine—so my suggestion is to ask your local librarian for one authoritative volume and the most popular one.

Two or three such books should help you determine whether or not you resonate to astrology.

Resources for Astrology

professionalastrologers.org
uraniatrust.org

Crystal Gazing, Scrying, Mirror Divining

A crystal ball with an even, shiny surface has traditionally served as a focus point for intuition and prophecy. Perhaps after a ritual in which the crystal is purified, the seer gazes into the ball. The surface becomes cloudy, then images appear. These visions aid in answering questions and seeing the future or the past.

The practice of crystal gazing grew out of the practice of bowl divining or scrying. In ancient times, the seer gazed into a bowl of clear water or the surface of a still pond to focus the mind and gain psychic knowledge. In one variation, mirror divining, one gazes into a mirror that is often surrounded by black cloth. A small mirror will serve the purpose, or a large one to see the whole self reflected. Doctor John Dee, a famous navigator and advisor to Queen Elizabeth I and her explorers, used a small glass hand mirror as a means of divination. It is on display in the British Museum.

Gazing into one's own eyes can be a powerful experience to gain access to the hidden reaches of the mind. Raymond Moody, the researcher who wrote *Reunions: Visionary Encounters with Departed Loved Ones*, put this ancient tool to modern use when he built the psychomanteum where people can communicate with their deceased loved ones.

Resources for Crystal Gazing, Scrying, Mirror Divining

Andrews, Ted. *Crystal Balls & Crystal Bowls: Tools for Ancient Scrying & Modern Seership.* St. Paul, MN: Llewellyn Publications, 1995.
Tyson, Donald. *Beginners: Tapping into the Supersensory Powers of Your Subconscious.* St. Paul, MN: Llewellyn Publications, 1997.

Dowsing, Pendulum

The ancient art of dowsing has traditionally been associated with water, as in water witching. The dowser walks along and carries either an L-rod, usually made of copper or iron, or a Y-rod, a forked stick that the dowser holds by the "ears" of the Y. When he or she walks over the underground water, the long part dips, raises, or twists to indicate finds.

Some dowsers need no tool at all. The action of the arm is sufficient to indicate where water is or where lost objects are. Practitioners are often very much in touch with the fact that they are keying into their own subconscious wisdom and prompting from spirit sources like guides and masters. Some even rid homes of ghosts.

Before asking a question of the L-rod or Y-rod, the dowser must decide what the movements will mean. For example, a left-to-right swing means yes and a back-and-forth swing indicates no. Or circling to the right means yes and circling to the left no. Some use an alphabet chart to spell out words, much like a Ouija board.

Research indicates people are sensitive to electromagnetic fields. Whether or not that ability is at work in dowsing is somewhat unclear. More important, when dowsers walk over a dowsing zone of water or whatever is being dowsed, some experience physical changes such as increased heart rate and less skin resistance. Sometimes they feel physically ill when stepping on the target. Research continues and looks positive.

The pendulum is rarely used outdoors as it gets jiggled around too much for accuracy; it is best for dowsing maps, books, and pregnant ladies' bellies. You can make your own pendulum from a small ball or crystal. Simply attach a chain or string of six-to-eight inches length. The pendulum can serve individual purposes. You can ask it if you'll get your promotion or whether your sister's baby will be a boy or girl, then wait for the answering swing. The trick is to keep your hand still so that you're not consciously moving the pendant. That way your subconscious mind or perhaps guiding spirits can influence its movement.

Resources for Dowsing, Pendulum

Hansen, George P. "Dowsing: A Review of Experimental Research," *Journal of the Society for Psychical Research*, Vol. 51, No. 792, October 1982, pp. 343-367.
Schultz, David Allen. *Improving Your Life Through Dowsing.* One World Press, 2000.
Dowsers.org

I Ching

Sometimes called *The Book of Changes*, created over five thousand years ago in China, *I Ching* is a system of divination popular in Asia as well as in western culture.

Form a question you want answered, with a yes or no answer like *Should I attend college?* or something like *What is keeping me from finding a lover?* Take three pennies and toss them three times. The Chinese use yarrow stalks. Keep track of the number of heads and tails you toss. Then transpose the numbers to hash marks and calculate the shape of a hexagram according to a formula. Once you have the shape of your hexagram, look it up in the *I Ching* and read the message, which is generally several paragraphs long and requires interpretation. Your throwing of the dice influences which hexagram you produce, and in that regard your subconscious belief system and intuition come into play.

Some other traditional divination methods are stitchomancy, the technique of choosing a book randomly and opening to any page to find guidance, and bibliomancy, the technique of selecting a random passage from scripture These are not offshoots of *I Ching*, but traditional divination methods in their own right. If you're curious about *I Ching*, you'll find beginner information on the web. You can buy computer software and books to develop the skill needed to understand the method then let your psychic energy guide your interpretations.

Resources for I Ching

Murphy, Joseph. *Secrets of the I Ching.* New York: Parker Publishing Co., 1970.
Facade.com
Zhouyi.com

Ouija Board

A Ouija board offers the opportunity for contact with spirit essences. It's actually a toy that consists of a board with an alphabet and numbers on it and a planchette, a plastic or wooden pointer. Two or more people sit around the board, ask a question of Spirit, then put their fingers lightly on the planchette. It will move from letter to letter, spelling out the words of the answer to the question.

The Ouija board has a bad reputation because of its game quality. Some people have claimed bad spirits or tricksters came through and caused harm. After use, some people say they are being haunted. Perhaps the device induces psychokinesis (PK), the ability to move physical objects by thought. If so, some poltergeist effects may occur that could seem like haunting. Usually teens are involved in poltergeist activity, and they often are the ones daunted by the Ouija board.

Arthur Hastings gives some cautions about channeling on a Ouija board or with automatic writing. His concern is that altered states might present you with portions of your mind that you find unpleasant.

Edith Fiore also warns against using the Ouija board and automatic writing, séances, and mediumship because possessing spirits can gain control or enter our aura. She says we're inviting trouble and laments the lack of training for mediums in the United States, unlike many foreign countries, such as Brazil. Our culture doesn't teach us to honor mediums or revere occult practices. If it did, we would have greater understanding of the forces we might urge into action with the Ouija board.

The direst warnings come from Joe Fisher:

> The Ouija board attracts earthbound spirits more readily than any other inanimate device… mediums were taking huge risks in allowing themselves to become the unwitting accomplices of questionable discarnate attentions… of the lower astral realm.[46]

I don't use a Ouija Board personally because I can't get past the doubt that my own subconscious is operating the planchette. Should you decide to risk it, you might think differently.

Resources for the Ouija Board

Fiore, Edith. *The Unquiet Dead: A Psychologist Treats Spirit Possession.* New York: Ballantine Books, 1987.
Fisher, Joe. *The Siren Call of Hungry Ghosts: A Riveting Investigation into Channeling and Spirit Guides.* New York: Paraview Press, 2001.
Hastings, Arthur. *With the Tongues of Men and Angels: A Study of Channeling.* New York: Holt, Rinehart, and Winston, 1991.
allabouttheoccult.org/ouija-board.htm

Rune Stones

Runes are letters of an alphabet used by Germanic tribes, including Scandinavians and Anglo-Saxons, up until about one thousand years ago. Scholars believe the several versions of runic alphabets have a common source in the Indo-European tribe that was the source for most civilizations in the Western world today. In any event, Germanic runes are very old.

Somewhere along the way the alphabet letters took on symbolic meanings, and seers scratched them onto stones and used them to scry or divine the future. The alphabet, called Elder Futhark, contains three sets of eight runes, for a total of twenty four. Some runes are recognizable; for example, Berkano looks like our B, Hagalaz like our H, and Uruz our U turned upside down. Those three sound respectively like Bear-kawn-oh, B-Birch goddess, meaning birth, fertility, new growth, desire; Haw-gaw-laws, H-Hail, meaning wrath, destruction, trials; Ooo-rooze, U-Ox, meaning strength, energy, freedom, wisdom.

Rune stones seem exotic but have a familiar feel to them, smooth but uneven and a bit wild. Maybe it's race memory, but I like them best. As a divining tool, I prefer runes to any other although I'm still a beginner.

One method of casting runes goes like this: phrase a question, then think about it while you mix the runes in the bag. The conscious focus on the question allows your unconscious mind to select the most meaningful runes. Draw them out in a predetermined pattern, such as a line or a cross and lay them face up. You can do something as simple as three in a row, representing past, present, and future. Layouts go from simple to very complicated with the stones thrown on a patterned cloth that has layers of meaning, representing the ego, the world around us, and spiritual forces. After throwing runes on the cloth, read the meanings and draw intuitive conclusions with personal significance.

Another kind of runecasting is based on the work of P. M. H. Atwater. These runes date back over twelve thousand years to the area of the Crimea and are a feminine form of casting. The practitioner uses her or his intuitive skills to augment the simple throw of the runes.

You can buy runes in most New Age bookstores or online. Generally, directions come in the box.

Resources for Rune Stones

Atwater, P. M. H. *Goddess Runes* at cinemind.com/atwater/ godbooks.html
facade.com

Tarot

A card game several hundred years old, tarot came to be used for divining despite condemnation by the Catholic Church as evidence of the devil. Tarot is a tool for accessing the subconscious. With symbolic, allegorical drawings, the faces of the cards invoke subconscious knowledge and put the card reader in touch with his or her psychic dimensions.

The traditional deck consists of seventy-eight cards. Twenty-two major arcana or trump cards represent soul processes or journey segments of the person's life. Fifty-six minor arcana with four suits—wands, pentacles, swords, and cups. Forty pip cards (ace through ten of each suit) represent minor situations in the person's life. Sixteen court cards (page, knight, queen, and king of each suit) represent people in the person's life.

Each card has special meaning in regular position and a different one in reversed position, generally the opposite but not necessarily bad. For example, one card may mean *public* when in regular position and *private* when reversed. Further subtleties arise from the positions of the cards in relation to each other.

Once a client has posed a question for the reading, the tarot reader shuffles the cards and spreads them out in a variety of formations, the most popular of which is called a Celtic cross. Then he or she reads the cards, attaching traditional meanings to the intuitive process.

Often a good set of instructions comes with the tarot deck. If not, invest in one good book. That will be enough to make you feel comfortable with the technique. After you've done some readings for yourself and others, you might have a great enough interest to invest in lessons. On the other hand, if you like to play cards anyway, you may take to tarot like a natural. Tarot has become the most popular divination tool in modern America.

Resources for Tarot

Bunning, Joan. *Learning the Tarot: A Tarot Book for Beginners.* Red Wheel/Weiser; 1998.

Hollander, P. Scott. *Tarot for Beginners: An Easy Guide to Understanding & Interpreting the Tarot.* St. Paul, MN: Llewellyn Publications, 1995.

Louis, Anthony. *Tarot Plain and Simple.* St. Paul, MN: Llewellyn Publications, 2000.

facade.com

Chapter Twelve

Possibilities

"May the force be with you."

Obi-Wan Kenobi in *Star Wars*

<u>Mind over Matter</u>

Psychic experiences require us to leave the physical to go into the mental, emotional, and spiritual. With the circular motion that all such exploration involves, we return to the physical. Loving care of the body is critical. Even when we leave it one day, I've got a hunch we'll still honor it and remember our time in the physical with tender regard.

The Gallup Poll showed the greatest belief in psychic or spiritual healing or the power of the mind to heal the body: up from forty-six percent in 1990, fifty-four percent of Americans believe and nineteen percent are uncertain. Highly educated Americans are more likely to believe in such healing than the less educated.

At the time of my problems with arthritis, I used many of the therapies described below. I didn't really know which to choose and longed to discuss the matter with the rheumatologist. I made enough comments to realize he disapproved, so I relied on reading books.

There's empowerment for the patient in managing some aspects of his or her treatment. That can happen when medical doctors honor and consult with alternative therapists and include the patient in the process. Andrew Weil of the University of Arizona has been in the forefront of bringing awareness to physicians as well as to the public.

Happily, change is occurring in this area. According to the March/April 2008 issue of *AARP Magazine*, in some places in the United States wellness centers are opening with the mission of interfacing traditional medical treatments with "time-tested, well-researched alternative treatments such as meditation, yoga, acupuncture, healing touch, and herbal therapy... a movement experts say is finally, after more than a decade of prodding from patients, gaining acceptance among the nation's top physicians and medical schools."[47]

Once this wave spreads across our country, we'll have to overhaul other aspects of the medical establishment. One of the inconsistencies of our government is that it has funded over eighteen thousand research studies. Several prove the effectiveness of such treatments as acupuncture, but the treatments aren't covered by Medicare and other insurance plans. Go figure.

Here's a palette of alternative therapies that are safe and beneficial.

Prayer

It's no surprise that a majority of Americans believe in healing prayer; otherwise, no one would ever pray for healing for self or others. And it works. That's been proven in many a church, many a hospital room, and even in scientific laboratories.

Several studies done in recent years confirm that sick people who have prayers said for them heal faster and better than people who do not. Anyone would believe that because of the power of suggestion, but how about fungi and bacteria in petri dishes in laboratories? They grow faster or slower, depending on the intentions of the person praying over them.[48] No power of suggestion there. The National Institutes of Health have helped fund some of this research.

It's not even necessary for a person to know prayers are being said for him or her. What is important is the intention of the person praying. Positive outcomes result from positive prayer, and negative outcomes result from negative prayer.

All evidence points to the potency of prayer. Love, concern, and compassion combine to hinder illness and augment wellness. Debra Williams, in summarizing experiments on prayer, concludes: "Though the faithful will always believe that there need not be any physical evidence of the power and effects of prayer, science has come a long way toward showing just that—prayer is real, and it works."[49]

The intention of consciousness on its surroundings still works, whether we call that prayer, intention, magic, voodoo, or any other name.

The choice to help others in the process of developing psychic ability affirms life and offers potential rewards in personal satisfaction. Several varieties of energy healing are popular. Following is a partial list that can start you on the search for a method of developing and using your intuitive potential.

Many systems have sprung from the belief of Chinese medicine that the body is a bio-electrical system. Energy healing systems treat the space around the body as well as the body itself. The body clearly has some interface with the air around it, with an arbitrary boundary between the two. Rub your arm then watch the hair stand up on it. You can feel the electricity around your body.

The process used to treat this area once was known as aura cleansing and still is in New Age circles, but the general population reacts negatively to the name. Fear of words is a common human ailment. Energy healing sounds much less scary.

With some techniques the healer places his hands over the physical body and only touches the energy body or aura, also called the subtle body. By whatever name, we're talking about the space around our physical body; that area is an electromagnetic envelope, which can be photographed by Kirlian cameras.

Resources for Prayer

Williams, Debra. "Scientific Research of Prayer: Can the Power of Prayer Be Proven?" 1999 PLIM Retreat, *1999 PLIM Report*, Vol. 8 No. 4.
officeofprayerresearch.org — Unity International participates in research.
nccam.nih.gov/news/newsletter/2005_winter/prayer.htm
nih.gov — National Institutes of Health
plim.org/prayerdeb

Reflexology

With reflexology, foot massage, pressure on certain points on the foot transmits healing and relaxing effects to other parts of the body. Symptoms of headache, irritable bowel syndrome, pre-menstrual cramps, and several other ailments respond to reflexology. Some believe the pressure points relate to acupuncture points. Others suggest the massage itself releases endorphins or lactic acid.

Resource for Reflexology

reflexology-usa.org

Reiki

From Japan, reiki means spiritually guided life force and involves the transfer of energy. The healer lays his or her hands on the patient in a prescribed method that conforms to the chakras. The process energizes the chakras and promotes healing of both the physical body and the aura. Proponents claim improvements in almost all areas of disease, both physical and emotional. Healers must be taught and licensed.

Resources for Reiki

Reiki: Universal Life Force Energy. VHS, ART Productions, 1998.
iarp.org — International Association of Reiki Practitioners
reiki.org

Therapeutic Touch

An American nurse, Dolores Kreiger, and an American psychic named Dora Kunz, president of the Theosophical Society of America, combined their talents to create the therapeutic touch method. They took the teachings of Qigong masters and turned them into a method of healing now used in many hospitals and sometimes paid by health plans.

Kreiger wrote a book that teaches a pattern of passes over the body, designed to interface with the aura, soothing, cleansing, and repairing it. The practitioner, who doesn't have to be a nurse, can touch the body or keep the hands a few inches away. In either case, research studies have documented reduction of stress and pain.

During my convalescence from arthritis, I had the good fortune to experience therapeutic touch, which reduced the swelling and gave me much pain relief.

A Canadian organization works to spread this method. In fact, the nurse who helped me was a winter visitor to Arizona from Canada. That's one of the perks of living in the desert. We get to meet interesting people from all the cold places.

Resources for Therapeutic Touch
Kreiger, Dolores. *Accepting Your Power to Heal: The Personal Practice of Therapeutic Touch.* Bear & Company, 1993.
therapeutictouch.net

Healing Touch

A similar method of aura cleansing and energy charging, healing touch includes the use of color, gemstones, and other tools. Many American nurses are practitioners.

Resources for Healing Touch
Brennan, Barbara Ann. *Hands of Light: A Guide to Healing Through the Human Energy Field.* New York: Bantam Books, 1988.
healingtouch.net
healingtouchinternational.org

Acupuncture, Acupressure

These two methods are variations on the same theory of medicine from ancient China. The theory holds that our vital energy, life force, *chi, ki, qi,* pronounced chee, flows through fourteen paths or meridians of the body. Illness restricts the flow. Excitation of certain points where energy flows allows healing to occur. Practitioners prick with needles in acupuncture or apply pressure with thumbs or fingers in acupressure.

At first glance, such an approach toward health might seem odd, particularly to those of us brought up in the allopathic tradition of medicine. Allopathic medicine treats disease by introducing an agent, generally a drug that has a counteractive effect. Homeopathy introduces a minute bit of the actual disease-causing agent, for example, smallpox inoculation.

Chinese medicine has at its heart the belief that the life force can be balanced or unbalanced. Yin is feminine, yang masculine. They represent the cycle of change in human life: full or empty, hot or cold, summer or winter. Good health involves keeping the two forces in balance according to our basic constitution. The Chinese call that balanced condition our original body and face before life and learning took a toll on us. The interplay of events, emotion, and desire change our original body and face. The practitioner can restore them to balance.

Although I've not experienced acupressure, I'm certain it works because of the benefits I've gained from acupuncture. All in all, acupuncture turned out to be an extremely effective tool for me while overcoming arthritis.

Once when I had laryngitis and had lost my voice for several days, I returned for two acupuncture treatments. My voice came back while I lay on the table. Some people say acupuncture isn't real, but they're wrong. It's as real as drug therapy, but I prefer it because it has no side effects except for an occasional sense of high energy or exuberance.

Practitioners generally combine acupuncture or acupressure with Chinese herbs or other herbs. My acupuncturist recommended I take olive leaf extract for the laryngitis, not too scary, since it's been researched in America and found beneficial. They sometimes recommend the third prong of Chinese medicine, Qigong exercise and meditation.

Although effective use of acupuncture and acupressure requires medical knowledge, intuition comes into play in diagnosis and placement of the needles. State laws vary on licensing requirements. Also, some insurance companies cover treatment; some don't.

The World Health Organization recognizes acupuncture and traditional Chinese medicine's ability to treat over forty-three common disorders including:

- Gastrointestinal Disorders, such as food allergies, peptic ulcer, chronic diarrhea, constipation, indigestion, gastrointestinal weakness, anorexia and gastritis.

- Urogenital Disorders, including stress incontinence, urinary tract infections, and sexual dysfunction.

- Gynecological Disorders, such as irregular, heavy, or painful menstruation, infertility in women and men, and premenstrual syndrome (PMS).

- Respiratory Disorders, such as emphysema, sinusitis, asthma, allergies and bronchitis.

- Disorders of the Bones, Muscles, Joints and Nervous System, such as arthritis, migraine headaches, neuralgia, insomnia, dizziness and low back, neck and shoulder pain.

- Circulatory Disorders, such as hypertension, angina pectoris, arteriosclerosis and anemia.
- Emotional and Psychological Disorders, including depression and anxiety.
- Addictions, such as alcohol, nicotine and drugs.
- Eye, Ear, Nose and Throat Disorders.
- Supportive therapy for other chronic and painful debilitating disorders.[50]

The National Institutes of Health have funded research on acupuncture, so it's going main stream. Most studies show positive gains without the side effects that drugs often produce. Only some of the claimed categories have research behind them, but soon many more will.

Resources for Acupuncture/Acupressure

Teeguarden, Iona Marsaa. *Acupressure Way of Health: Jin Shin Do.*
New York: Japan Publications, 1978.
acupuncturealliance.org
pulsemed.org

Geomancy, Feng Shui

Geomancy studies the ways spirit and place can intersect to enhance people's lives and aid spiritual growth. It is based in geometry, called sacred geometry by practitioners.

Geomancy, including divining with ley lines and other physical aspects of the earth, allows a freedom of thought that lets intuition emerge. It has a more playful aspect than some of the other divining tools. If we truly want intuition to emerge as a working factor in our lives, we have to lighten up and not take ourselves too seriously.

A popular form of geomancy, Feng shui, the Chinese version, influences *qi*, energy, to entice good fortune, love, and happiness into your life and to heal space. Movement is a key to the idea, whether in clothing, architecture, interior décor, or garden arrangement. Things that swing, fly, tumble, sway, or lilt help move *qi* through space.

Colors have important considerations as well, yellow for health, white for children and family, red for money. Choices of colors depend on areas you want to cultivate or downplay. The idea is to enhance the environment for experiences you want and avoid those you don't. Websites, books, and computer software teach the basic principles so you can do feng shui for your home or work site. The Feng Shui Society, a non-profit organization that accredits courses and lists practitioners, will help you find a practitioner or become one yourself.

It's fun to read about the ideas and figure out little touches to make your home and grounds more energy friendly. I've added a fountain, hanging crystals, geraniums, and other little decorative touches, including windsocks in front and back of the house. I ended up taking down the fountain because it attracted annoying little black bugs, but all the other feng shui items make the house breezier and lighter, more fun to be in.

Resources for Geomancy & Feng Shui

Kennedy, David Daniel and Lin, Yun. *Feng Shui for Dummies.* John
     Wiley and Sons, 2000.
fengshuisociety.org.uk
geomancy.net
geomancy.org

Yoga

Most exercise programs—walking, running, aerobics, weight training—produce good physical conditioning and stress reduction. Should you want to increase your psychic potential in the process, you can practice yoga. Along with conditioning and reduced stress, yoga increases creativity, intuition, and generally attunes a person to psychic manifestations.

Yoga in its very name means to join the body, mind, and spirit. It arose from the ancient Hindu tradition of India but has been used by other groups, both with and without a religious focus. It came to the United States over a hundred years ago and has become quite popular. Yoga combines *prana*, breath control, with stretching and holding the body in different poses for a short period of time. With the body calmed, the mind can become still, a prerequisite for meditation. In fact, yoga classes often end with a short meditation. Most junior colleges and city programs offer yoga classes. In the absence of a class, videos and DVDs work well.

Many scientific studies have documented yoga's benefits. They include easing heart disease and high blood pressure, pain, headaches, diabetes, depression, and an assortment of ills, large and small. That's on the physical level. On the psychic level, many meditators on whom studies of cosmic consciousness have been done regularly practice yoga. Ken Wilbur in *One Taste* says that "psychic experiences are often the gateway to the next level, the subtle; and in kundalini yoga, the practitioner rides these bodily currents to their source in the... radiance of light at and beyond the crown of the head."[51]

Resources for Yoga

Wilbur, Ken. *One Taste*. Boston: Shambala, 2000.
americanyogaassociation.org
yoganetwork.org

Tai Chi

Popular enough in America for a feature in an arthritis drug commercial, tai chi combines dance, martial art, and meditation. Its movements are fluid and highly structured. Practice generally lasts thirty to forty minutes and is best done with a teacher because of the intricate routines. Like yoga with *prana*, tai chi focuses on the movement of *qi*, the life force or breath of life that flows through the body.

Tai chi has particular use for arthritis and other degenerative diseases. Studies both in China and in the States have confirmed its benefits. Realizing results with an illness or with meditation requires a commitment of time, probably a year of daily practice, although you'll begin to feel better within weeks if you've not been exercising at all.

Resources for Tai Chi

taichinetwork.org
thetaichisite.com

Qigong

Qigong is the granddaddy of all the Chinese imports—not only tai chi but also karate, kung fu, aikido, and other martial arts descended from qigong. Far more popular in China than its offshoots, qigong focuses on moving fresh *qi* through the body. In *The Way of Qigong,*

Kenneth Cohen defines qigong as "a wholistic system of self-healing exercise and meditation, an ancient, evolving practice that includes healing posture, movement, self-massage, breathing techniques, and meditation."[52]

There are many tributaries of qigong, such as reiki, therapeutic touch, and healing touch. While practicing qigong one begins to feel the energy flowing through one's own body, particularly in the hands. Energy can be passed to another in a healing way whether by touching or not. In fact, some practitioners of other disciplines say it's better not to touch the body of the client because the goal is to infuse the aura with fresh, healing energy, then the body will heal itself.

My therapeutic touch nurse loaned me Cohen's book. An American teacher, Cohen makes videotapes and DVDs that are easy to follow. I found his teaching and the practice of qigong most beneficial.

Cultivating psychic ability through physical exercise like qigong seems natural. That there is healing in people's hands pleases me, too. In the past people who claimed to see auras were often the objects of derision. The situation has to change with scientific research that verifies intuitive knowledge.

Resources for Qigong

Cohen, Kenneth S. *The Way of Qigong: The Art and Science of Chinese Energy Healing.* Ballantine, 1999.
Nqa.org — National Qigong Association
qi.org

Psychokinesis

Psychokinesis (PK), the ability to move physical objects by the power of one's mind is at the same time one of the most unbelievable of psychic phenomena and one of the most highly researched and proven. Several examples follow:

D. D. Home in the 1800s, a world-famous medium, could levitate people in their chairs, cause furniture to rise, even go out a window himself headfirst and return feet first. He never charged for any of his hundreds of séances and performed in daylight so scientists could investigate. In a lifetime of mediumistic work, no fraud charge was ever proven against him.

Although Home had the best reputation, scientists investigated many other mediums because of their popularity during the nineteenth century.

Additionally, many people declared saints in the Catholic Church received that honor because people saw them levitate. Other reasons for conferring sainthood included instances of PK such as miraculous healings and causing objects to float in the air.

Current discussion of PK divides it into two categories: small instances called micro and large ones called macro. Following are examples of micro PK:

- J. B. Rhine's experiments with dice throwing at Duke University showed that the desire to make certain numbers come up had an influence on the way the dice fell.

- Instances of faith healing by the laying on of hands or through the use of magical potions happen outside the confines of the laboratory in evangelists' tents or in the homes of Voudon practitioners or witches.

- Helmut Schmidt invented the electronic coin flipper and asked subjects to try to influence the way the coins fell by use of their minds only. He had successful trials.

With random number generators, a whole new area of PK testing came into being, most notably with the Princeton Engineering Anomalies Research (PEAR) program, headed by Dr. Robert G. Jahn. Under rigidly controlled laboratory conditions, people could influence the random number sequences at a level far beyond chance. Interestingly, men did better than women.

That program closed in 2007 with new work carried on in subsequent directions at the International Consciousness Research Laboratory, icrl.org, whose objective is to explore human/machine interactions.

Meanwhile work at Princeton continues with the Global Consciousness Project.

Here is the purpose quoted from their website:

The Global Consciousness Project (GCP) is an international effort involving researchers from several institutions and countries, designed to explore whether the construct of interconnected consciousness can be scientifically validated through objective measurement. The project builds on excellent experiments conducted over the past 35 years at a number of laboratories, demonstrating that human consciousness interacts with random event generators, apparently "causing" them to produce non-random patterns.

Events that gain the attention of the world show up on the graphs. You can see the fluctuations of such events as Nine Eleven, New Year's Eve, the Obama Inauguration, even the current financial crisis.

These studies are ongoing. Their website has the latest updates at noosphere.princeton.edu.

Some notable instances of large or macro PK include:

- The Israeli Uri Geller has performed for scientists and lay audiences since the 1970s. He bends spoons and other types of metal with the power of his mind. Knowledgeable people, from Astronaut Edgar Mitchell, Margaret Mead, and Wernher Von Braun to psychic investigators Arthur C. Clarke, Putoff and Targ, have observed Geller and verified his abilities. On the other hand, Geller has been caught faking without acknowledging he used magician's tricks to accomplish his results. As a result, there's an ongoing argument about his integrity and abilities just as there is for other psychics. There's always the possibility of fraud, and a gifted person with a negative agenda can fool even high-profile psychic researchers. When in doubt, read both sides.

- The Miami events of 1967 are typical of many poltergeist cases. Warehouse workers became concerned that they had a ghost because products flew off the shelves when no one was touching them. Parapsychologists who investigated determined the ghost-like activity only happened in the presence of a young shipping clerk, Julio Vasquez, a Cuban refugee. Julio was having family problems and even attempted suicide. Subsequently he was arrested for theft. The "hauntings" stopped when he went to prison. The parapsychologists determined Julio had been moving the objects with his mind.

- Ted Serios is credited with having accomplished the feat of creating pictures on film by the use of his mind. It's easy to fake photographs, as has happened with so-called photos of UFOs and crop circles. For good or ill, the public has often discounted claims made by Serios.
- At the moment of the death of a loved one, oftentimes a picture will fall, a clock will stop, or some other unusual physical incident will take place.

Varying degrees of proof have come to bear on these phenomena. However, reports of PK continue to occur. It's safe to say there are people, including some scientists, who will never accept this phenomenon as a fact. PK requires some healthy skepticism. Gullible people can be taken in by magicians, con artists, and gamblers.

Maybe Uri Geller's spoon bending isn't particularly important in the broad perspective of world activities, but the fact that anyone can bend spoons with his mind confounds our view of how the world works. The media are quick to pounce on stories like his and equally as quick to expose failures or frauds. Acceptance of PK is slow to come, but if we are to develop into a greater culture, we must remain open to the possibility.

Physicists say that, in the study of electrons, the observer modifies the outcome simply by observing. We may not understand the great impact of our thoughts on the world of matter. Indeed, we may participate far more actively than we realize in the creation of our world.

I am reminded of Seth, who, speaking through the medium Jane Roberts, often said, "You create your own reality." Such a simple statement, but so complex in its ramifications. If we belief that we do help create the world around us, and evidence from both philosophy and science indicates that we do, then it's incumbent on us, as citizens of earth, to make ourselves the best we can be. To grow spiritually is often an end product of our searches into the psychic.

Resources for Psychokinesis

Radin, Dean. "For Whom the Bell Tolls," *Noetic Sciences Review*, March-May, 2003.
deanradin.blogspot.com/2007/02/debunking-debunkers.html

noosphere.princeton.edu – Global Consciousness Project
urigeller.com
skepdic.com/geller.html

Mystical Awareness

In the introduction to the English translation of the *Bhagavad-Gita*, Aldous Huxley delineates the Perennial Philosophy. These are the four fundamental beliefs that can be found in all major religions of our time as well as the Pre-Christian nature religions and the beliefs of shamans throughout the world in the present and in the past. These ideas bridge cultural, geographical, and historical barriers.

The Perennial Philosophy

The Perennial Philosophy represents the core religious beliefs of humans:

1. The physical world and conscious beings are manifestations of a Divine source.
2. Humans can unite with the Divine through direct intuition.
3. Humans are composed of an ego and an eternal Self, which is divine.
4. The purpose of human life is to come to unitive knowledge of the Divine.

Given the first three tenets, there are some ways to address the fourth: to come to unitive knowledge of the Divine. For me that includes developing my psychic abilities. It seems to me it's possible to work on that with some techniques we use alone and techniques we can apply with others.

Some individual techniques include:

Meditation Techniques

- One-pointedness or mindfulness meditation where you keep returning your focus to a mantra or phrase. Many people use the Sanskrit phrase *Om Mani Padme Hum*, which means (sort of) I salute the mind, which has reached the lotus of the heart. It is said in the Tibetan language to mean the true sound of truth and is used to quiet and center the mind. You can read more about it at dharma-haven.org/tibetan/meaning-of-om-mani-padme-hung. htm.

- Breathing exercises where you are simply following the breath as it goes in and out, watching it, so to speak. Other methods involve active control of the breath, such as breathing in through one nostril and out through the other. The purpose is to quiet the mind and the body, allowing thoughts to cease so that you may remain poised and alert in the moment.

- Contemplative prayer, part of the Christian tradition, not prayer in the sense of asking for anything. It is quieting the mind and focusing one's thoughts on God or love or joy or on a phrase such as "Be still and know that I am God." Psalms 46:10

- Insight meditation with formal practice. The idea is to attend to each aspect of self as it arises. For example, if your shoes are too tight, notice that until it fades. If you remember an argument with someone at work, notice that until it fades. If you feel angry or tired, notice that until it fades. The purpose is to become relaxed, to relieve suffering, and to increase self-understanding. You can read more at dharma.org.

- Discursive meditation, used in many Christian contemplative orders and the main method of modern Druid orders. One chooses a topic on which to meditate and carries on an internal conversation on it, following where it leads but always returning when the mind wanders off the topic.

Once you've decided to give one method a try, you may encounter the same kind of obstacles as with journal writing. You have to assess for yourself whether you can manage the quiet time it will take to meditate, at least twenty minutes of total privacy each day, and a place where you can be alone.

Teacher or Not

The East Indian tradition, from which much of the West's knowledge of meditation has come, considers a teacher essential to spiritual development. On the other hand, Americans are chronic do-it-yourselfers. You'll need to determine whether you want to try meditation privately. If so, there are many, many books available from the supermarket checkout lane to Amazon.com to your local bookstore.

Meditation practice and ideas are rather individualistic and lend themselves to independent practice.

You might take a class at a local church for a small fee. There are also many schools devoted exclusively to meditation, with or without psychic experiences as a focus.

The Maharishi Mahesh Yogi taught meditation throughout the world and established teaching centers where people can learn the techniques. His organization has sponsored or been part of many research projects that show the advantages of meditation. His website lists:

- Improved Mental Abilities: Increased intelligence, increased creativity, improved learning ability, improved memory, improved reaction time, higher levels of moral reasoning, improved academic achievement, greater orderliness of brain functioning, increased self-actualization.

- Improved Health: Reduced stress and anxiety, reduced hospitalization, reduced incidence of disease, reduced need for out-patient medical care, reduced health care costs, reduced use of alcohol and drugs, improved cardiovascular health, reduced physical complaints, increased longevity.

- Improved Social Behavior: Improved self-confidence, reduced anxiety, improved family life, improved relationships at home and at work, increased tolerance, improved job performance, increased job satisfaction.[53]

Dr. Jon Kabat-Zinn, who ran the Stress Reduction Clinic at the University of Massachusetts Medical Center, recommended two approaches for healing or good health. First, one should establish the pattern of daily withdrawal for a time, such as twenty minutes, to go inside oneself and become quiet. In addition, one should learn to become aware of one's thoughts without judging them, the practice of mindfulness.

Sitting for Development

To sit for psychic development means to make a conscious effort to increase your psychic abilities. It's important to find a group with an informed leader.

Determine how much of your psychic development you want to do on your own and how much in a group. If you have supportive family or friends, you may feel comfortable with journal keeping and meditation alone. Otherwise, a development group will very likely benefit you. Find a local group where you can share your experiences and learn from those of other members.

Formal groups run by organizations carry the imprint of the beliefs of the sponsoring body, of course. Many churches offer classes on meditation and sometimes on psychic awareness; however titles may vary, depending on how open the group is to the paranormal.

Spiritualist churches are very open, of course, and offer courses on spiritual development in which they include psychic development. Many mediums host ongoing psychic development groups. So do practitioners of Wicca. You can consult your local New Age directory.

Informal groups are generally hard to find unless you start them yourself. The group I participated in evolved from a writing group where some of the members had an interest in developing their ESP. We decided in advance which area we'd like to work on each time we met. We covered remote viewing, past life regression, healing, meditation, tarot cards, and several other activities. The person who led the group sometimes had to study appropriate material so that our practice was worthwhile. Leadership and hosting rotated, and we kept snacks to a minimum. The focus was psychic development, not a social hour.

If you're willing to talk about your desire to start a group, you'll probably find others with a similar interest just about anywhere, including your place of employment. Often libraries run programs on psychic phenomena. If so, attending may result in new friends who would like to start a group. Presenters at such events make good sources for finding qualified group leaders.

You can join the Institute of Noetic Sciences at ions.org. They have local groups and online groups where you might find people with common interest. In fact, if you do an Internet search for psychic development groups, you will find many opportunities. I'm not personally recommending any of them except Noetic Sciences.

I have also had good experiences with churches who are members of the National Spiritualist Association of Churches at nsac.org. Not, I'm sure, that the others aren't equally reliable—I've just had no experience with them. If there is a website with a base in your hometown, you may as well invest in a phone call. You might be able to find something of interest that way.

Keeping a journal, saying affirmations, meditating, and sitting for development lend dignity and importance to our psychic experiences. We're not only telling our family and friends that we're trying some new ways of being, we're also telling our own right brain that it's okay to manifest these subtle experiences. We're reprogramming ourselves to tune in more to our souls.

Whatever we pay attention to grows. You will have more psychic experiences if you put these processes into practice. Be ready for an E-ticket ride.

Cosmic Consciousness

Mystical states do not arise from learning or culture but seem to arise independently of them, according to Robert Forman in *The Innate Capacity: Mysticism, Psychology, and Philosophy*. Mystics say they encounter consciousness itself or awareness itself in the ultimate unity. Jung and other psychologists maintain that these states are innate, intrinsic to human nature. Each of us longs for the religious or mystical because we are in touch with the unconscious that longs to become conscious, with the unmanifest which longs to become manifest.

Yogis use the word om as a bridge between the two states in yoga practice. It's not just yogis who attempt to achieve cosmic consciousness. That is also the goal of such far-flung endeavors as astral travelers, clairvoyants, Wiccans, tarot readers, the mystic brotherhood, Christian mystics, believers in theosophy—seekers of all stripes. What exactly are they seeking? They do not all call it by the same name, but they seek cosmic consciousness.

Although primarily known as a philosopher, Ken Wilbur has mastered meditation and achieved cosmic consciousness. He says: "This constant consciousness through all states—waking, dreaming, and sleeping—tends to occur after many years of meditating... You still have complete access to the waking-state ego, but you are no longer only that."[54]

The human brain can produce four types of brain waves, which get progressively longer: beta waves as in thinking, alpha as in reading, theta as in dreaming, and delta as in sleeping. Normally, when monitored by an electroencephalograph (EEG) machine, a device for measuring electrical activity in the brain, people tend to produce one or two brain wave patterns at any given time.

A meditation researcher and friend of Wilbur hooked him up to an EEG machine and showed that his brain produced delta waves while awake. He could produce theta waves on demand.

Concurrently, Dr. Lynne I. Mason did an experiment with several meditators who claimed to have attained transcendent or cosmic consciousness. Like Wilbur, their brain wave patterns showed a distinctive pattern: theta and alpha brain waves while also producing delta. This research proves meditators and others who claim to have achieved high states of bliss are experiencing a state of consciousness most of us do not access.

Wilbur wrote his book *One Taste* in the hope of encouraging more people to meditate. He describes his own method: "Upon waking, or upon passing from the dream state to the waking state, look directly into the mind, inquire directly into the source of consciousness itself—inquire 'Who am I?'"[55]

We started out at the beginning of this book with the hope of increasing psychic awareness. Clearly, when we step on that path, we head into an area of spiritual development with many other positive outcomes, including satisfaction, even joy. Wilbur describes his own bliss this way:

> The feeling of Freedom has no inside and no outside, no center and no surround. Thoughts are floating in this Freedom, the sky is floating in this Freedom, the world is arising in this Freedom, and you are That... You are the world, as long as you rest in this Freedom, which is infinite Fullness.[56]

With no personal experience in this state of mind, I can resonate to Wilbur's description as a goal. I also remember my brief sojourn in a lucid dream where I momentarily felt the expansiveness he speaks of.

If you have had a peak experience, you probably have an inkling too of what might be enjoyed.

Religion Versus Spirituality

To the mystic the search for the Divine ends in love. For the psychic the search for the divine ends in knowledge of truth beyond the senses. These two paths toward spirituality overlap because a psychic can have peak experiences and mystics sometimes have visions or exhibit other psychic abilities. Spirituality is the baseline from which religions arise. Because humans desire to know the nature of reality and experience oneness with the Divine, they embrace religions.

In Roger Walsh's *Essential Spirituality: The 7 Central Practices to Awaken Heart and Mind,* religion means "concern with the sacred and supreme values of life." Spirituality he calls "direct experience of the sacred." The goal of spiritual practice is "awakening... to know our true self and our relationship to the sacred."[57]

The final tenet of the Perennial Philosophy states the belief: The purpose of human life is to come to unitive knowledge of the Divine.

By comparison, the seven practices that Walsh suggests serve as chapter titles:

1. Transform your motivation: reduce craving and find your soul's desire.
2. Cultivate emotional wisdom: heal your heart and learn to love.
3. Live ethically: feel good by doing good.
4. Concentrate and calm your mind.
5. Awaken your spiritual vision: see clearly and recognize the sacred in all things.
6. Cultivate spiritual intelligence: develop wisdom and understand life.
7. Express spirit in action: embrace generosity and the joy of service.

Faith in Yourself

Predictions of a hedonistic future with people genetically coded to experience cosmic consciousness might seem far-fetched, but they aren't much different from the counter-culture of the Sixties and its focus on spiritual and psychic experience through drugs and alcohol.

Misguided as these approaches might have been, they reflected a basic desire for spirituality shared by all human beings. We're programmed to grow spiritually in the same way our bodies are programmed to grow from babyhood into adulthood.

Religions can help us chart our course. Hearing of the experiences of others, including such a thing as reading this book, can help us. But, finally, we all are accountable for ourselves.

Whether we come into spiritual maturity depends on our faith in ourselves and our persistence. We do the best we can to move along the path.

What we each attain for ourselves fans out into the larger consciousness. What we do for ourselves to grow spiritually moves every human being a bit closer because we all feed into the collective unconscious. The Global Consciousness Project at Princeton University attempts to prove just this:

> When millions of us share intentions and emotions the GCP/EGG network shows small but meaningful differences from expectation. This suggests that large scale group consciousness has effects in the physical world. We need to know about this, and learn to use our full capacities for creative movement toward a conscious future. [58]

The words of the scientists echo the words of the poet, both attempting to name the meaning and thus contain it. Alfred Lord Tennyson said:

> Quite frequently from boyhood, when I have been
> alone... this has come upon me through repeating my own
> name to myself silently, till all at once, as it were out of the
> intensity of the consciousness of individuality, individuality
> itself seemed to dissolve and fade away into boundless
> being, and this is not a confused state but the clearest, the
> surest of the surest, utterly beyond words—where death
> was an almost laughable possibility—the loss of personality
> seeming no extinction, but the only true life.[59]

I hold a thought in consciousness, a prayer of love and light for you in your psychical and spiritual exploration. May it be rich and joyous.

Resources for Mystical Awareness

Anderson, Alan C. et al. *New Thought: A Practical American Spirituality.* Herder & Herder, 1995.

Ballou, Robert O. *The Portable World Bible.* Penguin Books, 1972.

Borysenko, Joan. *The Ways of the Mystic: Seven Paths to God.* Carlsbad, CA: Hay House, Inc., 1997.

Castleman, Michael. Blended Medicine: The Best Choices in Healing. Rodale, 2000.

Chopra, Deepak. *How to Know God: The Soul's Journey into the Mystery of Mysteries.* New York: Harmony Books, 2000.

---*Ageless Body, Timeless Mind: The Quantum Alternative to Growing Old.* New York: Three Rivers Press, 1998.

---*The Seven Spiritual Laws of Success: A Practical Guide to the Fulfillment of Your Dreams.* San Rafael, CA: Amber-Allen Publishing, 1994.

---*The Third Jesus: The Christ We Cannot Ignore.* USA: Harmony Books, 2008.

The Holy Qur'an, Arabic Text, English translation and commentary by Maulana Muhammad Ali. Ahamadiyyah Anjuman Isha'at Islam. USA: Lahore, Inc., 1995.

A Course in Miracles. USA: Foundation for Inner Peace, 1983.

Cousineau, Phil, Ed. *The Soul of the World: A Modern Book of Hours.* HarperSanFrancisco, 1993.

Cramer, Todd and Munson, Doug. *Eckankar Ancient Wisdom for Today.* Minneapolis, MN: Eckankar, 1995.

Crute, Sheree. "The Best Medicine," *AARP The Magazine,* March/April 2008, 66-71.

Darling, David. *Soul Search, A Scientist Explores the After Life.* New York: Villard Books, 1995.

Dass, Ram. *Be Here Now.* Crown Publishing, 1971.

--- *Journey of Awakening.* New York: Bantam, 1985.

Desautels, L. L. "The Alchemy of Words," *Science & Spirit,* Volume 13 Issue 4, July August, 2002.

Forman, Robert K. C. *The Innate Capacity: Mysticism, Psychology, and Philosophy.* New York: Oxford University Press, 1998.

Holmes, Ernest. *The Science of Mind.* New York: G. P. Putnam's Sons, 1988.

Houston, Jean. *The Possible Human.* Los Angeles: J. P. Tarcher, Inc. 1982.

Huxley, Aldous. "Introduction to Bhagavad-Gita," *Bhagavad-Gita.* Translated by Swami Prabhavananda and Christopher Isherwood, Signet, 2002.

Kubler-Ross, Elisabeth. *On Death and Dying.* New York: Touchstone, 1997.

--- *On Life After Death.* Berkeley, CA: Celestial Arts, 1991.

Levine, Stephen. *A Gradual Awakening.* New York: Anchor Book, 1989.

---*Who Dies? An Investigation of Conscious Living and Conscious Dying.* New York: Anchor Books, 1982.

McTaggart, Lynne. *The Intention Experiment.* New York: Simon & Schuster, 2007.

Noetic Sciences Review, 1986 to Present, Institute of Noetic Sciences, 101 San Antonio Road, Petaluma, CA 94952. (Now entitled *Shift.*)

Melfi, Anne. "Superconscious States," *Aquarius.* Atlanta, Georgia, September, 1997.

Murphy, Michael. *The Future of the Body: Explorations Into the Further Evolution of Human Nature.* New York: Tarcher, 1992.

The Open Bible, New American Standard Bible. Nashville: Thomas Nelson, Publishers, 1979.

Pearce, Joseph Chilton. *The Crack in the Cosmic Egg: Challenging Constructs of Mind and Reality.* USA: The Julian Press, 1988.

Rinpoche, Sogyal. *The Tibetan Book of Living and Dying.* HarperSanFrancisco, 1994.

Schwartz, Gary E. *The G. O. D. Experiments.* New York: Atria Books, 2006.

Targ, Russell and Katra, Jan. The Scientific and Spiritual Implications of Psychic Abilities," *Articles, Links & References.* espresearch.com/espgeneral/doc-AT.shtml.

Teasdale, Wayne. *The Mystical Heart: Discovering a Universal Spirituality in the World's Religions.* Novato, CA: New World Library, 1999.

Tennyson, Hallam. Alfred Lord Tennyson, A Memoir, Greenwood
   Press, 1969.
Walsh, Roger. Essential Spirituality: *The 7 Central Practices to
   Awaken Heart and Mind.* New York: John Wiley & Sons,
   Inc., 1999.
Weil, Andrew. *Spontaneous Healing.* USA: Ballantine Books, 1996.
Wilbur, Ken. *One Taste.* Boston: Shambala, 2000.
---*A Theory of Everything: An Integral Vision for Business, Politics,
   Science, and Spirituality.* Boston: Shambhala, 2000.
Williams, Debra. "Scientific Research of Prayer: Can the Power of
   Prayer Be Proven?" 1999 PLIM Retreat, *1999 PLIM Report,*
   Vol. 8 No. 4.
Zukav, Gary. *Seat of the Soul.* New York: Simon & Schuster, Inc.,
   1989.
aarpmagazine.org
drweil.com
beliefnet.com
eckankar.org
findthechurch.org — New Thought Centers and Churches
healingchannel.org Integral-inquiry.com
icrl.org – International Consciousness Research Laboratories
theintentionexperiment.com — a site with "a series of scientifically
   controlled, web-based experiments testing the power of
   intention to change the physical world"
nccam.nih.gov — National Center for Complementary and
   Alternative Medicine
nih.gov — National Institutes of Health
noosphere.princeton.edu — Global Consciousness Project
pulsemed.org
religioustolerance.org
sacred-texts.com
unityinternational.org
wholehealthmed.com

(Endnotes)

1   Newport and Strausberg, *Gallup Poll*, June 8, 2001. All poll results throughout the text refer to this article.

2   Guggenheim and Guggenheim, *Hello from Heaven*, 231.

3   Stevenson, "Six Modern Apparitional Experiences," 352.

4   *Ibid.* 361.

5   Schwartz with Simon, *The Afterlife Experiments*, 247.

6   Morse with Perry, *Transformed by the Light*, xii-xiii.

7   *Ibid.*, 80-81.

8   Grossman, "Who's Afraid of Life and Death? 34.

9   Targ and Katra, *Miracles of the Mind*, 8.

10   *Ibid.*, 76.

11   LaBerge and Rheingold, *Lucid Dreaming*, 4.

12   Castaneda, *The Art of Dreaming*, viii.

13   Desautels, "The Alchemy of Words," 14.

14   Cook, *Freeing Your Creativity*, 23.

15   Slate, *Astral Projection*, 148.

16   Cramer and Munson, *Eckankar*, 19-20.

17   Orloff, *Second Sight*, 267.

18   Virtue, *Messages from Your Angels*, 227.

19   Charlton, "Peak experiences," 10.

20   Pahnke, "The Psychedelic Mystical Experience in the Human Encounter with Death," 4.

21   survivalafterdeath.org.uk/researchers/james.htm

22   Zammit, "Xenoglossy," 3.

23   "How can I stop the voices in my head?" psiresearch.org.

24   Funkhauser, "Dreams and Déjà vu," 1-9.

25   Hastings, "What Is Channeling?" 10.

26   Schwartz and others, "Accuracy and Reliability," 1.

27   Hastings, "What Is Channeling?", 10.

28   Fisher, *Hungry Ghosts*, 291.

29   Krippner, "Psi Research," 2.

30   Fiore, *The Unquiet Dead*, 123.

31   Franklin, "Midsummer Magic," 2.

32   Guiley, *Mystical and Paranormal*, 337.

33   Laszlo, *Science and the Reenchantment of the Cosmos*, 35.

34   Clark, *Strange and Unexplained*, xxvi.

35   Ring, *The Omega Project*, 168.

36   Mack, *Abduction*, 43.

37 *Ibid.* 413.
38 Ring, *The Omega Project*, 168.
39 Bodine, *A Still, Small Voice*, 48.
40 Rhea, "Training Psychic Intuition," 6.
41 Lundstrom, "A Wink from the Cosmos," 4.
42 Roberts, *The God of Jane*, 119.
43 Lundstrom, "A Wink from the Cosmos," 1.
44 Chopra, *How to Know God*, 256.
45 Kershner, "Success in Hypnosis," 1-2.
46 Fisher, *Hungry Ghosts*, 272-277.
47 Crute, *AARP Magazine*, 66.
48 Williams, "Research of Prayer," 5.
49 Ibid.
50 Acupuncturealliance.org.
51 Wilbur, *One Taste*, 146.
52 Cohen, "The Way of Qigong," 4.
53 Tm.org
54 Wilbur, *One Taste*, 51-53.
55 Ibid., 74.
56 Ibid., 257.
57 Walsh, *Essential Spirituality*, 3-4.
58 Noosphere.princeton.edu.
59 Tennyson, Alfred Lord Tennyson, A Memoir, 320.

Author Notes

Special thanks and much gratitude to:

- The people who allowed me to use their stories whether with a name or a pseudonym, especially Betty Joy, Susan Shelton, Vijaya and Dan Schartz.
- The leaders and the members of my psychic development groups for allowing me to learn and grow with them.
- My family now—Brandy, Brock, Stephanie, Barby, Emily, Aaron, Josh, Tearle, Trena, and Rick—for love and support. This book more than any other of mine challenged the wisdom of allowing a family member to be a writer.
- My father, Howard Fesler, my mother, Beulah Crosley, and her whole Crosley family in whose loving midst I grew up.
- Bryan for finally having a psychic experience of his own.
- Emmons and my other guides for setting the bar so high.
- My friends Nancy Brehm and Jacque Beatty for taking the psychic journey with me.
- The ministers and practitioners at Unity and Religious Science who taught me.
- The mediums and psychics who shared their gifts with me.
- The students, teachers, and staff at Carl Hayden High School for trusting and believing in me even when I didn't trust and believe in myself.
- The librarians at the Glendale and Phoenix city libraries for reference skill and accommodation.
- My writers' critique group members in both fiction and nonfiction for helping me improve my craft, especially Mike MacCarthy.
- The editors and publisher at Twilight Times Books for turning my manuscript into a beautiful book.

About the Author

At the age of seven, Toby lost her best friend, Marcia, in a car accident. Three months later, Marcia peeked over a cloud and said she liked her new world. Toby's family dismissed the episode as mere imagination, and she grew up distrusting her own perceptions.

Unable to reconcile this and other psychic experiences, such as precognitive dreams and seeing astral forms of people, she became a lifelong student of the paranormal. Her personal library contains over four decades of volumes from Bridey Murphy and J. B. Rhine in the Sixties to current studies by the Institute of Noetic Sciences and the American Society for Psychical Research. Her dream journals span the same time period and serve as resources for her life and work.

Repeated psychic experiences forced Toby to learn some coping strategies. She sat in development groups and experimented with techniques like psychometry, automatic writing, and dream analysis. As she came to terms with her nature, she wanted to share what she'd learned to help others with any self-doubt or concerns about their sanity.

Toby taught high school speech and drama and college English. Now her primary interests rest in understanding her psychic abilities and writing projects that incorporate that learning. A mother of two and grandmother of three, Toby lives in Arizona where she serves as president of Arizona Authors Association.

She is the author of several novels including a reincarnation series entitled *The Alma Chronicles* as well as two textbooks, *Program Building: A Practical Guide for High School Speech and Drama Teachers* and *Seeds for Fertile Minds: Eight Curriculum Integration Tools* with Betty Joy."

Resources in Print (alpha order)

Alien Encounters: Mysteries of the Unknown. Alexandria, VA: Time-Life Books, 1992.

Altea, Rosemary. *The Eagle and the Rose*. New York: Time Warner, 1995.

Anderson, Alan C. et al. *New Thought: A Practical American Spirituality*. Herder & Herder, 1995.

Andrews, Ted. *Crystal Balls & Crystal Bowls: Tools for Ancient Scrying & Modern Seership*. St. Paul, MN: Llewellyn Publications, 1995.

Assagioli, Roberto. *Psychosynthesis: A Collection of Basic Writings*. The Synthesis Center, 2000.

Bach, Richard. *Illusions*. USA: Delacorte Press, 1980.

Ballou, Robert O. *The Portable World Bible*. Penguin Books, 1972.

Barasch, Marc Ian. *Healing Dreams: Exploring the Dreams That Can Transform Your Life*. New York: Riverhead Books, 2000.

Bardens, Dennis. *Ghosts and Hauntings*. New York: Ace Books, 1973.

Barron, Frank, Alfonso, Montuori, and Barron, Anthea, Ed. *Creators on Creating: Awakening and Cultivating the Imaginative Mind*. New York: Putnam Book, 1997.

Bem, Daryl J. "Ganzfeld Phenomena." In G. Stein (Ed), *Encyclopedia of the Paranormal* (pp. 291-196). Buffalo, NY: Prometheus Books, 1996.

Berger, Ruth. *They Don't See What I See*. Red Wheel/Weiser, 2002.

Bernstein, Morey. *The Search for Bridey Murphy*. Garden City, New York: Doubleday & Co., Inc., 1956.

Bhaktivedanta, A. C. Swami Prabhupada. *Coming Back: The Science of Reincarnation*. Los Angeles: The Bhaktivedanta Book Trust, 1982.

Bodine, Echo. *A Still, Small Voice: A Psychic's Guide to Awakening Intuition*. Novato, CA: New World Library, 2001.

Borysenko, Joan. *The Ways of the Mystic: Seven Paths to God*. Carlsbad, CA: Hay House, Inc., 1997.

Bowman, Carol. *Children's Past Lives: How Past Life Memories Affect Your Child*. New York: Bantam Books, 1998.

Brennan, Barbara Ann. *Hands of Light: A Guide to Healing Through the Human Energy Field*. New York: Bantam Books, 1988.

Brinkley, Dannion. *At Peace in the Light.* New York: Harper, 1996.

Bunning, Joan. *Learning the Tarot: A Tarot Book for Beginners.* Red Wheel/Weiser; 1998.

Butler, W. E. *How to Read the Aura.* Wellingborough, Northamptonshire: The Aquarian Press, 1982.

Campbell, Joseph. *The Hero with a Thousand Faces* , 3rd Ed. Novato, California:New World Library, 2008.

Cameron, Julia. *The Artist's Way: A Spiritual Path to Higher Creativity.* New York: Putnam's Sons, 1992.

Castaneda, Carlos. *The Art of Dreaming.* New York: HarperCollins Publishers, 1993.

Castleman, Michael. Blended Medicine: The Best Choices in Healing. Rodale, 2000.

Charlton, Bruce G. "Peak experiences, creativity and the Colonel Flastratus phenomenon." *Abraxis* 1998 Volume 14, 10-19.

Cheetham, J. H. and Piper, John. *A Shell Guide to Wiltshire.* London, Faber & Faber, 1968.

Chopra, Deepak. *How to Know God: The Soul's Journey into the Mystery of Mysteries.* New York: Harmony Books, 2000.

---*Ageless Body, Timeless Mind: The Quantum Alternative to Growing Old.* New York: Three Rivers Press, 1998.

---*The Seven Spiritual Laws of Success: A Practical Guide to the Fulfillment of Your Dreams.* San Rafael, CA: Amber-Allen Publishing, 1994.

---*The Third Jesus: The Christ We Cannot Ignore.* USA: Harmony Books, 2008.

Clark, Jerome. *Encyclopedia of Strange and Unexplained Physical Phenomena.* Detroit: Gale Research, Inc., 1993.

Cohen, Kenneth S. *The Way of Qigong: The Art and Science of Chinese Energy Healing.* Ballantine, 1999.

Cockell, Jenny. *Across Time and Death: A Mother's Search for her Past Life Children.* Fireside, 1994.

Cohen, Sherry Suib. *Looking for the Other Side.* New York: Berkley Books, 1997.

Cole, G. D. H. and Postgate, Raymond. *The British Common People: 1746-1946.* London: Methuen, 1961.

Conway, D. J. *Advanced Celtic Shamanism.* Freedom, CA: The Crossing Press, 2000.

Cook, Marshall J. *Freeing Your Creativity: A Writer's Guide.* Cincinnati: Writer's Digest Books, 1992.

A Course in Miracles. USA: Foundation for Inner Peace, 1983.

Cousineau, Phil, Ed. *The Soul of the World: A Modern Book of Hours.* HarperSanFrancisco, 1993.

Cramer, Todd and Munson, Doug. *Eckankar Ancient Wisdom for Today.* Minneapolis, MN: Eckankar, 1995.

Crookall, Robert. *Case-Book of Astral Projection, 545-746.* Secaucus: NJ: Citadel Press, 1972.

Crowley, Vivianne. *Phoenix from the Flame.* London: The Aquarian Press, 1994.

Crute, Sheree. "The Best Medicine," *AARP The Magazine*, March/April 2008, 66-71.

Dalichow, Irene and Booth, Mike. *Aura-Soma: Healing Through Color, Plant, and Crystal Energy.* Carlsbad, CA: Hay House, Inc. 1996.

Dane, Christopher, *Possession.* New York: Popular Library, 1973.

Darling, David. *Soul Search, A Scientist Explores the After Life.* New York: Villard Books, 1995.

Dass, Ram. *Be Here Now.* Crown Publishing, 1971.

---*Journey of Awakening.* New York: Bantam, 1985.

Denning, Melita and Phillips, Osborne. *The Llewellyn Practical Guide to Astral Projection.* St. Paul, MN: Llewellyn Publications, 1980.

Desautels, L. L. "The Alchemy of Words," *Science & Spirit*, Volume 13 Issue 4, July August, 2002.

DuBois, Allison. *We Are Their Heaven.* New York: Simon & Schuster, 2006

Eadie, Betty. *Embraced by the Light.* California: Gold Leaf Press, 1992.

Edwards, John. *Developing Your Own Psychic Powers.* Carlsbad, CA: Hay House Audio, 2000.

Ellis, Pete Berresford. *The Druids.* Grand Rapids, MI: Wm. B. Eerdmans Publishing Co., 1995.

Ellwood, Gracia Fay. *Psychic Visits to the Past: An Exploration of Retrocognition.* New American Library, 1971.

Emerson, Ralph Waldo. *The Complete Essays and Other Writings of Ralph Waldo Emerson.* New York: Random House, 1950.

Falkus, Malcolm and Gillingham, John, Editors. *Historical Atlas of Britain.* New York: Continuum, 1981.

Fiore, Edith. *The Unquiet Dead: A Psychologist Treats Spirit Possession.* New York: Ballantine Books, 1987.

Fisher, Joe. *The Siren Call of Hungry Ghosts: A Riveting Investigation into Channeling and Spirit Guides.* New York: Paraview Press, 2001.

--- *The Case for Reincarnation.* New York: Bantam, 1985.

Forman, Robert K. C. *The Innate Capacity: Mysticism, Psychology, and Philosophy.* New York: Oxford University Press, 1998.

Franklin, Ann. "Midsummer Magic," *New Worlds*, NW022.

Funkhauser, Arthur. "Dreams and Déjà vu," *Perspectives*, Vol. 6, No. 1.

Garfield, Patricia. *Creative Dreaming.* New York: Ballantine Books, 1974.

--- *The Dream Messenger: How Dreams of the Departed Bring Healing Gifts.* New York: Simon & Schuster, 1997.

--- *The Universal Dream Key: The 12 Most Common Dream Themes Around the World.* New York: Cliff Street Books, 2001.

Goldberg, Bruce. *The Search for Grace.* St. Paul, MN: Llewellyn Publications, 1997.

Graham, Helen. *Color Therapy Then and Now, Parts I and II.* Ulysses Press, 1998. Article Index available at innerself.com

Greshom, Yonassan. *Beyond the Ashes: Cases of Reincarnation from the Holocaust.* Virginia Beach, VA: A. R. E. Press, 1992.

Grossman, Neal. "Who's Afraid of Life and Death?" *Noetic Sciences Review*, Number 61, September-November, 2002.

Guggenheim, Bill and Guggenheim, Judy. *Hello from Heaven.* New York: Bantam, 1997.

Guiley, Rosemary Ellen. *Harper's Encyclopedia of Mystical and Paranormal_Experiences.* HarperSanFrancisco, 1991.

Hamilton, William F. III. *Alien Magic: UFO Crashes, Abductions, Underground Bases.* New Brunswick, NJ: Global Communications, 1996.

Hansen, George P. *The Trickster and the Paranormal.* Xlibris, 2001.

--- "Dowsing: A Review of Experimental Research," *Journal of the Society for Psychical Research*, Vol. 51, No. 792, October 1982, pp. 343-367.

Hastings, Arthur interviewed by Jeffrey Mishlove. "What Is Channeling?" *Thinking Allowed Series*, 1995.

--- *With the Tongues of Men and Angels: A Study of Channeling.* New York: Holt, Rinehart, and Winston, 1991.

Head, Joseph and Cranston, S. L. Ed. *Reincarnation: An East-West Anthology.* Wheaton, IL: The Theosophical Society, 1962.

Higham, Charles. *Charles Laughton: An Intimate Biography*. New York: Doubleday & Co., 1976.

Hollander, P. Scott. *Tarot for Beginners: An Easy Guide to Understanding & Interpreting the Tarot*. St. Paul, MN: Llewellyn Publications, 1995.

Holmes, Ernest. *The Science of Mind*. New York: G. P. Putnam's Sons, 1988.

The Holy Qur'an, Arabic Text, English translation and commentary by Maulana Muhammad Ali. Ahamadiyyah Anjuman Isha'at Islam. USA: Lahore, Inc., 1995.

Houston, Jean. *The Possible Human*. Los Angeles: J. P. Tarcher, Inc. 1982.

Huxley, Aldous. "Introduction to Bhagavad-Gita," *Bhagavad-Gita*. Translated by Swami Prabhavananda and Christopher Isherwood, Signet, 2002.

Jansen, K. L. R. "Using ketamine to induce the near -death experience: mechanism of action and therapeutic potential. *Yearbook for Ethnomedicine and the Study of Consciousness*. Issue 4, 1995 (Eds C. Ratsch; J. R. Baker); Berlin, pp 55-81.

Kalweit, Holger. *Dreamtime and Inner Space: The World of the Shaman*. Boston: Shambhala, 1988.

Karlsen, Carol F. *The Devil in the Shape of a Woman*. New York: W. W. Norton & Co., 1987.

Kautz, William H. and Branon, Melanie. *Channeling: The Intuitive Connection*. San Francisco: Harper and Row, 1987.

Kennedy, David Daniel and Lin, Yun. *Feng Shui for Dummies*. John Wiley and Sons, 2000.

Kitel, Lynne D. *The Phoenix Lights*. Charlottesville, VA: Hampton Roads, 2004.

Knight, J. Z. *A State of Mind, My Story: Ramtha: The Adventure Begins*. New York: Warner Books, 1987.

Korff, Kal K. *The Roswell UFO Crash: What They Don't Want You to Know*. New York: Prometheus Books, 1997.

Kraig, Donald Michael. "The World of Magick," *New Worlds* NW023.

Kreiger, Dolores. *Accepting Your Power to Heal: The Personal Practice of Therapeutic Touch*. Bear & Company, 1993.

Kubler-Ross, Elisabeth. *On Death and Dying*. New York: Touchstone, 1997.

--- *On Life After Death*. Berkeley, CA: Celestial Arts, 1991.

LaBerge, Stephen. *Lucid Dreaming*. Los Angeles: J. P. Tarcher, Inc., 1985.

---and Rheingold, Howard. *Exploring the World of Lucid Dreaming*. New York: Ballantine Books, 1990.

Laszlo, Ervin. *Science and the Reenchantment of the Cosmos*. Rochester, Vermont: Inner Traditions, 2006.

Lautz, William H. and Brandon, Melanie. *Channeling*, San Francisco: Harper and Row, 1987.

Levine, Stephen. *A Gradual Awakening*. New York: Anchor Book, 1989.

---*Who Dies? An Investigation of Conscious Living and Conscious Dying*. New York: Anchor Books, 1982.

Levitan, Lynne and LaBerge, Stephen. "Other Worlds: Out-of-Body Experiences and Lucid Dreams," *Nightlight* 3 (2-3), 1991.

Louis, Anthony. *Tarot Plain and Simple*. St. Paul, MN: Llewellyn Publications, 2000.

Lundstrom, Meg. "A Wink from the Cosmos," *Intuition Magazine*, May, 1996.

Mack. John E. *Abduction: Encounters with Aliens*. New York: Scribner's Sons, 1994.

MacKenzie, Andrew. Appa*ritions and Ghosts*. New York: Popular Library, 1971.

Maslow, Abraham. *Religions, Values, and Peak Experiences*. The Viking Press, 1970.

---*Future Visions: The Unpublished Papers of Abraham Maslow*, edited by Hoffman, Edward. Thousand Oaks, CA: Sage Publications, 1996.

McMoneagle, Joseph. *Remote Viewing Secrets: A Handbook*. Charlottesville, VA: Hampton Roads, 2000.

McTaggart, Lynne. *The Intention Experiment*. New York: Simon & Schuster, 2007.

Melfi, Anne. "Superconscious States," *Aquarius*. Atlanta, Georgia, September, 1997.

Mitchell, Edgar D and White, John, Ed. *Psychic Exploration: A Challenge for Science*. New York: A Perigee Book, 1974.

Monroe, Robert A. *Journeys Out of the Body*. New York: Anchor Press, 1977.

Moody, Raymond. *Reunions: Visionary Encounters with Departed Loved Ones*. New York: Ivy Books, 1993.

Morse, Melvin. *Closer to the Light: Learning from Children's Near-death Experiences*. New York: Ivy Books, 1990.

---*Parting Visions: Explorations of Pre-death Visions and Spiritual Experiences.* New York: Harper, 1994.

---*Transformed by the Light: The Powerful Effect of Near-Death Experiences on People's Lives.* New York, Villard Books, 1992.

Moss, Robert. *Conscious Dreaming.* New York: Crown Trade Paperbacks, 1996.

Murphy, Joseph. *Secrets of the I Ching.* New York: Parker Publishing Co., 1970.

Murphy, Michael. *The Future of the Body: Explorations Into the Further Evolution of Human Nature.* New York: Tarcher, 1992.

Newport, Frank and Strausberg, Maura. "Americans' Belief in Psychic and Paranormal Phenomena Is up Over Last Decade," *The Gallup Organization,* June 8, 2001.

Newton, Michael. *Destiny of Souls: New Case Studies of Life Between Lives..* St. Paul, MN: Llewellyn Publications, 2000.

---*Journey of Souls: Case Studies of Life Between Lives Between Lives.* St. Paul, MN: Llewellyn Publications, 1994.

Noetic Sciences Review, 1986 to Present, Institute of Noetic Sciences, 101 San Antonio Road, Petaluma, CA 94952. (Now entitled *Shift.*)

The Open Bible, New American Standard Bible. Nashville: Thomas Nelson, Publishers, 1979.

Orloff, Judith. *Emotional Freedom: Liberate Yourself from Negative Emotions and Transform Your Life.* New York: Harmony Books, 2009

--- *Second Sight.* New York: Warner Books, 1996.

---*Positive Energy.* New York: Three Rivers Press, 2005.

Osis, Karlis. "Life After Death," *ASPR Newsletter,* Summer, 1990, Volume XVI, Number 3, pp. 25-28.

Ostrander, Sheila and Schroder, Lynn. *Psychic Discoveries Behind the Iron Curtain.* Englewood Cliffs, NJ: Prentice-Hall, Inc., 1970.

Pahnke, Walter N. "The Psychedelic Mystical Experience in the Human Encounter with Death," *Psychedelic Review,* Number 11, 1971.

Pearce, Joseph Chilton. *The Crack in the Cosmic Egg: Challenging Constructs of Mind and Reality.* USA: The Julian Press, 1988.

Radin, Dean. "For Whom the Bell Tolls," *Noetic Sciences Review,* March-May, 2003.

Reiki: Universal Life Force Energy. VHS, ART Productions, 1998.

Rhea, Kathlyn, interviewed by Jeffrey Mishlove. "Training Psychic Intuition," *Thinking Allowed Series,* 1998.

Rhine, Louise E. *ESP in Life and Lab: Tracing Hidden Channels.* New York: The Macmillan Company, 1967.

Rieder, Marge. *Mission to Millboro.* Grass Valley, CA: Blue Dolphin Publishing, Inc., 1993.

Ring, Kenneth. *Heading Toward Omega: In Search of the Meaning of the Near-Death Experience.* New York: William Morrow & Co., 1985.

Rinpoche, Sogyal. *The Tibetan Book of Living and Dying.* Harper San Francisco, 1994.

Roberts, Jane. *Seth: Dreams and the Projection of Consciousness.* Walpole, New Hampshire: Stillpoint Publishing, 1986.

--- *The Nature of Personal Reality.* Englewood Cliffs, NJ: Prentice-Hall, Inc., 1978.

--- *The God of Jane: A Psychic Manifesto.* Englewood Cliffs, NJ: Prentice-Hall, Inc., 1981.

--- *The Unknown Reality: Volume One of a Seth Book.* Englewood Cliffs, NJ: Prentice-Hall, Inc., 1977.

--- *The Unknown Reality: Volume Two of a Seth Book.* Englewood Cliffs, NJ: Prentice-Hall, Inc., 1979.

Roman, Sanaya and Packer, Duane. *Opening to Channel: How to Connect with Your Guide.* Tiburon, CA: H. J. Kramer, Inc., 1987.

Ross, Anne. *Pagan Celtic Britain.* Anne Hutchison Radius, 1997.

Ryerson, Kevin. *Spirit Communication: The Soul's Path.* New York: Bantam Books, 1989.

San Felippo, David. "Religious Interpretations of Near-Death Experiences," a Doctoral Candidacy Essay, September 17, 1993.

Schmicker, Michael. *Best Evidence: An Investigative Reporter's Three-Year Quest to Uncover the Best Scientific Evidence for ESP, Psychokinesis, Mental Healing, Ghosts and Poltergeists, Dowsing, Mediums, Near Death Experiences, Reincarnation, and Other Impossible Phenomena That Refuse to Disappear.* Second Edition. San Jose: Writers Club Press, 2002.

Schultz, David Allen. *Improving Your Life Through Dowsing.* One World Press, 2000.

Schwartz, G. E. R. and others. "Accuracy and Replicability of Anomalous After-Death Communication Across Highly Skilled Mediums." *Journal of the Society for Psychical Research,* Volume 65.1, January, 2001.

---with Simon, William L. *The Afterlife Experiments: Breakthrough Scientific Evidence of Life After Death.* New York: Pocketbooks, 2002.

Sheldrake, Rupert. *Dogs that Know When Their Owners Are Coming Home.* New York: Three Rivers Press, 1999.

Sherk, Warren. *Agnes Moorehead A Very Private Person.* Philadelphia: Dorrance & Company, 1976.

Slate, Joe. H. *Astral Projection and Psychic Empowerment.* St. Paul, MN: Llewellyn Publications, 1998.

Stearn, Jess. *The Search for a Soul: Taylor Caldwell's Psychic Lives.* New York: Doubleday, 1973.

Steiner, Rudolf. *Reincarnation and Karma: Two Fundamental Truths of Human Existence.* USA: Anthroposophic Press, 1992.

Stevenson, Ian. "Six Modern Apparitional Experiences," *Journal of Scientific Exploration.* Vol. 9, No. 3, Autumn, 1995, 351-366.

Schwartz, Gary E. *The G. O. D. Experiments.* New York: Atria Books, 2006.

Schwartz, G. E. R. with Simon, William L. *The Afterlife Experiments: Breakthrough Scientific Evidence of Life After Death.* New York: Pocketbooks, 2002.

Schwartz, Stephan A. *Opening to the Infinite.* Buda, TX: Nemoseen Media, 2007.

Shroder, Tom. *Old Souls: The Scientific Evidence for Past Lives.* New York: Simon & Schuster, 1999.

Summers, Montague. *The History of Witchcraft.* New York: Carol Publishing Group, 1984.

Stevenson, Ian. *Children Who Remember Former Lives: A Question of Reincarnation.* Revised Edition. MacFarland and Company, 2000.

---*Twenty Cases Suggestive of Reincarnation.* New York: American Society for Psychical Research, 1966.

---Where Reincarnation and Biology Intersect. Westport, Connecticut, Praeger, 1997.

Stone, Ganga. *Start the Conversation: The Book About Death You Were Hoping to Find.* New York: Warner Books, 1996.

Talbot, Michael. *The Holographic Universe.* New York: Harper, 1991.

Targ, Russell and Haray, Keith. *The Mind Race: Understanding and Using Psychic Ability.* New York: Villard Books, 1984.

---and Katra, Jan. *Miracles of the Mind: Exploring Nonlocal Consciousness and Spiritual Healing*. Novato, CA: New World Library, 1999.

---*Limitless Mind: A Guide to Remove Viewing and Transformation of Consciousness*. Novato, California: New World Library, 2004.

Teasdale, Wayne. *The Mystical Heart: Discovering a Universal Spirituality in the World's Religions*. Novato, CA: New World Library, 1999.

Teeguarden, Iona Marsaa. *Acupressure Way of Health: Jin Shin Do*. New York: Japan Publications, 1978.

Tennyson, Hallam. Alfred Lord Tennyson, A Memoir, Greenwood Press, 1969.

Tyson, Donald. Beginners: Tapping into the Supersensory Powers of Your Subconscious. St. Paul, MN: Llewellyn Publications, 1997.

Varela, Franciso J., Ed. *Sleeping, Dreaming, and Dying: An Exploration of Consciousness with The Dalai Lama*. Boston: Wisdom Publications, 1997.

Virtue, Doreen. *Messages from Your Angels: What Your Angels Want You to Know*. Carlsbad, CA: Hay House, 2002.

Walsh, Roger. Essential Spirituality: *The 7 Central Practices to Awaken Heart and Mind*. New York: John Wiley & Sons, Inc., 1999.

Webster, Richard. *Spirit Guides and Angel Guardians: Contract Your Invisible Helpers*. St. Paul, MN: Llewellyn Publications, 2001 Weil, Andrew. *Spontaneous Healing*. USA: Ballantine Books, 1996.

Whitton, Joel L. and Fisher, Joe. *Life Between Life*. New York: Time Warner, 1986.

Wilbur, Ken. *One Taste*. Boston: Shambala, 2000.

---*A Theory of Everything: An Integral Vision for Business, Politics, Science, and Spirituality*. Boston: Shambhala, 2000.

Williams, Debra. "Scientific Research of Prayer: Can the Power of Prayer Be Proven?" 1999 PLIM Retreat, *1999 PLIM Report*, Vol 8 No. 4.

Zukav, Gary. *Seat of the Soul*. New York: Simon & Schuster, Inc., 1989.

Websites and web-based articles (alpha order)

aarpmagazine.org

adb.online.anu.edu.au/biogs/A040457b.htm — Richard Hodgson

acupuncturealliance.org

afterlife.com

allabouttheoccult.orgallisondubois.com

americanyogaassociation.org

ancient-wisdom.co.uk

angels-online.com

angelshop.com/encounters

angeltherapy.com

aspr.com — American Society for Psychical Research

assap.org — a London research group

astralvoyage.com

Atwater, P. M. H. *Goddess Runes* at cinemind.com/atwater/godbooks.html

awakening-intuition.com

Ballentine, Brian. "Ezra Pound and the Occult." cwru.edu/artsci/engl/
    VSALM/mod/ballentine/resources/occult.html

beliefnet.com

bestpsychicmediums.com

bioholography.org

Boeree, C. George. "Carl Jung," ship.edu/~cgboeree/jung.html

blavatsky.net

boundaryinstitute.org

catholic.net

catholic.org

castleofspirits.com

celticcrow.com

Corby, Dana. "Harry Potter and the Cuckoo's Egg" witchvox.com/
    words/words_2003/e_harry01.html

---"In the Big Rock Candy Coven" at newwiccanchurch.net/redgarters/
    rg_itbrcc.htm

---"The Mohsian Tradition" at witchvox.com/trads/trad_mohsian.html

cropcircleconnector.com

cropcircleresearch.com

crystalinks.com

cufos.org — Center for UFO Studies

dailygalaxy.com/my_weblog/2007/06/cetacea-mind-be.html
deanradin.blogspot.com/2007/02/debunking-debunkers.html
deanradin.com – psi research
des.emory.edu/mfp/james.html
dharma.org
drweil.com
ebook.lib.hku.hk/CADAL/B31417310/index.html – text of *The Adventure*
eckankar.org
edgarcayce.com
ehe.org — Exceptional Human Experiences
espresearch.com
facade.com
fengshuisociety.org.uk
findthechurch.org — New Thought Centers and Churches
firstamendmentcenter.org
fst.org — First Spiritual Tempe
Funkhauser, Arthur. "Three Types of Déjà vu." home.cc.umanitoba.
      ca/~mdlee/dejavu.htm
Fry, Gill. "Encounters with Angels: Interview with Emma Heathcote."
      netowne.com/angels-christian/angels/encounters.htm
gardening.about.com/od/totallytomatoes/qt/Red_Mulch.htm
geomancy.net
geomancy.org
ghost-hunters.tv
ghostresearch.org
ghoststudy.com
haunted-places.com
healingchannel.org
healingtouch.net
healthsystem.virginia.edu/internet/personalitystudies — Ian Stevenson
horizonresearch.org
huna.com
hypnosis.org
hypnosis.com
iands.org — International Association for Near-Death Studies
iarp.org — International Association of Reiki Practitioners
iarrt.org — International Association for Regression Research and
      Therapies
icrl.org – International Consciousness Research Laboratories

noosphere.princeton.edu — Global Consciousness Project
nqa.org — National Qigong Association
nsac.org/spiritualism.htm — National Spiritualist Association of
     Churches
nuforc.org — National UFO Reporting Center
oberf.org — Out of Body Experience Research Foundation
officeofprayerresearch.org — Unity International
oraclegatherings.com
organicconsumers.org/corp/tsunami.cfm
outofthepsychiccloset.com
paralumun.com
paranormal.about.com
parapsi.com
parapsychology.org
pni.org — Pacific Neuropsychiatric Institute
psychicscience.org
plim.org/prayerdeb
powerful-psychic-reading.com/psychometry.html
professionalastrologers.org
psiarcade.com
psiarcade.com/gaia
psiexplorer.com
psiresearch.org
psychedelic-library.org
psywww.com/asc/hyp/faq5.html - hypnosis and mind control
pulsemed.org
qi.org
reflexology-usa.org
reiki.org
religioustolerance.org
rhine.org
sacred-texts.com
sethcenter.com
seti.org — SETI Institute
shamaniccircles.org
shamanism.org
sheldrake.org/papers/Animals/animals_tsunami.html
skepdic.com
spr.ac.uk - British Society for Psychical Research

sri.com — Stanford Research Institute
stephanaschwartz.com
sunnyway.com
survivalafterdeath.org
taichinetwork.org
Targ, Russell and Katra, Jan. The Scientific and Spiritual Implications
    of Psychic Abilities," *Articles, Links & References*. espresearch.
    com/espgeneral/doc-AT.shtml
theintentionexperiment.com
themystica.com
therapeutictouch.net
thetaichisite.com
todancewithangels.com/contacts.html — Dr. Peebles channels
trvuniversity.com — Technical Remote Viewing University
twilighttimesbooks.com
ufoevidence.org
unityinternational.org
uraniatrust.org
urigeller.com
web.mit.edu/newsoffice/2007/deja-vu-0607.html
webspace.ship.edu/cgboer/jung.htmlwhatismetaphysics.com
wholehealthmed.com
windbridge.org
Wiseman, Richard and O'Keeffe, Ciaran. "A Critic of Schwartz et al.'s
    After-Death Communication Studies, *Skeptical Inquirer*,
    November, 2001. csicop.org/si/2001-11/mediums.html
witchvox.com
witcombe.sbc.edu/earthmysteries/EMIntro.html
worlditc.org — World I T C, the New Technology of Spiritual Contact
yoganetwork.org
Zammit, Victor. "Xenoglosssy," *A Lawyer Presents the Case for the
    Afterlife*. Available on line: victorzammit.com
Zhouyi.com — I Ching

Toby Fesler Heathcotte

Don't miss any of these
other exciting SF/F books

➢ Angelos
(1-933353-60-0, $16.95 US)

➢ Jerome and the Seraph
(1-931201-54-4, $15.50 US)

➢ Monkey Trap
(1-931201-34-X, $19.50 US)

➢ Shadow Worlds
(1-933353-79-1, $16.95 US)

➢ The Elixir
(1-933353-03-1, $16.95 US)

Twilight Times Books
Kingsport, Tennessee

Order Form

If not available from your local bookstore or favorite online bookstore, send this coupon and a check or money order for the retail price plus $3.50 s&h to Twilight Times Books, Dept. GB609 POB 3340 Kingsport TN 37664. Delivery may take up to four weeks.

Name: _____

Address: _____

_____

Email: _____

I have enclosed a check or money order in the amount

of $_____

for _____ .

If you enjoyed this book, please post a review
at your favorite online bookstore.

Twilight Times Books
P O Box 3340
Kingsport, TN 37664
Phone/Fax: 423-323-0183
www.twilighttimesbooks.com/